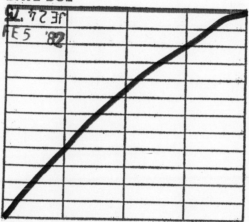

The Ripe Harvest

EDUCATING MIGRANT CHILDREN

The
Ripe
Harvest
EDUCATING
MIGRANT CHILDREN

EDITED BY
ARNOLD B. CHEYNEY

 **University of Miami Press**
CORAL GABLES, FLORIDA

Thrust in thy sickle, and reap;
for the time is come for thee to reap;
for the harvest of the earth is ripe.

Revelation 14:15

Contents

Foreword

MIGRANT CHILDREN have very little visibility in the scheme of education. They are ephemeral—beginning and ending in a day. This literally happens all too often in schoóls around the country. They come and go, rootless, with little or no concern shown by local communities. In Miami during the tourist months, which are concurrent to the growing season, very few persons realize that several thousand migrants are around. Thousands of tourists and Dade Countians daily travel up and down U.S. 1 to the Florida Keys, never realizing they are within several yards of a great host of people who supply them with potatoes, tomatoes, avocados, strawberries, and beans. Migrants and their children are the unseen producers in America.

This book has been written because of the dearth of information available that would help classroom teachers improve their understanding of migrant children and deal with the problems peculiar to them as individuals. Prospective teachers need a source of information that would help them before they enter the classroom. Teachers who have these children in their classes need to test their experiences against the knowledge and understandings of others who have put considerable time and thought to this area of study.

This compilation of original articles was gathered because it was thought that a scholarly approach to migrant education incorporating practical applications was needed. Much of what has been written in the past has not focused on meeting the problems faced by a teacher with a large class who on any given Monday receives two or three children without records who have a language background that is less able than that of the rest of his class (perhaps bilingual but poor in both languages) and no appreciable interest in this strange place—the school.

This book has been written at the end of one decade and the beginning of a new with the hope that the opinions offered will serve as a setting and foundation to make credible judgments for future educational designs and programs. It is not, of course, the answer but a beginning to the answers that must come forthrightly in order to save a portion of society from the slavery of being kept by the majority.

The writers of this volume would be the first to shed any aura of expertness in migrant education which might be alluded to them. Migrants, like the American people in general, are of various creeds, colors, and nationalities. They are black, white, yellow, American Indian, Mexican American, Puerto Rican, Cuban, French Canadian, and Canadian Indian. They live and travel as singles, families, small groups, large groups, and a number are stabilizing and coming under the title of seasonal agricultural workers. Some are offshore workers and wetbacks. They live in tents, in small shacks, cars, trucks, trailers, dormitories, and comfortable and not so comfortable houses. To be an all encompassing "expert" in migrant education is not possible.

The writers were given loose general areas in which to write, with the added freedom of developing their themes as they saw best. This they did in terms of pages written and style. But, if there is any thread that runs consistently throughout, it is that migrant children are individuals with individual needs and aspirations. Not unlike all children, I might add.

The book has been divided into two main sections and a chapter which looks to the future. Part I—Human Considerations—serves as a background for understanding the migrant child in terms of individuality, self-worth, culture, health, and intellect. Part II—Curricular Considerations—is based on the understanding the teacher has of Part I and includes developing curricula through the child's experiences, his language and social experiences, and a knowledge of how to diagnose his capacities in terms of strengths and weaknesses.

The reader has an obligation as have the writers. The obligation lies not in accepting the ideas as presented but to grapple with them intellectually, put those that can be accepted into workable solutions and continue, or at least begin, a pragmatic concern for a group of children who need not only a sympathetic awareness on our part but an educational lift so they can make choices as to their future.

Arnold B. Cheyney

Coral Gables, Florida
January, 1972

PART I

Human
Considerations

CHAPTER 1

Significant Factors
in the Migrant Experience

BILLIE DAVIS

Billie Davis views the challenge of educating migrant children from the perspective of having been one. Her insights take on a relevance that those of us who have only applied our educational knowledge to the problem cannot perceive. She sees the following factors significant in the migrant experience: marginality (surrounded by others but not able to be a part of the group); mobility (always "starting over"); nonmaterial appeal (an interest in reading, learning, loving God, enjoying poetry); culture items (the unfairness of lessons containing concepts such as curtain rod, lavatory, and ladle when there are none in the experience); and contributing (the key to becoming an accepted member of society).

Mrs. Davis is a nationally known speaker for educational organizations, schools, colleges, clubs, churches, and Sunday school conventions. She speaks with the student's viewpoint of public education. Her article "I Was a Hobo Kid," which appeared in the *Saturday Evening Post* and was reprinted in the *Reader's Digest,* has done much to defend the effectiveness of modern public education.

She received her B.A. degree at Drury College where she graduated *summa cum laude.* Her course work for her master's degree is completed in sociology at the University of Missouri. Presently, she works directly with older migrant youth who are in the High School Equivalency Program (HEP) at the University of Miami.

"You don't look like a migrant."

"How did you happen to get out of the migrant stream?"

The fact that remarks and questions such as these are addressed to a former migrant worker by scholars in the field of migrant education intimates the existence of a need and desire for more understanding of the migrant child as a person.

The chapters which follow in this book attempt to effect understanding within the framework of the various disciplines and sciences that have proved to be reliable and useful to educators. The specific purpose of this initial chapter is to add dimension to the thoughts of the various authors by giving the reader a glimpse into the life and memories of one migrant child.

Probably the purpose can be accomplished best through the use of a simple first-person recital, in which references to theory and interpretative comments are kept to a minimum. Before proceeding, I should mention some factors which may influence any application of the material: (1) My experiences as a migrant took place during the 1930s, ending during World War II. (2) My father was white, a product of rural midwestern poverty, and although he had little formal education his imagination and intellect may have surpassed that of most of his peers. (3) My family ties were neither "extended" nor very strong. We were so loosely knit that I felt no binding obligation and no great security in my family. These facts are pertinent, since they place the incidents in historical perspective and give some justification to the treatment of the experiences as typical of the migrant status rather than the result of ethnic influence.

I was born in the hopyards of Oregon and with the seasons and years I followed the fruit and vegetables throughout the western valleys. There were peaches and plums, and then sweet white grapes and cotton in the San Joaquin, potatoes in Shafter, more fruit along the coast, dates and beans and carrots in Coachella, and on to the vast Imperial for vegetable crops.

Occasionally there would be a great adventure when my capricious father would stop the old jalopy at a junction, throw a penny into the air and cry, "Heads we go east!" Then there were sugar beets in Colorado, maybe a harvest of wheat in Kansas, and down south for the cotton.

We lived in tents, in rows of one-room shacks provided by the growers, and sometimes in government camps. The eldest child, living in the cramped confines of such quarters, I knew the most intimate details of family life and economy. I watched the children being born, usually without outside attendants. Eight were born besides me, and two of them died before my eyes.

I pulled long bags of cotton down the thorny rows, carried

boxes or "lugs" of fruit, climbed trees, and dug into the black earth with my hands. I stood in the rain to hold a piece of tin over the fire while Dad cooked mush and Mom cared for the little ones in the crowded tent.

I knew all about the big depression; that the government is full of graft; that rich people work the poor to death and then kick them in the teeth; that some sassy lout a little way up the ladder is always trying to lead you around by the nose; and a poor man's got no chance.

Sometimes, when we wandered too far from the main stream and were caught with nothing to pick or if Dad was just fed up with doing another man's dirty work, we made willow baskets and crepe paper flowers to sell. This was my department, for which the folks trained me from infancy. The earliest thing I can remember is selling baskets and flowers. I was instructed to go up one side of a street and back down the other throughout the town, knocking at every door and entering every place of business, asking, "Would you like to buy a basket today? They are twenty-five cents apiece."

It was the basket peddling that made me conscious of the pattern of life in a settled community and the contrast between this and my own life style, dress, language, and total condition. The difference was so obvious that I began to conceive of the towns-folk as "real people" and of us as "campers." I never used the word "migrant" to describe myself, though I knew that we were called variously "migratory workers," "farm labor," "transients," and "oakies."

Because my job was to call at every building, I became conscious, too, of the public buildings and facilities in the town pattern. Because I was taught to meet strangers and speak to them, I became far more articulate than most of my acquaintances in the camps. Possibly they asked within themselves the same questions I did. I am reasonably sure that many of them did. But I asked the questions out loud, and I had more opportunities than they to seek answers. Gradually I learned of a life where there were schools, churches, libraries, and parks, and even learned something of how these were provided through community cooperation and taxation. Eventually I was peeking through windows and doors, and finally I gained the courage to enter a library, a church, and a school.

We moved often, and evidently the enforcement of attendance regulations was lax in most of the communities (especially where undesirable types were likely to crowd the classrooms at certain seasons), so I was past eight years of age before I went to school. Then it was because I coaxed my parents into submission, took my sister by the hand, and walked into a school building, impelled by both curiosity and determination to learn how to read. After that, all of the children in my family went to school by bits and starts until most of us were able to con school systems out of high school diplomas. Although my experience does not fit the pattern which many outside scholars find in the lives of migrant children, it is by no means unique in its essential components. My subsequent observations and studies have led me to the firm conclusion that several of the factors are generally significant and relevant to the understanding and education of migrant children today.

Marginality

Much of what is said in these pages is true of disadvantaged populations in general. Many of the factors are prevalent in the slums and ghettos. The migrant situation deserves special consideration, however, because the proportionate significance of various factors may deviate strikingly. For example, children of the ghetto may come to feel alienated from the larger society, but the migrant child may never feel integrated into any society at all. From my viewpoint as a migrant child, the most characteristic element of. my life may be summarized in a brief sentence: I did not belong.

Our games of pretend centered almost always around this theme. When I played with a tiny plastic doll (not only were toys expensive, but they were a nuisance to carry, so even if someone gave us a toy we could not keep it unless it were small), I would pretend that we were "real people." I remember clearly the exact words I uttered as I sent my child, brushed and starched, like the kids who lived in houses, out to play: "Now don't go down to the camps and play with those dirty kids. You might catch the lice!"

I overheard conversations in the town. "Dirty gypsies, probably steal chickens and have the lice. Low class people like that. Not a thing you can do. Never appreciate anything. Give 'em something and they'll tear it up."

Often, when my sister and I had been successful in selling our baskets, we would find a school building, and, if there were no children there, we would walk about the grounds, just pretending that we were "school kids," pretending that we belonged to that other world through which we walked as foreigners.

Once as we played on the swings in a park, we heard a child say to another, "Mother says we have to go home when the six o'clock whistle blows. We're having company for supper." After that, on numerous afternoons in the parks and school grounds of perhaps a dozen states, I repeated the words to my brothers and sisters, loudly, so that kids from the houses could hear. It sounded so like real people. And my brothers and sisters copied me: "Mother says we have to go home when the six o'clock whistle blows . . . "

Habitually I ducked into stairwells and doorways to avoid a direct meeting with a group of school kids, and I learned to walk far around little stores where they gathered, sucking on lollipops and jawbreakers and stringing out bubble gum in that smart-alecky way. I was white and spoke English and yet I recognized that I was very different. (How much greater is the problem of the child who is more different still!)

There were times when I felt angry and frustrated and bitter. I am sure I could have been led into violent and destructive action if a leader had appeared. Occasionally I threw rocks at the school kids, and once I tore the lace off the beautiful dress of a child who called me a dirty peddler. But greater than anger and bitterness was the desire to be like the others. I really did not want to fight them. I wanted to join them.

Undoubtedly this accounts for much of the eagerness with which I looked forward to attending school. I believed that in school one could learn how to read, which would somehow open magic doors to the world of real people. Ironically, after I started to school I became even more alienated. Now I was a kind of traitor to my own people. My parents, threatened in their position as I made ideals of the teachers, scoffed and ridiculed and even punished me. I was scolded for saying "thank you," slapped for refusing to say "ain't," and sent to bed hungry for putting ideas into the heads of the little ones.

At school I was a curiosity. Older than my classmates and accomplished in some areas beyond any of them, I was behind where it counted most. I had to guess at the material they had covered before I arrived. They told in oral reports of music and dancing lessons. They baked cookies, competed in talent shows, drew pictures, and knew the names of movie stars.

"I can start a fire in the rain with only one match." Should I venture to say it? They would laugh.

If I were quiet, I was dull. If I talked, I was pushy and awkward. Sometimes I would become so eager to show that I did know something that I would butt in out of turn. It sounded loud and rude. It seemed to me that the others could shout each other down in a conversation and no one minded, but when I tried, they all stopped talking and stared.

So I learned to live in two worlds. I became a compromising, marginal type personality. Soon I could move from one role to another with considerable skill and even began to derive a certain pleasure from the experience. I came to realize that belonging nowhere has a positive side: You can learn to get along anywhere.

It is imperative that anyone who would understand the migrant child be able to comprehend the full significance of this tendency to adapt and compromise. Much that is taken for lack of motivation, dishonesty, and lack of ambition or initiative may be related to this mechanism.

The teacher must recognize the positive aspect and seek to guide the child in such a way that the ability to adapt becomes an asset. As for me, I was lucky enough to find a not uncomfortable niche, somewhere between the campgrounds and the town. Later I could think of myself as a bridge for my people. The wide range of sympathies, appreciations, and pleasures that compose the person I was to become is a legacy not to be despised.

Now I know that my parents were undergoing an experience similar to mine. They were ambivalent in their attitude toward the institutions of the town. On one hand they wanted their children to have a chance. They understood something of the value of education. They would declare loudly to every case worker, "We want to keep the kids in school." And they meant it when they said it. Still, school made deep inroads into their way of life. It limited freedom to travel and robbed the family of wage earners. It alienated them from their children and undermined their authority. They, too, had to learn to negotiate the uncertain route along society's margins.

Some of my efforts to join the world of real people were rather pathetic and others were humorous. There is no way of knowing how many attendance officers I have sent in circles of confusion by giving false addresses on registration blanks. And in some cases even a fine new accumulative record system would have failed to serve my best interests, because I changed my name. It seemed the last straw to have a boy's name on top of being a new kid. In spaces marked "Father's Occupation" I let my imagination run free. I would justify "carpenter" by explaining to myself that anyone who used a hammer and nails was a kind of carpenter; and "landscaping" might refer to anyone who worked with plants, and sometimes my father mowed lawns, too. And "salesman" was appropriate because of the basket business.

Mobility

All of the foregoing maneuvers, as well as the tendency to compromise rather than to rebel, are related to yet another significant factor in the migrant experience: Mobility.

The individual migrant today may have more or less mobility, depending upon the situation in which he makes his living. If he is a member of a crew that follows an essentially established route month after month, then he may be living in a mobile ghetto. His associations may be almost permanent and the society in which he lives almost as closed as it would be if he lived in the slums of a city.

For most migrants, however, there is some possibility of change and regrouping, and even of joining and leaving the migrant stream. For these, the mobility may provide a significant degree of hope for the future, or an avenue of escape from disagreeable situations or associations.

When I was a child the inertia which deprives the modern migrant of some of the possible advantages of mobility had already begun to set in. But there was the push of misfortune behind us, too, and the tug of hope toward a better tomorrow over some near horizon. In those days we thought that almost anything might be left behind. A man hit the road to escape discomfort or disaster. There was something of the pioneer spirit left among us. Almost anything might be discovered, if your luck held out.

These elements have been eroded by changing social and economic forces, but their traces are inherent in the very idea of migrant activity. There are definite vestiges, for example, of the tendency to escape responsibility. This is a logical response to mobility. Whatever operates or exists in a given location, did so before the arrival of the migrant, and will do so after his departure. He has invested nothing and he expects no returns.

In my experience, however, it was obvious that migrants could assume responsibility and took pride in doing so where motivation was stimulated. My father had a double standard for the treatment of property. When we camped by a river or in a clump of trees beside the highway, he cleaned up the camp meticulously before leaving. He made a rake from two sticks, with nails for the prongs. Sometimes we children made such rakes in our play and helped to clean the camp. But if we stayed in a shanty provided by the "rich" owners for whom we worked, or in a government camp, no raking was done. Nature could expect our cooperation, but the bigwigs could do their own dirty work.

From the viewpoint of the teacher, the products of mobility which I have suggested (failure to assume responsibility, a tendency to escape, and a tendency to look for greener pastures farther on) may seem to be negative values. From the viewpoint of the migrant child, it is not so. For one thing, the child of the road is likely to be more free of fatalistic frustration than is his brother in the permanent ghetto. I think it worked this way for me—like the old motto, "This too shall pass away."

"If nothin' opens up here, we'll git on," I heard the men declare. Then Dad would tell a story which somehow seemed very important. It wasn't at all funny to me, but the men laughed, the kind of bitter laugh of a loser getting ready to try again. "There was this hungry baby crying and crying. The mother said, 'Hush-a-bye, hush-a-bye. Daddy will sell the spare tire and then we'll travel some more.' "

I remember camping in El Paso. I would go with Dad to the riverbank to cut the slender willows from which we made the baskets. We would stumble upon groups of wetbacks who had made it across the river. We conversed in odd mixtures of Spanish and English. They asked about the chances of finding work. They wanted to make money and get a break for their kids.

"This is a big country," my dad would agree. "You may hit it lucky. Quién sabe?"

I knew what they had left across the river. I understood the driven, haunted look they cast behind, and I felt with them the strange compulsion toward the unknown road ahead. Although their descendants seem like truckloads of futility, going out to the fields, and indeed they are left today with few options, I cannot forget the fact that is basic to their existence as migrants: They have believed in some possibility of escape and in some modicum of hope for the future. Just understanding this will give the teacher a keener insight into the needs and potentialities of their children, and may inhibit a tendency to permit stereotyping.

As we grew older my sister and I would play a "starting over" game to prepare ourselves for entrance into a different school. We invented new personalities and sometimes new names for ourselves. Somewhere we became acquainted with the concept "first impression," and for a certain period we were convinced, or pretended to be, that our failure to make friends was to be blamed upon a bad "first impression." We laid elaborate plans for the impressions of the future, but mostly we forgot them, and went blundering in, as inept as ever, to stammer clumsily before the first adult we met, "We'd like to go to school here, please."

I was sure I could make friends if I could start to school on a first day when everyone else was starting, too, but never once did I get an opportunity to test the theory. In fact, I never did learn how to make friends; but there was always the possibility that I would. In the next school.

Nonmaterial Appeals

The migrant situation is basically an economic one, and undoubtedly the problems it has generated could be solved if enough
money could be used judiciously. Yet to believe that nonmaterial
goals do not appeal to hungry and alienated individuals is to be
deluded by middle-class values and standards of achievement. My
own attitudes can be explained, in part, by the looseness of my
family ties and by the experience of selling baskets. They are none
the less valid as examples, for they indicate the presence of specific needs and the possible merit of further investigations into the
subject of motivation.

When you sell baskets, you notice buildings. You discover the
configuration of a town and come to realize that there is a repetition of pattern: a business district, with perhaps a large building at
the center, garages, warehouses, apartment houses, factories, poor
homes, and rich homes. Scattered among the stores and houses
you find the "public buildings," schools, churches, libraries and
parks. The curiosity of childhood decrees that if you walk among
these buildings often enough, you will venture inside someday. At
least that is what happened to me.

First I tried a church. A fascinating new world opened before
me. It was clean and beautiful. I sat in a polished pew and looked
at the stained glass windows. There was nothing to buy or sell. I
returned, cautiously, when the real people were entering, and no
one evicted me. I listened to the music and the sermon. Before
long I had discovered the Sunday School, where special small
chairs were provided for children and there were stories, handi-
crafts, and sometimes orange juice.

Nothing that has happened to me since has impressed me more.
I liked the chairs, especially the red ones. I liked to play with clay
and crayons. I liked to hear how God loves children, and how
Jesus walked around from place to place with a lamb in His arms
and no house to live in. I cherished the story of how He blessed
the children and considered each one very important. I was quick
to accept the attractive idea that there is something fine and high
and beautiful to live for. It made more sense than the goal I had
known, which was to sell enough baskets or pick enough fruit to
keep the kettle filled with mush or beans.

There was practically no social experience in these early ventures. I would peek into a room until someone offered me a chair. Usually the teacher would ask my name but little else. The situation was structured and the time was short, so a child could be allowed to participate quietly in some of the activities without getting involved. Afterward I would run away. My parents did not know where I had been.

Then there was the library. I asked a lady who bought a basket, and she told me that it was filled with books, which the people of the town kept there for the use of all. It was difficult to imagine such a situation. How did they organize it to take turns with the books? How could they make each one pay his part so that no one was cheated? Why did they want all those books anyway? I asked others, and pieced together for myself the story of the free public library.

The first library I entered was a small one which consisted, it seems, of a general reading room, a big desk, tables and chairs, and bookshelves against every wall. There was no one there except the lady at the desk.

"Can I help you?" she asked.

I stood frozen.

"Did you want something, little girl?"

"I want to see the books."

She allowed me to walk around the room, looking at the shelved books. Then she let me sit at one of the tables and look at pictures in a magazine. I became an ardent fan of the public library. It was a place to rest when you were tired. It was quiet and cool or warm according to your needs. It belonged to everyone.

Most of the migrants I have known, no matter what their ethnic background, have been either religious or very superstitious, or both. Often they have had what we called a "code" or set of values to which they adhere rather consistently.

My dad had his own idea of prayer, which he called "saying the codes," and it would have shocked my Sunday School teachers considerably. Dad claimed that he hated cops, laws, government, red tape, schools, churches, teachers, maps, clocks, calendars, and big business; but when no one was pushing him, he could rationalize his position and outline a sort of philosophy of life.

As a teenager, sometimes I tried to defend his values to others.

There was a teacher whose judgments of my family seemed unfair to me. "My Dad lives by a different code," I insisted. But the teacher could not understand.

Affluent sons of the sixties and seventies who have scorned their parents' round of profit-making activities and have dashed off rebelliously to live, bearded and unwashed, in a hippie pad, for flowers and for love, have no monopoly on the altruism of adolescence. Kids were like that in the fruit camps.

We were finishing our mush one morning when the black limousines came to take some of the campers to vote. They had been here long enough, they boasted, to sign up for Mr. Roosevelt. "We're glad to vote for Mr. Roosevelt," they fawned, entering importantly through the heavy doors that were held open for them, "We know which side our bread is buttered on."

"Yeah, butter," scoffed one of the young people who had dropped by to await the school bus with us. "First you gotta have bread."

He poured some water into the empty condensed milk can, held his thumbs over the holes to shake down any milk that might have clung to the sides, and sucked the milky water from the can. The rest of us ran our fingers over the tin plates and licked off the last few grains of corn meal.

"We sure won't vote for butter," we agreed, perhaps still under the spell of a patriotic assembly. "When we are old enough to vote, we'll sure not vote for butter."

Sometimes a teacher fastens the learning experience to a distant goal which the child sees no need to achieve; and so the edge is dulled and learning is made more difficult. Perhaps it would be fun to learn, just for the knowing.

There was a Latin American girl who coveted a high school diploma because it was an impressive document which she wished to display on the walls of her shack in the migrant camp. The idea so outraged the instructor that the learning experience was destroyed for both student and teacher.

I never really lost sight of some acceptable, middle-class goals as I fought my way through school. I wanted a job, a house, and good clothing. But entangled with these was the thread of a more abstract desire. I wanted to share in the creation and perpetuation of the ideas and institutions that I had discovered along the streets. In the meantime there were satisfactions and achievements that could be measured neither in terms of economics nor statistics: I could read and learn, love God, and enjoy poetry, even if I lived in a tent.

Culture Items

No expert in measurements knows better than I the wishful thinking inherent in the concept of culture-free testing. I have sat with cold, damp hands, holding my breath, hoping the teacher would not call on me. The assignment was an English lesson in how to explain a process. The list of processes from which we were to choose did not contain one with which I was remotely familiar. There were such items as: pressing a garment, washing the china, setting up a croquet game, playing Ping Pong or tennis. I did not have the courage to choose a different item nor to explain my dilemma to the teacher.

In my early years I never entered a house. Constantly I stumbled over such terms in lessons and tests as: windowsill, staircase, curtain rod, cabinets, highboy, lavatory (until I learned to use a dictionary, I never understood which of the fixtures this referred to), drawer pull, mantle, casters, ladle, light cord. We had no electric lights until I was in high school, except in the government camps, where they were turned on and off from a main switch. We never had a telephone, vacuum sweeper, washer, toaster, refrigerator, radio, or floor lamp.

We never had a private bathroom, or a kitchen sink, or an oven. I never owned a tricycle, bicycle, or pets (stray dogs are a separate category). We did not "go on vacations," "have company," "take lessons," or "pack luggage." We had no front yard, backyard, next door, or neighborhood. We did not sweep or shovel walks. We had no shelves, attic, cellar, or basement. For years I owned no hairbrush, toothbrush, nail file, or pajamas. I could go on. In short, the ordinary middle-class world was strange to me and its terms frightened me.

I rejected opportunities to learn because I was ashamed to admit that I did not know. When I entered a new environment where all those present seemed to be participating in an activity, I had no way to judge the level of accomplishment of the others. They seemed to know everything, and I alone was ignorant.

One of my most painful experiences in this regard was my failure to understand musical notes. It was customary in many schools to teach the names of the notes: do, re, mi, and so on. The children sang the note names instead of the words in the music book and tapped with their fingers the number of "beats" which each note was to receive.

None of this made any sense to me. I could not discover the key to such statements as, "The last note to the right is called 'do.' " What was it to the right of, and why was it called "do" at times and not at others? A word, like *cat,* made sense. It was *cat* no matter where you saw it. But music notes kept changing names, even though they retained the same form, as far as I could discern. I could not ask the meaning of these things when all about me the children tapped competently. The music teacher hurried in and out. It seemed she frowned at me sometimes. I tried to tap and move my lips at the same intervals as did the child beside me. Somehow I made it through the grades without ever being forced to admit that I had no idea what was going on.

I faced similar problems in math, when the educators tried to make the examples practical. (Practical for kids who lived in houses, belonged to Scouts, baked cookies, and owned bags of marbles.) I could subtract two from twenty-four. But when it came to telling how many cookies would be left if mother baked two sheets of a dozen each and Bobby ate one off each sheet, then I was intimidated into saying I did not know.

In the upper grades the obstacle came with "current events" and literature and music appreciation assignments requiring the use of mass media. How could I admit that I had no radio in my home? When there was a radio assignment I had to decide whether to be absent, pretend that I had forgotten the assignment, or try to glean enough information from the others to fake a report. If a newspaper were required, I might find one in a library, beg, or steal one, or look over someone's shoulder. It was never as simple as the teacher made it sound.

Since I tended not to be rebellious and I liked most of the school work, I was seldom a discipline problem in the schools. My only troubles in this area resulted from my curiosity concerning the ways of real people. Once I was punished for stealing from lunch boxes. Actually, I had no intention of stealing. I stayed in the building at recess, which was against the rule, because I was new and afraid to face the kids. The lunch boxes in the cloak room where I hid were attractive and interesting. I decided to look into one. It contained sandwiches wrapped in waxed paper, carrot sticks, and a little jar of dessert. It was neat. I closed the box carefully and opened another. Soon I was carried away and was bent on examining every lunch before the bell rang. A teacher caught me and sent me right in to see the principal. It was hardly stealing. I put everything back meticulously—except one irresistible cupcake.

One trip to the office did not deter me forever. I examined lunch boxes several times after that. Also, I tried on coats, gloves, and galoshes.

For some forgotten reason I was left alone one day in an office and got into trouble for trying to make a telephone call. I felt about telephones as some people do about snakes—I was terrified by them yet fascinated. Someone came in before I could get the operator, but probably I would not have spoken to her if she had answered. I knew no one to call. I just wanted to say that I had used a phone.

The Need to Contribute

No fact I ever learned in school as a child, or later in courses designed to explore philosophically or scientifically the being and behavior of man, has more directly influenced my understanding of myself and others than a "memory verse" I learned in Sunday School. "It is more blessed to give than to receive," the teacher quoted, and then added her interpretation, "It is happier to give."

Later I was surprised to find that the quotation is taken popularly as a kind of utopian concept from some world beyond the nitty-gritty experiences of real existence. I heard it that day in

Sunday School as I am sure it was meant to be understood, from the viewpoint of the reluctant receiver who longed for the opportunity to offer something that someone else would consider valuable. The "blessed" and "happier" people drove up in black cars and hoisted from them overflowing baskets and bundles of food and nearly-worn-out clothing. They stood behind the windows at the Farm Labor Aid and picked their way cautiously among the shacks and tents to deliver relief checks. Always I stood with my family, receiving: ashamed, embarrassed, unhappy, and unblessed. Or I ran to hide and to cry or to rage against the injustice of a world where some people get to do all the giving.

We have thought of our society as one where the goal is to acquire and have amused our sociology classes with tales of primitive tribes where social status derives from giving away quantities of goods; but our charity balls and tax deductions for gifts are typical of many indications in our society of the need to express something (power, status, worth, acceptance in the human family) by acts of giving. The interests of affluent young people turn to giving. They feel cheated when they are forced exclusively into the position of receivers and begin a frantic potlatch of rebellion, trying to give away a style of life, identity, their love, and their bodies.

The failure of some teachers to develop satisfactory relationships with migrant children can be traced to their inability to understand the need of the child to contribute. The teacher believes that he has become far more sophisticated than the do-gooder who takes a basket of food to the campgrounds. He is proud that he can think not only in terms of helping the child, but also in terms of "helping him to help himself." He frames this thinking in academic terms, such as development of self-concept, self-actualization, and internalization of values.

What he may forget is that the child needs opportunities to express his progress in practical actions, and that the most meaningful and satisfying of these is not demonstration of skill and knowledge nor evidence of modification of behavior in relationship to the accepted norms, but rather a chance to contribute or share what he has with others. It is not enough to give a child a fish, nor to teach him to fish, you must give him a chance to teach someone else. You must let him know that you believe he can.

The special relevance of this concept to the teaching of migrant children is that there is a tendency for those who work among the "disadvantaged" to overlook the fact that these individuals are capable of making contributions to society. The dedicated teacher of disadvantaged children may be inordinately absorbed in applying his own knowledge and satisfying his own need to give.

The whole question of giving and receiving is an interesting and profound one which could bear a great deal more investigation. In a society which has come to grips with its social problems to the extent that ours has, it is unfortunate that few individuals seem conscious of this basic issue. To many professional persons, as well as to sincerely motivated nonprofessionals, "lack of appreciation" for help that is offered seems downright sinful. Failure to "take advantage of opportunity" is interpreted as laziness or "lack of motivation."

Many would-be benefactors of society, social planners and educators who believe that they have isolated needs and procured the means of meeting some of them, discover that it is most difficult to give what they have to offer, whether it is a material gift or an "opportunity" in some area of personal or social development. The intended receiver is either arrogant and demanding, or he does not know how to use that which is given to him, or he refuses to receive it because he is proud or ashamed.

Among the migrants I knew there were some from each of the above categories. Most of us would take material gifts, because we were hungry and destitute. But we hated it, and we hated those who gave. We never analyzed our feelings, or imputed any definite motivation to the givers. We just hated them, and some of us hated ourselves for lowering to receive their offerings.

When I peddled baskets, frequently I refused to take money without delivering my wares. "You keep the basket," a kindly gentleman would say, offering me a quarter. "No," I would insist, "You can put it in your office."

On the other hand, my father took a certain delight in getting all he could from the relief office, the Salvation Army, or any other institution that seemed organized to give out money, food, or clothing on an impersonal basis. We applied for "grants" at the

Farm Labor Agency and "clothing orders" and "surplus commodities" whenever we could. I heard the men comparing notes and laughing about the day's haul.

I went to school in "clothing order" shoes and carried "surplus commodities" in my lunch, but I resented any attempt on the part of the teachers to pry into my material world or to offer me material gifts. School was in a separate compartment, I felt somehow, although I do not remember verbalizing my sentiments.

Once I fainted at school and the doctor said I was undernourished. The teachers arranged to have a bottle of milk in the refrigerator in their lounge. I was to go there between classes and drink milk twice a day. The teachers were discreet. They suggested an hour when the lounge was likely to be unoccupied. Of course we had no refrigerator or icebox at "home." Seldom had I tasted "bottle milk" since we had to use canned or powdered. Most of that went for the babies. Fresh cold milk was a treat. But each day I went to the teachers' lounge twice and poured a glass of milk down the sink. Sometimes I was tempted to sip just a little, but even though no one saw me, and even though I wanted the milk, I poured it down the sink.

No individual influenced me in a special way or brought a dramatic turning point into my life, but there were several whose words and actions I remember, though I cannot tell their names nor the places where I knew them. Among these unforgotten ones is a teacher who knew about the happiness of giving.

Evidently she noticed something about the way I held the book in reading class and decided to arrange for an eye examination. She did not send me to the clinic or to some impersonal organization. She took me to her own oculist, not as a charity case, but as a friend. It is easy to tell the difference when you have been a charity case all your life and hardly ever a friend.

Indeed, I was so intrigued with the activity that I did not realize exactly what had happened until one day at school she gave me the glasses.

Then I began to protest, embarrassed, "I can't take them. I can't pay for them."

She told me a little story: "When I was a child, a neighbor bought glasses for me. She told me that I should pay for them someday by getting glasses for some other little girl. So you see, the glasses were paid for before you were born."

Then the teacher said the most welcome words that anyone had ever said to me.

"Someday you will buy glasses for another little girl."

She saw me as a giver. She made me responsible. She believed that I might have something to offer to someone else. She accepted me as a member of the same world she lived in. I walked out of that room, clutching the glasses, not the recipient of charity, but a trusted courier.

This is the teacher a migrant child needs—one who can bridge the gap between his past and his future and pull him into the mainstream of society where he can accept his heritage and be motivated to perpetuate it. It is not begging the symbol too much to believe that this teacher and others like her gave me the right to call my own a way of life which was paid for before I was born, and placed confidently into my unkempt hands the responsibility for making it available to others.

CHAPTER 2

Developing
a Sense of Self-Worth

CAROLYN GARWOOD

Dr. Garwood sets the stage of her chapter on developing a sense of self-worth among migrant children by using Maslow's hierarchy of needs. Migrant children must be given the awareness of alternative responses to situations. Mutual trust and openness between teacher and students through a variety of activities will help communicate to migrant children their sense of worthiness and acceptability. Finally, to be truly effective, the teacher must constantly search for knowledge about himself.

Dr. Garwood has been a consultant to several migrant programs and various migrant education workshops in Florida. She has directed several training institutes for professional educators from schools with multicultural student bodies. She has taught at Syracuse University and the University of Missouri, where she received her Ph.D. in counseling psychology. Dr. Garwood is a professor of education and chairman of the Department of Educational Psychology at the University of Miami.

THE SEARCH for those educational experiences that will best provide the child of the migratory workers with the skills and understandings that will enable him to build a happy and productive life is both challenging and complex. It must involve the recognition by the classroom teacher of certain basic laws of behavior.

A Theory of Motivation

Learning is behavior change. In order to facilitate learning then, we must ask the questions, "What energizes behavior? " and

"What triggers the human organism to action? " Maslow (3) conceptualizes an answer in his theory of a hierarchy of human needs. Man's needs determine the response he will make to any stimulus in his environment.

Maslow's model of human behavior might be viewed as a ladder with the rungs representing needs arranged from the lowest order to the highest. Until one meets the needs at the lower end of the ladder he has little or no inclination or energy for attempting to work on those at a higher level. Observations of the child in the classroom based on this theory will frequently provide the teacher with valuable insights as to the most appropriate approaches that will allow the individual to become involved in a meaningful way in learning activities.

The first or lowest rung on the imaginary ladder represents physiological needs, those things which are necessary to maintain adequate physical functioning such as food, water, and sleep. A child who has had no breakfast before beginning his school day or who has not had an opportunity for adequate rest will demonstrate little, if any, motivation to work on higher level activities.

The need for safety, both physical and psychological, occupies the second rung. In our society physical safety is not frequently threatened and even in a farm labor camp minimum protection from the elements is provided. Perceived threats, however, may be felt by children who witness physical violence among adults. Of more concern to the classroom teacher is the desire for psychological safety. Many children are afraid to take risks, afraid to put themselves in a position where failure is a possibility. The child who refuses to attempt a task may be doing so because if he tries and fails, he will have exposed himself to all that failure can mean in a classroom. The student who says, "I'm just a C student," may be protecting himself because if he tries for something more than a C and doesn't make it, he'll see himself as less worthy. Combs (1) illustrates this phenomenon with the analogy of a poker game in which the player with the most chips can dare to risk the most. The child with the most success experiences can dare to risk the possibility of failure; the one who has never experienced success must attempt to meet his need to protect his psychological self by not daring, not trying.

If the basic needs of the individual are met on these first two levels, he is freed to work on the next rung, the need for belongingness and affiliation. Through the provision of a safe climate for learning in which each child is considered a vital contributing member, the classroom teacher can enable each youngster to meet this need.

The next level or rung of the ladder illustrates the need for self-esteem, the need to feel that one is a worthy person, the need to see oneself as able to cope. It is on this level that many youngsters seem to be stopped and yet until they satisfy this need they will not be able to move on to the final rung of the ladder on which they can work on the need for information and knowledge, the need to appreciate the beauty of life around one, the need to be all that one can be.

The child who has had a limited number of experiences to prepare him for the activities of the classroom and whose life is considerably different from that known by the authority figures with whom he comes in contact may seem to be unmotivated, uninvolved. It is the thesis of this article that he may be expending so much of his vital energy in attempting to maintain himself as an individual that he has little if any left to use in learning to read, to manipulate numbers, or to relate meaningfully to his classmates.

A Perceptual Model

Let us examine a model of human behavior that will help to illustrate the significance of this concept. Each individual lives in a psychological life space which contains everything—every person, every feeling, every dream—that he knows. This is his reality and it determines his behavior—all of his actions, every choice he makes. While he may not be able to tell you at any one time what makes up his life space, or his perceptual field, you can get an idea of how an individual's world looks to him by closely observing him. Those things which he approaches, chooses, moves toward are the things he values; on the other hand, if he attacks or runs from a thing in his world you will know it is a thing of threat, a frightening object. And, remember, his behavior is determined by his reality, by how things look to him.

There are many things in a life space; everything that a person knows, everything that he feels. But there is one thing there that is more important than anything else and that is the individual himself—the I, the ME, the MYSELF. And the most important determinant of how a person behaves, of what choices he makes, of what he values and what he fears is how he sees himself, his self-concept, his self-image. The kind of person he thinks he is is the kind of person he will be.

If he sees himself as a stupid person, he will act stupidly. Gertrude Noar tells the story of the kindergartner who, when asked a very simple question, answered, "I don't know." When queried further, he stated, "I'm a turtle; turtles don't know nothin'." The child saw himself as incapable, his designation within the classroom confirmed his perception, and he behaved accordingly.

The individual who sees himself as a "misfit," one who cannot cope in social situations, will be frightened by activities that require him to interact with others. The one who feels he is not worth very much will organize his world to be that of a worthless person.

We can understand a person's behavior and provide activities designed to change it only by knowing how he sees his world and how he sees that most important thing in his world, himself. This we can best learn by sensitively observing him, his choices, his values, his fears.

It is important to remember here that no two people have the same reality; no two people see the world in exactly the same way. Each individual brings a different constellation of experiences to any point in time, and any quite similar experiences can have quite different meanings to different individuals. It is extremely important that teachers of children whose cultures differ from the norm constantly bear that in mind. Statements such as "There is nothing of which to be frightened here," "Anyone could do this," and "This is nothing about which to cry " may be absolutely true in the reality of the teacher, but they may be false and distorted when seen through the eyes of the child. These differing perceptions of a situation explain why individuals behave differently, make different choices, choose different responses to an identical stimulus.

If an individual could live within his own life space, and it was the only thing with which he had to deal, he would not experience conflict. But society has rules, regulations, and demands and the individual's ability to meet them determines the rewards he will receive. This is necessary not only to understand how the individual sees himself and his world but also to attempt to change these perceptions when they result in self-defeating behavior.

Classroom Implications

How can we change the way an individual sees himself and his world? We must provide an atmosphere that convinces him through the things that we do that his fears and feelings are important, that he is a worthy individual. Telling him so will not suffice because we behave in terms of our feelings and not of our knowing. The adult who is frightened and uneasy from the time he purchases a ticket for a trip by air until the wheels of the jet settle safely on the runway at its destination is little consoled by reading figures about flight safety. The child who perceives the classroom as a place of great threat will not change his perceptions by being told that nothing can hurt him there. He must experience the feeling of acceptance, of safety, of freedom to be who he is.

In order to provide this experience the teacher himself must honestly believe that each child is an acceptable human being without qualification. This does not mean he is acceptable if he reads well, if his face is clean, or even *if* he tries, but that he *is* an acceptable person. This does not mean we accept his inadequacies in social skills, his lack of knowledge, and his academic deficiencies as final. It must be understood that we expect improvement, that we have faith in his ability to improve, and that together we will work toward that end.

The expectations that the teacher has of the individuals in his class may be the most powerful motivating force of all. The teacher who can communicate this positive expectation can change the student's perception of himself. Goethe once said, "When we take a man as he is, we make him worse, but when we take him for all that he could be, we advance him to what he can be."

The type of learning climate that allows for this sort of communication to take place is dependent on the quality of the interpersonal relationships that are created in the classroom. Those students who feel unworthy and frightened, who are unable to distinguish between self-defeating and self-enhancing behavior, learned to see themselves in this way because of experiences they have had with human beings which convinced them that they were *not* capable, *not* competent, and so *not* allowed to make choices. There is only one way to change these perceptions. We must provide every opportunity for them to have new and different kinds of experiences with human beings that will convince them of their worthiness and capabilities. These will only be successful if they are provided in an atmosphere of mutual trust and respect. This respect must be honest and it must be based upon truth. We must look for the strengths so that the respect can be sincere.

In developing an atmosphere conducive to this kind of growth it is extremely important that the teacher be aware of his own personality dynamics, of how he sees himself and his world. He must be sensitive to his own attitudes, values, and biases, and understand how these affect his interactions with other human beings because he becomes an instrument, a tool of vital significance in facilitating the growth of the students with whom he works.

Suggested Activities

Because of the differences in expectations and behavior between the world of the classroom and that which the migrant child experiences with his family, it is important that the teacher provide a consistently structured order in which limits are made very explicit. The child must know what is expected so that he will be able to choose acceptable responses to situations that arise. If the teacher is straightforward and direct and clearly defines what he expects, there will be more opportunity for the child to avoid mistakes. This can be done without a sense of threat and in an atmosphere of mutual cooperation.

Values can best be taught by relating them to the classroom situation. To say that people do not fight, for example, is unrealistic, for the migrant child has probably witnessed many violent encounters. However, he can well understand that there are other, more acceptable ways of handling disagreements at school.

We must remember that learning is a very personal thing and that it occurs only within each individual. Matching students by test scores, chronological age, or any other one variable will still result in a great variety of differences between youngsters because each one will learn differently. The trick for the teacher is to help each individual student find out what approach to learning works best for him.

Frank Reissman (4) suggests that role playing is an excellent technique for use with students for whom a physical style is most suitable; he had found through research, that after engaging in role playing, students have been more verbal in class. This approach helps students with limited experience to move from concrete situations into higher levels of understanding. Role playing is simply a trigger for more advanced learning; it does not replace more abstract activities. In addition to assisting youngsters to verbalize more freely, role playing can be used in developing interpersonal understanding. It is an ideal method for assisting a student to "stand in the other person's shoes; to look out the other guy's window."

Students must be helped to accept their feelings and to express them in acceptable ways. Anger, hurt, elation must be recognized, discussed, and handled and never ignored or rejected. To reject one's feelings is to reject the most significant part of his person. To learn to deal with feelings, which are such a significant basis of behavior, is a very important part of becoming an educated person.

The teacher of the migrant child must be aware of behavior that is the result of cultural expectations. Such behavior can ordinarily be modified by the provision of new experiences that provide the child with alternative ways of responding to a situation. We must be careful not to strip away behavior patterns that may be serving the child in some way without making sure that he has learned other satisfying and effective ways of meeting the situation.

Gathering Information

Specific techniques for garnering more information about children, particularly those who engage in consistent self-defeating behavior, may be helpful. These methods of observation are designed to assist the teacher in seeing the world through the child's eyes, so that the teacher can better understand the migrant child's perceptions of himself and his world. One suggestion is to observe the child carefully and then ask oneself the question, "How must one feel to behave that way?" This may assist one to sensitively "tune-in" to what the child is communicating.

The device of incomplete paragraphs, in either oral or written exercises have been used successfully by some teachers. These paragraphs might begin, "Some day—————," "If only—————," "I wish—————," or "School—————." A story can be related without giving an ending and the students can discuss possible endings. Discussing the consequences of the various alternatives can make this a significant learning experience as well as an information-gathering device.

Although arranging a meeting time is often difficult every effort should be made by the teacher of the migrant child to meet and talk with the parents. While some interpretation of the objectives of the school will probably be needed, this opportunity should be viewed primarily as a chance to gather information. The parent should be encouraged to talk. If the teacher can determine how the parent sees the school, his children, himself, and his world, he can have a pretty good idea what perceptions the child has and where possible distortions exist.

Another project that can provide the teacher with valuable insights while increasing the child's sense of awareness of himself as a unique individual is the preparation of booklets with titles such as "Who Am I?" "Just Me," or perhaps "Mary." These can be constructed in ingenious ways that illustrate those aspects of the child and his world which he considers important. Discussions of similarities and differences can help to point out individual strengths.

In some classrooms the use of mirrors in assisting students to develop a sense of personal identity has proved very successful. Mirror images may be used as subjects for discussion, for composition, or for creative art work. Similar use of large color photographs of individual children has been very effective.

In using the developing sense of self to implement meaningful learning experiences it is necessary to begin early to acquaint the migrant child with a much broader picture of the world of work than he has seen. We now know that vocational choice is not really a choice at all but a series of choices—a developmental process. Information and attitudes concerning these choices must begin with the development of respect for the work which the student knows. Projects, classroom speakers, and field trips should be planned to meet this first important objective. As a student progresses through his school career he should receive ever increasing opportunities to acquire new information that will increase his awareness of the many available work opportunities.

If we could successfully accomplish these two goals (the development of a realistic attitude about self and an accurate and broad view of the world of work) our concerns about realism of choice and aspiration level would be solved. It is only after an individual accepts himself for all that he can be with his unique pattern of strengths and weaknesses that he is ready to make a wise choice. It is imperative that we reduce the number of individuals who spend their allotted days by default rather than by their own choosing because they have not been provided with information and skills to enable them to see and benefit from alternatives.

It has been pointed out that the critical choices of individuals are not chiefly mathematical, scientific, or historical. They are, rather, choices of values, choices involving the use of time, energy, or money, choices of friends, choices in receiving and expressing ideas. Information on which these important choices can be made and the skills necessary for engaging in the decision-making process must become increasingly a part of the content of our educational program if this program is going to prepare individuals for a productive life.

Additional Suggestions

In developing a classroom climate that is nonthreatening and growth producing, it is necessary that the teacher attempt to bring order and meaning to each new experience. We must not expect the child, particularly the one from a limited environment, to make translations of one experience to another or to understand the usefulness of one activity to past or future ones. Direct teaching on the meaning of rules, activities, and language must be a constant part of the learning experience if the child's level of understanding of the total effort is to be increased. Not only is this necessary for the most meaningful involvement in the ongoing activity, but it is mandatory if the child is to use this present learning to increase the number of responses available to meet future situations.

When a feeling of "Let's talk about it" exists in the classroom, an open honest exchange is always available to increase knowledge or to correct misunderstandings. The teacher will find that this atmosphere is just as valuable when she does not understand as when the students do not. In addition, it can correct distorted perceptions before they produce self-defeating responses by the child.

We must find materials with which the migrant child can identify. In addition to using the child himself as subject matter, it is important to focus on the world that is familiar to him. Many teachers have found that a camera is a valuable tool which can be used to provide material which has meaning. The child is not limited to this environmental teaching material, but it can be valuable as a means of getting the child involved in his own learning. Once that occurs movement from this basic point can be made in many directions. If it does not occur, on the other hand, other types of experiences may have very limited significance.

It is important to remember that the child is constantly learning something about himself and his world. He learns what he lives. The teacher's expectation of him and his perception of that expectation will influence significantly his aspiration level and consequently his involvement in classroom activities. Again, it must be repeated, this must be more than a verbalized, "You can do better." The teacher must honestly believe that this is true and must communicate this belief to the student.

Some teachers find that encouraging youngsters to help each other can be a positive step in developing confidence. Not only does this enable the helper to feel useful, but the child being helped may also understand a concept more quickly when it is communicated in peer language.

Recognizing individual areas of accomplishment is a continuous task of the teacher as is making these accomplishments visible to the individual himself and to his peers. At times it may be necessary to begin with something like superior performance on the jungle gym or the ability to paint a very colorful picture. The developmental results of reinforcement can be expected to encourage the child to widen his pattern of accomplishment as he feels capable of coping adequately in one area.

As the child learns to accept and like himself, he will be increasingly more accepting of others. The teacher who can communicate a feeling of acceptance and worthiness to each student with whom he comes in contact, will find those students communicating this same feeling to each other. In the safe climate established in this kind of classroom, learning can take place freely and without fear.

As the child learns more about himself, he will become aware that he can accomplish some tasks easier and more effectively than other tasks. We must help him learn to utilize his strengths and minimize his weaknesses and to understand the importance of these factors in the life decisions he will make.

Not only is this knowledge of individual worth important, but also a knowledge of the child's subgroup, his subculture, should be stressed. Kurt Lewin (2) has said, "The child who has insight into his group status, particularly if it is a disadvantaged one, is better able to cope with this status in a positive manner." The teacher whose subculture differs from that of his students must make every effort to understand this different group (particularly its strengths) in order to assist his students to develop this insight. A knowledge of the contributions of various subgroups may be imparted through every area of the curriculum.

Summary

One of the most vital needs of the human organism is the need to see oneself as a worthy person, to think well of oneself. This need must be met before an individual can be free to expend his energy on learning, aesthetic appreciation, and personal growth.

Because of the limited number of experiences related to school-like activities which the migrant child has had when he enters the classroom, he feels incapable and unable to cope. The number of alternative responses to any one stimulus which he knows are extremely limited. He may be aware of only one response, and that may not be an acceptable one in a classroom situation.

In order to allow him to become involved in his own learning, in his own growth, it is necessary to communicate to him a sense of worthiness, of acceptability. This can best be accomplished in a classroom atmosphere in which mutual trust based on an open and honest relationship between teacher and student exists.

In addition to utilizing a variety of activities designed to increase the self-knowledge and self-acceptance of his students, the most effective teacher will be one who also engages in a constant search for knowledge about himself. In this way he can be aware of and in control of the messages he communicates to his students about who they are and what they can hope to be.

References

1. Combs, Arthur. "What Kind of People Do We Want?" Speech given at A Training Institute for Teachers and Counselors of Multi-Cultural Schools, University of Miami, March 1964.

2. Lewin, Kurt. *Resolving Social Conflicts.* New York: Harper & Row, 1948.

3. Maslow, Abraham. *Motivation and Personality.* New York: Harper & Row, 1954.

4. Reissman, Frank. *The Culturally Deprived Child.* New York: Harper & Row, 1962.

CHAPTER 3

Developing
an Understanding of Culture

ALFRED M. POTTS

Dr. Potts' purpose in this chapter is to help the teacher in his understanding about culture so he might better serve the migrant child. He points out that the migrant child is "cultured" and that the teacher must identify the basic culture of each individual child and learn to know that culture. We must acculturate (influence migrant children into society's dominant cultural mold) while allowing for both undoing and doing in this educative process.

Dr. Alfred M. Potts has had wide and varied experience in migrant education as director of the Migrant Education Research Project and the Migrant Education Section of the Colorado State Department of Education, as professor of education and chairman of the Center for Cultural Studies, Adams State College, Alamosa, Colorado, and as director of the ERIC Clearinghouse on Rural Education and Small Schools, New Mexico State University, Las Cruces. He received his Ed.D. at Rutgers. His publications in various journals on migrant education are numerous. Dr. Potts is presently retired in Florida.

THE MIGRANT CHILD is insufficiently encultured in any culture. His culture learning is from a setting of limitations. The limitations may be due to any one of many causes.

The culture of his home may be only a remnant of a decaying subculture, outmoded because it cannot cope with complex conditions of the modern era. It may be simply a state of cultural poverty limited to the narrow needs of survival. It may be a conglomerate of elements from several cultures, disorganized due to lack of cohesion. The home culture may be one originally rich for a people in a particular time and place, but now in a state of disorganization because of transition into a more dominant culture.

The child's cultural intelligence status is likely more affected by his family's origin than by his family's migrant occupation or mobility. Engagement in migrant labor occupations is usually a result of limited culture and a concomitant lack of salable skills.

Whatever the culture of the child, the teacher who will benefit him must know how to discern the child's cultural possessions and limitations. This chapter is intended to aid the teacher toward fulfillment of his understanding *about* culture that he might better serve the migrant child. To reasonably know the content of a culture is quite another project of lifetime duration.

Knowing something of the structure of culture is essential to understanding the cultural status of any human. Though the traits of various cultures may differ, a perceptual ability can be developed to discern the attributes of a child of any background. If these few pages stimulate the reader to continuing investigation into educational anthropology, they shall have served their major purpose.

Culture

Culture is the ways of doing in a society. It is the concepts, the institutional processes, the format of the skills that guide a people in a particular time. Culture must be learned. It has been created by man in social group. Its purpose is to provide the principles and practices for smoother group operation. Its patterns of activity are designed to aid the group in performing with minimal friction toward the accomplishment of that society's life objectives.

Renewal of Culture

Educating its young is a major activity of every culture. Throughout the history of man, there has been recognition of the need to educate the new generation that it may carry on the society. A goal of education* is the passing of a society's culture on from one

*Education is acquisition of knowings, skills, and processes that develop ability for performance in a society's culture.

generation to another. Culture provides continuity and eliminates a need for each generation, through trial and error, to create a new way of life.

Cultures that remain static from generation to generation, that continue established practices without change, actually tend to retrogress in relation to cultures of other societies. The element of "renewal" is desirable in two respects. One is renewal of the culture by passing it on to the succeeding generation and the second is renewal by changes in the cultural forms to allow for more effective uses of technological advances and progress in human association (4).

Culture Today

Tremendous changes are being generated in the modern period of the American society. Physical sciences have led the way by production of technological machines and processes that create need for changed relational patterns among humans. The culture has become so complex, so interactive among geographically separated population groups, that isolated cultures within the population can no longer operate in a fully successful manner with characteristics that were developed for life in self-sufficient or low tempo times. Isolated cultural forms hinder exchange and association with the major group because of differences in principles and values, in practices for association, and in utilization of the material artifacts in common usage.

Multiple cultures, however, tend to strengthen a whole society by the stimulating effect of the differences. The maintenance of a pluralistic culture generally is deemed desirable. The principle of freedom of choice of one's culture is an established practice in the American political structure.

Intracultural conflict is centered in the problem of acceptance-rejection by the major culture group of the performances by a minority culture group. Historically, minority cultures operating within a dominant culture have tended to be assimilated by the major culture. This phenomenon can be understood when the desire for survival of the minority group is seen as a compelling force to acculturate.

One assumption about migrant peoples is that, like all Americans, they desire the ability to move upward in the economic and societal life of their country. Mobility of people in today's America has many causes. Mobility is both geographic and social. Movement from a migrant's rural, ethnic culture to an expansive culture entails vital changes and adjustments in forms of activity and in concepts and standards that regulate decision-making powers of the individual.

Acquisition of Culture

Much of culture-learning, particularly in the early years, is *nonconscious* learning. It is acquired by observation and copying, by informal direction of elders and peers, as well as by formal teaching. The *knowings,* repeatedly activated, become *internalized.* The acceptance and operation of these internalizations tend to create much of the fiber of humanness in Homo sapiens. Many are firmly fixed. Any changes that are required for living in a different cultural association may have to be made deliberately by the individual. Changes may be difficult to make; particularly so if the person is not well aware of the controlling cultural features which possess him.*

The culture of the United States, is, historically, in a state of development and emergence. The assembling in one vast territory of literally scores of cultures was cause for explosive conflicts between individuals and between groups. Gradually there have emerged practices for behavior and accomplishment that receive general acceptance by more and more people. In time, these become the basic patterns though always susceptible to varied adjustments and change. Ultimately, there may be a "United States culture" that is distinct from other ethnic cultures.† It may be

*Culturation is the process of acquiring culture. Encultration is the process of acquiring one particular culture, usually the culture into which a person is born. Acculturation is widely misunderstood. It refers most often to the acquisition by a person of a different culture than that already possessed, in which case he usually abandons elements of his first culture in favor of the adopted culture pattern. Less frequently it refers to the process of a culture itself undergoing change.

†Statement of Arnold Toynbee in New York City during his 1967-1968 visit to the United States.

more uniformly practiced than any of the cultures existent and active in the country at the present time.

To attain complete mastery of the total American culture would be impossible for any one person. Each person possesses only a portion of an existent culture. The combination that is internalized by each individual is the absorption from his particular life experiencing, whether it be learned from one or from multiple cultures. It has been secured from parents, relatives, playmates, neighbors, peers, teachers, street and social observations and perceptions. The culture acquired by an individual in large measure affects the operative abilities he will activate. It might be said that giving a human being a culture is about like superimposing an invisible aura about him that serves as a persuasive agent to operate within generally preestablished formats. An ability to initiate, to explore beyond the format, may or may not be one of the characteristics of the internalized culture. Among migrant peoples this ability is characteristically at a low level. Necessarily, the learning, whether formal or informal, has come from within the scope of the life in which the individual has existed. Migrants reared in limited cultural environments learn only that which their environments offer. The ability to observe and to question that which is seen outside of their immediate surroundings may not be developed because their culture does not allow them to explore and question.

Role of the Teacher

Recognition must be given to the degree and type of culture possessed by the teacher himself. To teach effectively one must: (1) have awareness of the meaning of the term "culture"; (2) be aware of the varied characteristics of the major and minority cultures exhibited by his pupils; and (3) possess a reasonably accurate understanding of his own culture. The latter is essential for understanding the contrasts of one's own enrichments, limitations, and possible biases when identifying and appraising the culture-possessions of the pupil. In adjudging another person's culture, a teacher might simply compare that person's characteristics to his own without true identification or proper analysis.

Knowing how to observe and determine the culture status of a child is one of the most valuable abilities of a teacher. Through observation of a child's activities an appraisal can be made of his active value system and his culture-influenced patterns of behavior. An analysis can indicate those areas in which there is need for complete learning and those areas where adjustments and changes in behavioral forms can improve the child's performance.

Superficial knowledge of isolated culture patterns is not enough to be wholly effective with insufficiently culturated children. The knowledges and observation powers must be adequate to produce functional understanding for creating a proper remedial learning program.

What is Culture?

Since Edward B. Tyler's initial defining of culture in 1872, there have been hundreds of definitions. An attempt to transmit the complete meaning of such a complex in a few sentences risks serious oversimplification. One must develop the idea of culture to understand the totality of the semantic. Let us begin the exploration with Tyler's definition: "Culture is that complex whole which includes knowledge, belief, art, morals, law, custom, and other capabilities acquired by man as a member of society."

Culture includes all that is man-created. "Man-created" is not the same as man-made. Man creates the ideas, the patterns, the disciplines, values, and standards, the institutional forms that become the central guides for lifeways in a society. He created formulas for utilization in common everyday practices as well as for many less frequent activities. Examples of these ideas and forms are the common handshake for use in greeting and seating arrangements for diplomats at an international conference.

Man facilitates his work and play by following already established "rules of the game," thus alleviating a need for new decisions on "how to do" each time he enters into a different situation. The culture has preestablished the how, so the decision may be simplified to merely choosing the form and variation to use. Again the handshake in example: between two men the form to select may be a full, firm grasp with barely a movement of the hand; between male and female, in a given circumstance, the most acceptable form may be for the female to offer her hand first and the male to respond by a relatively light grasp and movement of the hand.

Differentiation between culture and the products of culture (artifacts) may serve in delineating and defining the *idea* of culture. In creating an automobile formulas are established for building the parts, assembling them, and utilizing the product. The completed automobile is a product of culture. The elements in the manufacture and in the utilization that have become part of the American culture are the formulas for making the steel, the glass, the tires, the instructions for assembly, and the ways for operating and utilizing the completed machine. The machine, unrelated to man's control, cannot perform cultural activities. As an artifact of culture, man puts it to purposeful use. It is the use forms, created and activated by man, that become part of the culture.

Use forms include "drive on the right side" as a standard culture pattern in the United States. When one is driving the auto on the right side of a road, this culture pattern is in active state. When there are no cars on the road, the "pattern" is inactive and unseen but the "drive on the right" culture still exists and man has ready access to it. When the car with man's guidance is activated on the right side, the culture exhibited is the man-guided activity pattern; the automobile is an auxiliary agent.

Culture is a huge concept. As it must be learned by each new generation, the school's task of choosing which portions should be formally taught is an awe-inspiring challenge.

Return to Acquisition of Culture

It is generally accepted that an influential sector of a person's culture is learned in early childhood. This suggests that much of culture learning in this period is acquired by nonconscious learning. There is little freedom of choice on the child's part. The type of culture in which he exists is the determinant of that portion of personality development that can be attributed to cultural conditioning. In later youth and adult years, when ability to exercise freedom of choice is more prevalent, the individual attempting to acculturate—to abandon certain influential fixations and replace them with others—may find the new type of performance feels artificial or unnatural. He may tend to revert to his "natural" way of doing. His "natural" way may be simply the way of his first cultural learning.

Culture is the chief external influencer of an individual's personality. The manner of dressing, the type of individual and group activities, forms for interpersonal relationships, the creation and utilization of artifacts, and the objectives, philosophies, and values that constitute the standards for decision-making are derived from a culture.

A person is both fettered and freed by his culture. The limitations are due to the following of acceptable patterns, rather than initiating a new way of doing. The established patterns, while limiting the individual for a general good, may simultaneously be allowing great freedom. Greater individual liberty and freedom of choice is available in a more affluent and advanced culture simply because there are more numerous alternatives and variables from which to choose. Important to the exercise of the freedom-of-choice principle is teaching the child how to choose between the alternatives and variables of an enriched culture.

The migrant child is cultured. Out of whatever type of environment he comes to school, at whatever age, he already has acquired culture. His culture though may be partial, outmoded, imbalanced, or overweighted with elements of negative variables.

Geographic Origin

From whence comes the migrant child? Knowing the geographic location of origin can be an initial indicator of the affective culture of the child. The home bases of agricultural migrant workers are spread from coast to coast. A worker may come from a small subsistence tract in New Mexico, Colorado, Arkansas, or another state (14). He may be a resident of a border county of Texas or of one of the larger cities of that state. He may be a semitransient, claiming Florida or California as "home." He may have come from an uprooted sharecropper family or from a poor area of a small town. His ethnic culture background may be of the Spanish-

American of the Upper Rio Grande Valley or Mexican-American of the Lower Valley, Anglo-American from the mid-Mississippi region, Black-American from the southeastern states, or Indian-American from the Southwest. The ethnic culture background of the migrant family and child can be an indicator of the child's cultural heritage and conditioning.

The child may or may not go "on the road" with father, parents, or a family group. There may be some influences from "migrant mores" in his conditioning. The traits attributable to agricultural migrancy, however, may be of relatively recent origin and possibly cannot be reasonably separated as "migrant traits."

A few decades ago, there may have been proportionately more year-round transients in migrant work than there are today. Possibly the most itinerant group of migrant families of the present period are members of the East Coast migrant stream who winter and work the November-December to April-May period out of Florida migrant labor camps. The location of a camp, such as Belle Glade, is considered by some to be home base. These are the people who might be the most influenced by any elements of culture that could be attributed to migrancy. From this location the on-the-road season may take a family to one or several locations from Virginia to New York to a midwestern state. Some people of the West Coast stream move up and down the coast without an apparent home base. Most of today's migrant families, however, do have a "home." The home and origin environment are important as clues to the foundational operant conditioning of the child.

Dominant Versus Subculture

No person is expected to acquire all of the characteristics of his culture. In a population as large and pluralistic as that within the contiguous states, there are many subcultures. Throughout the population there exist patterns that, with minor variations, tend to constitute the dominant or the general American culture most activated throughout the whole population. No subgroups operate in complete isolation from dominant culture influences.

It is reasonable to suggest that there is not a distinct single migrant culture. There are cultural characteristics developed to cope with the mobility and other requirements of migrancy. But, these, as in urban or rural cultures, are, in a sense, superimposed upon the basic culture practices.

Experienced teachers of migrant pupils tend to first identify the basic culture of the child to know him well. It can be noted, too, that these teachers first and foremost accept the child as a child, thus establishing a conceptual basis that is soundly psychoanalytical.

Cultural traits are directors of thought and actions and even though internalized to become forceful motivators, they should remain under the conscious control of the individual. Culture is learned. Its elements can be reinforced or forgotten.

Role of the School

Whether the school does or does not deliberately accept responsibility for the teaching of "Culture," it does have that responsibility because, ipso facto, Culture is what it is teaching. A key to more successful culturation education is in the school's awareness of its real responsibility for creating opportunity for learning those portions of the culture that society assigns to it.

Do the skill and factual knowledge subjects, e.g., reading, arithmetic, history, comprise the means to education, or is there equal responsibility to aid the child in developing a value system and the forms of behavior common to the society? Will the pupil use the skill of reading for continued positive expansion of himself? The dichotomy of responsibility that has been created in the country's history is that the American family has retained the right to teach a child what to believe; it has delegated to the school a responsibility to teach skills and facts. Skills and facts, too, are ingredients of culture.

Major sources of learning are the teacher, from whom the child learns not only facts and skills but also beliefs, values, personal biases, and culture forms, and the family and peer group, which may transmit high quality or inadequate, poor quality, or extremely limited beliefs and mores to the young. If there is conflict or voids in the necessary learning, how then is the dilemma to be resolved for the greater benefit of the child? If the principle of separation is to be retained in our political culture, would it be logical to assume that a practice beneficial to the child would be a maximum exposure to the broad spectrum of culture as a reasonable preparation to his ultimate freedom of choice? Is the school an agency that should offer a complete exposure to learning opportunity, including the development of ability to examine beliefs?

Are migrant peoples the "disadvantaged"? In terms of contrast to the total population, many must be considered as insufficiently culturated. Underculturation may be due to lack of education in the dominant culture, or to possession of a subgroup culture that does not sufficiently meet requirements for productive performance.

The child, disadvantaged by either limitation, can be offered an expansive education effectively in the school facility. There must be reasonable recognition of what may be given to the child and what may be taken away if the curricula are formulated solely in a single culture. The school aim should be the preparation of an individual with abilities to perform at the level of his capabilities.

Cultural Transition

More rapid change is occurring in subcultures during this contemporary period than perhaps any other time of American history. A culture, such as the Spanish-American which was historically centered in the upper Rio Grande valley, is in continuous process of change. This Spanish-American culture was heterogeneously developed by adopting and adapting from Spanish, Mexican, and American Indian ways. The purpose of this culture was to sustain a people in low level subsistence in a locale far removed from the original source of economic and spiritual support.

Its values were adoptions and adaptions molded into a foundational value system, influenced by Western ecclesiastics, intended to pragmatically meet the needs of the rigorous realities of the place and times. Beginning a century and a quarter ago the Anglo-American forms impinged their influences into the isolated culture. Adjustments of the indigenous culture format were necessary to survival in the new Anglo association. Today, this Rio Grande culture possesses wide variations from community to community as its people adjust it to meet the needs of the intercultural relations over wider geographic areas.

In the process of a people undergoing cultural transfer, perhaps the most laggard element in a changing culture is its basic value system. Values are deep-rooted and constitute the conscience of a people. History has shown that in one life span single individuals can be quite completely acculturated, abandoning one culture and becoming operative in another. The time period usually extends over several generations for all members of a group to acculturate and identify well with another culture. The continued influence of the first culture, however decreasing, may be due to the carrying forward of first-culture values and their application to foreign culture forms. The more divergent are the values of the first culture from the values of the second, the greater the difficulty in acculturating.

During the period of cultural transition, people can become disoriented and undergo social instability due to either the lack of knowledge of the second culture forms or to application of the former irrelevant values. There are large segments of the migrant peoples at such stage of cultural disorganization. When both a culture and its people are in transitory state, the process of acculturation may be slowed considerably. Migrants of the Latin and Indian groups are perhaps the most affected by the phenomenon of changes in their historic cultures.

The Value Orientations

Humans have certain types of basic problems to meet and resolve wherever they live. A society creates its culture forms to meet these problems. There seems to be a set of foundational value orientations common to all cultures (6). These tend to serve as a framework upon which cultures are built. Conversely they may

serve the teacher as guides for identification of cultural characteristics possessed by children.

Florence Kluckhohn's definition of value orientations is clearly
stated: "Value orientations may be defined as evaluative principles
inclusive of both cognitive and affective elements which give order
and direction to human acts and thoughts in the solution of common human problems" (6, p. 1).

These orientations identify the major and necessary areas of
human concern to maintain a way of life. Dr. Kluckhohn suggests
that a society develops its culture forms for meeting these problems. To allow for deviant circumstances, it allows variable ranges
of the forms within which the society may operate. The variables
are controlled in both range and preference. In that manner, there
is developed a "rank ordering" of acceptability, with some practices more preferred, some accepted, and some less preferred to a
point of nontoleration. The degree of preference is determined by
judging the variable of the form with the objectives and values of
the culture.

Value orientations are not "values." They are a framework for
identification of the broad areas of human activities and for the
value systems that are developed for quality control of the activity
behaviors.

Utilizing value orientations as reference controls, a teacher may
construct a profile of a child's culture traits. Dr. Kluckhohn suggests these basic orientations: Human Nature; Man-Nature; Time;
Activity; Relational; Space.

Human Nature

The nature of Man is postulated on a range from evil, through a
mixture of good and evil, to good. Herein, the concern is for the
identifiable nature of a cultured human, rather than the philo-
sophic concern of the basic nature of Man. The teacher would try
to identify the conception of selfhood exhibited by the child. His
conception of self would tend to show the acceptances about
Man's nature upon which he operates. Are these conceptions internalized, thus strong controls, or are they superficial and con-
sciously controlled for accomplishment of immediate objectives?
The goal of observation is the identification of the child's opera-
tional values as related to self and to others.

Man-Nature

The range in a child's activities and expressed thoughts as they relate to his association with Nature (and Deity) can indicate whether his practices, attitudes, and values are in subjugation to Nature, in harmony with Nature, or directed toward mastery over Nature. These characteristics are identifiable in culture group activities that will often serve to illuminate the preferences of the individual.

A culture that submits placidly to Nature's ways tends to subjugate its activities to the will of Nature; one that attempts to adjust its practices to fit into the ways of Nature tends to harmony; but one that has intent to dominate or to change Nature for its own purposes attempts mastery. The following paragraphs describe cultures with each of the three orientations.

An early Rio Grande family planted a garden and "trusted in faith" for moisture and nutrients to promote growth. Drought persisted, the beans for winter food supply withered, the attitude toward resultant shortage of food was one of resignation. The shortage was considered a circumstance beyond their control.

The American Indian cultures, in the main, lived with practices in harmony with Nature. Animals were killed only according to need, all parts were utilized, lifeways were adjusted to the routines of Nature.

The dominant American culture places a first emphasis upon the mastery over Nature orientation. Changing the natural face of the earth by controlled crop production, covering vast areas with concrete and structures to satisfy needs, tunneling beneath rivers and through mountains indicate effort by man to gain control.

Time

The range of choices in time to which a culture may orient is over the past, the present, the future. As with other orientations there may be combinations and variables in application. The dominant middle American culture is primarily future oriented as shown by the promotion of desire for life preparation through education, planning and building for a better tomorrow. A present orientation suggests emphasis upon living for today, and a past orientation tends to revere, venerate, and duplicate from ancestry.

Activity

The modality of activity orientations suggests the creation of patterns that I have designated as Being, Being-in-Becoming, and Doing. The acceptances of a culture tend to promote the degree of action in first, second, and third priority. The concept of a sleeping Mexican undoubtedly originated out of the view that he was, in the main, influenced by the Being orientation. There remains in Latin cultures an emphasis upon what a person is, rather than what he does. Generally the culture orientation of the United States is Doing, thus, the hustle and bustle of constant activity throughout the society, and the oft heard question "What does he *do?*"

Relational

The relationship of man to man is shown in a culture's method of identifying individuals with the type of roles assigned to them. The father's brother becomes uncle to his brother's children. The father's responsibilities are defined in respect to relationship with his wife, mother, children, business associates, friends, and acquaintances. To reinforce established patterns, a society frequently imposes its expectations by writing them into law. The gregarious nature of man is regulated by the acceptability of the relationship variables.

Lineality is the practice of giving first preference to the members of the family line. Collaterality is associative emphasis upon those who parallel or are in some way side by side with a person or a group. Individualism places emphases of activity and role in the person and suggests importance of the single individual.

Space

The modes for allotting and utilizing geographic space are necessary to harmonious living. The practices for allotting space to a family for establishing a home is one space orientation of a culture. Space utilization can be a significant indicator of a family's cultural status. Migrants relate to space in a way somewhat similar to nomadic tribes by seeking subsistence where it can be found over an extended spatial area. Modern advanced cultures are now extending the space utilization concept into the air and beyond.

These six value orientations may offer a basic organization for a pragmatic analysis of a child's culture. In each of the orientation areas, man develops forms to accomplish his objectives. Values or standards are created as controls against which to measure activated performance. A portion of the range of standards becomes the desirable value scale, a middle portion would be acceptable or tolerated, and some portion would not be tolerated.

Migrant Child, School, Teacher, Society

Knowing the migrant child is an absolute essential to determination of the content and methods for his education. First and foremost, he is a child, so innate individual differences must be recognized. Like all children he must learn the arts of cultured living. Like all children he has existed and learned the ways of life—the knowings—that have been available in his environment. Every societal environment possesses its limitations for behavioral learning. Every environment has its own cultural richness and poverty. Paucity is a symbol of migrant environments.

An important factor with the migrant child is the types of limitations that have conditioned him in a too narrow sense and possibly limited his opportunity to create a questioning and exploratory intellect that would permit expansion through his own observations. He is a product of cultural influences that are characterized by their paucity and often by their outdated characteristics. His environmental education has produced two major areas of deficiencies. One area includes the limitations in quantity and quality of knowledge and the other the incentive to initiate his ability to perceive and reason.

The two generalizations about the migrant child's conditioning are critical for recognition by the school: the culture possessed by the child and the child's cognitive ability to see and recognize the unfamiliar beyond his own culture. About his cultural knowings, a responsibility exists to identify three things: (1) his knowings and skills that are "affirmative" in the sense of being true and within the variables of the culture's acceptance; (2) his knowings that are not true or not within the acceptable range of the culture; and (3) the skills and knowings (including behavior forms and values) that are not possessed but deemed desirable at a particular age or grade. Possibly, of the three, the most difficult for the school are those in the second group.

The teacher and auxiliary personnel are the agents of the school who must do the analyses and execute the programs. To be effective they must possess adequate understanding and have clear-cut directives for the school's objectives and purposes. Currently in American education, there is neither a clarity or in-depth definition of objectives and purposes to properly support the teachers' role with culturally disadvantaged children (13).

The school, as an institution, has great responsibility for certain determinants that are absolutely necessary for fulfilling its mission to the migrant child. It should restudy and determine what its responsibility ought to be in respect to transmission of beliefs. Generally, in contemporary nonparochial schools, there is passive toleration of programs that neither accept or reject the laissez-faire principle. The reality is that the teacher is a source, as well as an instrument, for belief transmission. There is much nondeliberate transfer of teacher-accepted beliefs. Does the method of passing a child around among teachers of innumerable and variant beliefs do the job of educating the child with self-determination abilities? The answer must be a loose no. Belief transfer is undoubtedly taking place, but there may be no development of the ability to accept or reject beliefs through an intellectual process actuated by the individual.

Cultural renewal requires transfer of its knowings and its patterns. But for positive change for good in the culture itself or within individuals, the people must possess intelligent abilities and processes for creating change. The migrant child needs the ability as a motivational force in creating change within himself, even though his readiness for growth may be only within his preestablished cultural limits. The predication that the individual creates the culture, activates it sociologically, and thus controls the format destiny of the ultimate group culture, dictates a need for possession of self-determination ability that can be activated within an acceptable cultural framework.

To fulfill the obligation to teach the society's culture, the school personnel must have an understanding of the meaning of culture. What is it, really? Begin by thinking of cultural patterns, forms, and ideas not as behavior but, rather, as the format or the pattern of the behavior. Lift it away from activated behavior. There it is; it cannot be seen, but somewhat like the harness hanging above the horses in a 1900 unlighted fire station, it is ready to be instantly put into a proper place and activated. The patterns are stored in men's minds, whether the pattern is the simple one of raising the hand in greeting or the complex one of getting into a spaceship for a trip to the moon; whether the intricacies of reading and writing or the manner of buying a ticket to get into a movie house. Mastery of the skill elements of a culture, as reading and writing, is acquisition of only segments of a culture. Without activation of other parts of culture, one element may be relatively useless. Reading is considered a useful skill because it is a tool for learning. If one does not activate the reading skill, it is useless to the learning process. A key then to motivating a desire to use the skill is development of the individual's ability to "see" and understand the desirableness of the rewards in reading.

Beyond the teaching of the skills, to which much effort is given by the school, what facts should be taught? Is the teaching of the organized mechanics of the language as important for lifetime use as teaching the cultural semantic of the sound symbols that are the language? To what extent is the school responsible for teaching the child the social behavior forms of its culture?

These matters and questions are raised here primarily to call attention to what is and is not done today and to reidentify some of society's responsibilities to its schools, so the teacher may know the expectancies of his role and the authority for fulfilling them.

The migrant child is classified as "disadvantaged." What constitutes his disadvantagement? What is "advantage"? What, then, is needed to put him in the advantaged group?

As used repeatedly, and often glibly, the inference is that any or all of the following may be observable in a disadvantaged child:

Characteristics that identify with a subculture that differs in values or behavioral forms from those of the dominant or the school's culture.

Insufficient understanding of any language.

Very limited knowledge of the world.

A store of negative knowledge that may be a liability. Some pseudo-knowledge acquired from his folklore society.

A distinctive, low ceiling appreciative sense, due to lack of understanding quality and numerical variation of worldly elements about him. A
value system incomplete in its orientations and scaled to relatively low
quality standards.

Not inability to learn but disinterest in learning what the society feels
he should learn.

The migrant child can be different from disadvantaged children
of other environments. The nature of the location of the influencing lifeways may have offered opportunity for significantly different learnings. A poverty tenement environment in a large metropolitan city, with its masses of people, noises, and urban visuals,
may vary greatly from a rural oriented, village poverty where individual association is paramount to group socialization and non-
identity. The structure of buildings, traffic conditions, relationship
to nature, contents of store windows, and observance of classes
and types of people may be at great variance. The migrant child
hears and sees about vegetable crops or attains experiences while
working in fields or gleaning food for the family after the harvesters have passed. "Big city" may have no meaning at all to the
migrant child. His folkways may be unsuited to necessities in a
society beyond his own group.

The amalgam of ideas is the matrix of human activity. One form
or another of communication is essential in activating culture.
There are many forms for communication and symbols are the
basis of most forms.

The cultural semantic of words, terms, and ideas must be taught
with multiple media. Words are man-created symbols—artifi-
cialities invented to represent ideas, products, and facts. To attempt explanation of the meaning of an abstract symbol with
other still poorly understood word symbols may result in a confusion of understanding. Time and repetition may be useful as
tools in teaching, but the repetition may be strengthening a fixa-
tion of half-understanding rather than whole understanding.

Caution is required in the use of the migrant child's experiencing to teach or reinforce truths on the basis of what he has seen.
The observation of what has been seen may be so distorted in the
child's representation that repetition serves only to fix part-truths.

One teacher utilized pictures, maps, diagrams, and verbalization to ascertain how many of her fifteen children had "seen" a famous, and huge, mountain when they had ridden by it. None was aware of the spectacle. The order of business with migrant children, from the beginning to the end of their school experience is to help them learn. Learning includes seeing the actuality as it is. It includes hearing the sound and understanding the symbol that is its representation in language. It is likely that the question with migrant children is not just how they learn, but also how in the learning process, they relate new facts to that knowledge and acceptance already possessed.

Summary

To create an effective educative process for migrant children, there must be special consideration of certain elements to compensate for the differences possessed by the children. The differences must be identified in each child.

Decision is mandatory on developing policy concerning the aims and purposes of acculturation versus enculturation versus culturation. Acculturation would tend to attempt the influencing of migrant children into society's dominant cultural mold, enculturation would tend to strengthen each of the respective cultures, and culturation, properly executed, would strengthen the ability of the individual to be selective of facets of his culture, therefore producing societal members able to maintain continuous renewal and vitality in the general culture.

The prime responsibility for the undercultured child rests with the society as the controller of the school's purposes. Default in this responsibility results in eclectic productivity in education programs, too often with unpredictable results in the child. Definitively expressed aims would enable the professional teaching representatives of the society to better tailor learning programs to each child, that he might evolve into an individual possessing the characteristics to create a society of continuing productivity, growth, renewal, and vitality.

The migrant child is a child. In his preparation for adulthood, it is necessary to know the characteristics of the mold in which he has been cast and the characteristics of the mold that is good for him. His educative process must allow for both undoing and doing. The crucible is how well the educative process is fitted to him.

References

1. Anderson, James G., and Johnson, William H. *Sociocultural Determinates of Achievement Among Mexican American Students.* Las Cruces: ERIC/CRESS,* 1968.

2. Angel, Frank. *Program Content to Meet the Educational Needs of Mexican-Americans.* Las Cruces, New Mexico: ERIC/CRESS, 1968.

3. Brown, Ina Corinne. *Understanding Other Cultures.* Englewood Cliffs, New Jersey: Prentice-Hall, 1963.

4. Gardner, John W. *Renewal in Societies and Men.* New York: Carnegie Corporation of New York, 1962.

5. Gromatsky, Irene. *Consumer Education for Mexican-Americans.* Las Cruces, New Mexico: ERIC/CRESS, 1968.

6. Kluckhohn, Florence Rockwood. *A Classification of Value Orientations.* Cambridge: Harvard University (An Occasional Paper), 1962.

7. Kneller, George F. *Educational Anthropology: An Introduction.* New York: John Wiley & Sons (paperback), 1965.

8. Landes, Ruth. *Culture in American Education: Anthropological Approaches to Minority and Dominant Groups in the Schools.* New York: John Wiley & Sons, 1965.

9. Los Angeles City Schools. *The Teaching of Values.* Los Angeles: Los Angeles City Schools, 1966.

10. Madsen, William. *The Mexican-American of South Texas.* New York: Holt, Rinehart & Winston, 1964.

11. Potts, Alfred M., and Sherman, Neil. *Learning on the Move.* Denver: Colorado Department of Education, 1961.

*ERIC/CRESS is an acronym for Educational Resources Information Center, a United States Office of Education system for storage and retrieval of recent educational literature. CRESS is a symbol of one ERIC unit—Clearinghouse on Rural Education and Small Schools. ERIC facilities may be utilized at any of the numerous depositories in the United States. The facility offers access to recent research reports, ERIC-prepared reports, and other valuable literature.

12. Potts, Alfred M. *Providing Opportunities for Disadvantaged Children.* Denver: Colorado Department of Education, 1964.

13. President's Commission on National Goals. *Goals for Americans.* Englewood Cliffs, New Jersey: Prentice-Hall (Spectrum paperback), 1960.

14. Segalman, Ralph. *Army of Despair.* Washington: Educational Systems Corporation, 1968.

15. Smith, Marguerite. *English as a Second Language for Mexican Americans.* Las Cruces, New Mexico: ERIC/CRESS, 1968.

16. Strodtbeck, Fred L., et al. *Variations in Value Orientations.* Evanston: Row, Peterson and Company, 1961.

17. Ulibarri, Horacio. *Educational Needs of the Mexican American.* Las Cruces: ERIC/CRESS, 1968.

18. Wilson, Herbert B. *Evaluation of the Influence of Educational Programs on Mexican-Americans.* Las Cruces, New Mexico: ERIC/CRESS, 1968.

19. Zintz, Miles V. *Education Across Cultures.* Dubuque: Wm. C. Brown Book Co., 1963.

CHAPTER 4

Health Problems Among Migrants

E. L. MATTA, JR.

Dr. Matta discusses the Migrant Health Services in Dade County, Florida, as background for what is and can be offered in other parts of the country. He then discusses the specific health problems these migrant children bring to school which can have a dilatory effect on their learning capability.

Dr. E. L. Matta, Jr., is state director for Maternal and Child Health in Puerto Rico and is on the staff of the Medical School and the School of Preventive Medicine of the University of Puerto Rico. He is closely aware of the health problems of migrants through his research and specialities of pediatrics and public health in the South Florida area. His teaching appointments have included New York Medical College and the University of Miami School of Medicine. He received his M.D. from Jefferson Medical College, Philadelphia, Pennsylvania.

ANY DISCUSSION of the health of the migrant farm worker must consider the meaning of health as defined by the World Health Organization—"a state of physical, emotional, and social well being"; the role of this minority group in our national, state, and local communities (1, 14, 20, 23); and the migrant agricultural worker as a member of a unique nomadic culture in our land.

The role of the nomadic farm worker in our nation has been established in our society by the fruit and vegetable industry. The ability to choose fruits and vegetables wisely, judge their quality, and direct their careful handling requires the expertise of an especially developed individual. Self-training from childhood and possible anatomicophysiologic adaptation to the bent-over position required for grueling, continual hours of work, help to mold this worker and enhance his efficiency.

The realization of the development of a unique migrant agricultural culture in our society is only now being accepted, studied, and nurtured intelligently. Up to now all efforts were directed toward conformity of the migrant family to our established, orderly, and lawful ways of life. The attempt at fitting a square peg in a round hole has been ineffective. Once we accept without reservations the presence of this special culture in our midst and its role in our agricultural and food industry, it is much easier to provide guidelines for health, education, welfare, and social services (4, 5, 13, 25). Of these four, education has led the way in the organization and implementation of school programs adapted to the migrant age child (7, 8).

Health services have been developed in many areas (2, 3, 9, 11, 18, 19, 22). In Dade County, Florida, the Dade County Department of Public Health has organized and established a special health service for the migrant agricultural family, which complements already existing health programs.

Welfare and social services are mostly undeveloped, limited, and fragmented. American communities are aware of the presence of migrant agricultural workers and usually rate them in the lowest scale of the social framework, on a par with gypsies and vagrants. Many of the agricultural communities realize the need for migrant workers and accept their role, but with a split personality type of understanding: "We are here, they come and go. What is good for our resident citizens is not necessarily available for these transient residents." Understanding, acceptance, and plain Christian charity are the cornerstones upon which a community must structure sound welfare and social programs.

Since health is a state of physical, emotional, and social well-being, the migrant agricultural worker must be provided for in all of these areas. Provision for health and education alone will not suffice. Welfare benefits and social services must be extended to these families by every community where they temporarily reside as they travel throughout the land.

A brief discussion of the characteristics of the migrant household will serve as reference background for the discussion of migrant health services and the health problems encountered. Studies show the migrant households to be quite large, averaging 3.8 persons per household with 7.1 percent consisting of 10 or more persons; 13.3 percent being single person households (13). A matriarchal type of home organization is found in many of the Negro migrant households. As to marital status, a study of 880 adult Negro farm workers showed 74.4 percent to be married, 13.9 percent single, 7.7 percent separated, and 3.5 percent widowed. These marriages may or may not be legalized, but the family groups are acceptable and functional. The Tex-Mexican and the Puerto Rican migrants are for the most part legally married. The male, be he father, uncle, or grandfather, is the head of the family or clan. He directs and controls the family affairs. Earl Koos identified the existence of two general types of families which he termed "stable" and "unstable" (13). The family members of the former were industrious, conscientious, conservative, and well fed. They practiced good personal hygiene, had their children in school, and attended church as frequently as possible. The family members of the second group were the opposite as to each characteristic. Over one-half (53.4 percent) of all the households were classified as "unstable." Multiperson households, with a matriarchal head, were the most "stable." The least "stable" were those without children.

Migrant Health Services in Dade County, Florida

For several years the Dade County Department of Public Health developed a comprehensive health service care program for the migrant farm workers in Dade County through a special grant by the Migrant Health Branch of the United States Public Health Service (16). It has provided for the health needs of the migrant population that begins arriving in Dade County in September, reaches its zenith with the peak of the season in January and February, and declines toward the summer. The primary objective of this project is to provide a comprehensive and coordinated program of clinical, nursing, and sanitation services to migrant farm workers and their dependents in Dade County.

Contributory and secondary objectives include the following:

1. Determination of the health needs of agricultural migrants in this area.

2. Meeting these needs with existing community resources when possible and filling some of the remaining unmet needs through services provided by this project.

3. Identification of other factors that affect health services for agricultural migrant workers in Dade County.

4. Establishment of standardized records and procedures to facilitate follow-up care through improved interstate and intrastate cooperation and communication.

5. Publication of results that may be deemed useful elsewhere.

6. Affording training opportunities for persons interested in the development of similar activities in other areas.

At present, such programs as the one next described are in existence in other counties throughout the nation. They are fragmentary and depend mostly on local community leadership in health, education, and welfare. Such programs require greater coordination and greater emphasis on continuity of medical care, regardless of where the migrant moves, before they can be truly effective and successful.

Medical and Dental Services

The staff of the Migrant Health Program consists of a director, one full-time medical director, one part-time dentist, one coordinator, one nursing supervisor, four staff nurses, and a clerk.

Family health service field clinics provide medical services in four locations. Two of these are in large migrant camps and two are in areas near large concentrations of migrant housing. Afternoon and evening clinics are held in all these centers. Immunization clinics are held at the end of the afternoon clinics, two sessions per month.

The migrant dental clinic is held two nights each week. This clinic is plagued by broken appointments, but by scheduling more patients than can be conveniently cared for, the dentist is kept busy.

Hospital Care

In addition to migrant family clinics, the Migrant Health Program has contracts with hospitals to see patients on an outpatient basis. Patients referred to one of these hospitals are those who need X-rays or more extensive laboratory testing than the program is equipped to do, or those who require hospitalization. One hundred and seventy-eight such referrals were made, or about 3.7 percent of the total attendance at the clinic sessions. This indicates that the provision of adequate field outpatient services to migrants can effectively reduce the number of hospital referrals and therefore the cost of medical care. As in other health programs, the medical care services located nearer to the home of the patient are definitely more effective and less costly. The patient is enabled to get treatment during the initial stage of an illness when it is most beneficial, and can get well much more rapidly than if he were critically ill. Failure of communities to establish such decentralized clinic services near the migrant camps can only result in a less effective program.

Other Health Programs

Regular maternal and child health services are available for migrant pregnant females and their children. In the Dade County area the Head Start program provided medical and dental screening services for the migrant children enrolled in such programs. The Maternity and Infant Care Project No. 515 (Children's Bureau) provides for comprehensive health care (prenatal, postnatal delivery, family planning) and consultation for mothers and infants during the first year of life. It includes outpatient hospitalization as required. Subsequent services are continued under supervision of the Migrant Health Program physician in the project clinic and by the public health nurses in the migrants' homes.

Another program providing comprehensive health services to migrant children under seven is the Children and Youth Project No. 636 (Children's Bureau). This project covers 99 percent of the migrant area. It provides for outpatient consultation and hospitalization as required. It will be able to provide for the comprehensive health care of the migrant children in the South Dade area.

As part of the tuberculosis control program of the Department of Health an annual X-ray survey was conducted with a mobile unit visiting twenty-two camps and several communities in South Dade. Three of seventeen new cases of tuberculosis were found in one family; one older case was discovered.

Nursing

The nursing staff of the Migrant Health Program consists of a supervisor and four public health nurses. This staff is supplemented by 18 public health nurses from the general health program who devote varying amounts of their time in providing services to the migrant families and the migrant school children. More than 40 home visits were made by a community health worker for the purpose of making repeat appointments.

The public health nurses made 2,908 home visits to migrant families, serving a total of 1,027 households. The largest number (1,426) were made on behalf of child health supervision. The next greatest number (945) were made on behalf of maternity and family planning. Visits on behalf of tuberculosis accounted for 227 of the total, and 280 home visits were made to acutely or chronically ill persons. Many of these were to follow-up on persons treated in the migrant family clinics. Three of the project nurses are assigned to large labor camps and to the family clinics which serve these camps. This has made for excellent continuity of medical care.

In addition to home visiting, the public health nurses visit regularly the schools and day care centers for migrant children. Problems discovered are referred to migrant clinics, regular Health Department clinics, or for follow-up in their homes. Each public health nurse acts as a health educator. The Health Department nutritionists contributed their services and skills to the program.

Sanitation

Sanitation services are provided by one sanitarian on a full-time basis, and two others on a part-time basis. Condition of camp housing is considered from acceptable up to very good. All houses must be weathertight to be approved. Many of these are frame houses with some form of composition siding such as composition-covered paper, composition shingles, or weatherboarding; others are cement block. All living units must be within 200 feet of flush toilets, hot and cold water, and facilities for washing clothes. All central facilities are so located that very few living units are as far away as 200 feet. Cold water outlets are available from 5 to 25 feet from each living unit. Sanitarians investigate sanitation complaints in any area.

All applications for permits to operate these camps must be approved by the Florida State Board of Health. There has been a continued decrease in the number of labor camps approved. This is due in part to the Health Department's continued pressure on operators to upgrade their facilities. This often results in many of the workers living in overcrowded private housing. In the state of Florida private housing is the responsibility of the Florida Hotel and Restaurant Commission and other housing authorities.

All plumbing facilities have modern pressure water systems and flush toilets. Two of the larger camps have municipal type sewage systems. All other camps have septic tanks. Garbage is kept in approved garbage cans and collected two or three times per week. Refrigeration has been a difficult problem due to the unwillingness of the migrant families to share facilities.

Food handling practices are from poor to excellent. They are usually good to excellent where there are no family groups, but it is almost impossible to get the family groups to use the facilities especially provided for the preparation of food. All house openings are well-screened at the start of the season, but many of the occupants either break the screens out or prop the doors and windows open.

There has been a strong educational campaign to convince growers and crew leaders to provide chemical toilets convenient to all workers in the fields. There is still much to be desired in providing handwashing facilities for food handlers. An adequate supply of portable water is available to all crews while working in the fields.

Health Education

Individual counseling by all of the public health nurses, sanitarians, and other staff personnel associated with the project continued to be the major educational program. Working under the guidance of the director of the Health Education Division of the Health Department, officials of the Community Action Program and the local Office of Economic Opportunity have continued their work along these lines with films and literature provided by the Health Education Division.

Health Problems

The migrant season in Dade County can be considered to last

nearly six months, November through April. Migrant families with children start to move into the agricultural area of South Dade early in September; by the end of May they have left for other regions. During the season the four migrant clinics are open, staffed, and equipped to provide services. All four are fixed clinics in or near the larger camps. There are no mobile clinic units. There are three afternoon sessions and four evening sessions. This day and evening service seems to fit into the migrant work patterns. These four diagnostic and treatment clinics are supplemented by services provided at two health centers and one dental clinic in the area. These latter facilities provide for more sophisticated medical evaluation, diagnosis, and treatment for pregnant females, infants, preschoolers, and schoolers, as well as treatment for such specific diseases as venereal disease and tuberculosis. Immunizations are provided at the health centers. The third link in this chain of medical care is composed of two public and three private hospitals, one of which is a children's hospital. These hospitals provide twenty-four hour coverage for emergencies and acute illness, and inpatient hospitalization if required. This triad of special migrant clinics, public health preventive and curative services, and hospital specialized services is essential in the provision of good medical care for migrant workers and their families. There is also a special ingredient inherent in the provision of adequate health services: the knowledge, experience, and professional interest of the physicians providing the medical care. This is the decisive factor as to the quality of care provided.

Specific medical conditions reported for a selected migrant season are discussed next. The total peak occupancy during this season was 5,780 migrants. The conditions are discussed in order of incidence.

Disease of the Respiratory Tract. There were 1,514 patients, 31 percent of all clinic patients, with infections of the upper respiratory tract. The main diagnoses under this system were: colds and asthma, 1,038; influenza and pneumonia, 79; and bronchitis, 280. There were many cases of asthma. Diseases of the respiratory tract, therefore, account for a third of the illnesses of this group of migrants. The lack of resistance to infection is probably due to subclinical malnutrition resulting from low intake of such basic nutrients as protein, iron, Vitamin C, and Vitamin A (18).

In schoolchildren one must emphasize that the presence of colds will be characterized by a much more prolonged illness with hanging-on sniffles and cough, because the child is unable to overcome the initial infection. Most colds last three to five days, but in these children the low-grade cold lasts much longer than usual and may be allergic in nature. Although poor nutrition is an important factor, the way of life, and the care of the children at home greatly affect the course of the disease. If they are not in the best health, they are liable to have recurring infections throughout the school year. It would be of interest to correlate the absentee rate in this group to the episodes of colds. This respiratory infection further decreases the appetite of the child, which in turn reduces his nutritional intake. This depletes his reserves and further diminishes his resistance to disease. This cycle must be broken if the child is to recover and improve in health.

Digestive System Disease. Gastroenteritis and enteritis constitute 74 percent of the digestive system diseases reported. Dental decay constituted about twenty percent of the conditions, with a few cases of gingivitis, or infection of the gums. Gastroenteritis and enteritis have a common denominator: infection by contaminated food. The lack of supervision of the smaller child while the parents are at work creates real problems in the prevention of gastrointestinal disease in this age group. Lack of refrigeration of foodstuffs is another important factor. Gastrointestinal infection can be critical and even deadly to the smaller child due to dehydration, secondary to vomiting and diarrhea. The establishment of day care centers that will provide for the daytime supervision of the child, proper feeding under adequate sanitary conditions, and good personal hygiene are measures that can prevent these diseases.

Infective and Parasitic Diseases. Infective and parasitic diseases made up about 11 percent of the total number of conditions reported. The chief diagnostic findings were athlete's foot and ringworm of the scalp due to two types of fungi (fluorescent and nonfluorescent). The nature of the migrant's work, the lack of adequate personal hygiene, and living under crowded conditions are factors that contribute to the presence and spread of these fungi. In children, the skin infection is mostly of the impetiginous "Florida sore" type. The seriousness of this skin condition must be emphasized. Kidney damage can result due to tissue sensitivity to the toxins of the staphylococcus and streptococcus present in the lesions. Rapid treatment is essential. Good personal hygiene is mandatory for prevention. The generous and frequent use of soap and water is the most effective preventive measure. Cleaning exposed skin areas with a soap of high hexachlorophene content is recommended. Since the younger children are left at home unguarded and playing around in the earth yards, they are subject to a high incidence of this contagious disease. These children in turn transmit the disease to those attending school. The treatment of the child in school, by itself, is not sufficient. He will be reinfected by his brother or sister at home. The entire family must be treated in order to eradicate the disease in any one family. Treatment of impetiginous "Florida sores," regardless of severity, must include oral antibiotics. Washing the infected sores and applying of bacteriocidal ointments are additional measures to insure prompt healing of the lesions.

Venereal disease was the second largest group in the infective and parasitic disease classification. The incidence of venereal disease is highest among the single males that come to work in the areas, with a predominance of gonorrhea (95 percent) over syphilis (5 percent). The progress report of a migrant syphilis casefinding demonstration project states that of 18,082 blood samples drawn, 916 were reactive, a reactor rate of 5 percent. From the 916 reactive blood tests, 47 lesion cases, 52 early latent cases, and 88 latent cases of syphilis were brought to treatment (9).

Ascaris was the most important intestinal parasite identified, although some cases of hookworm were reported. Poor personal hygiene is an important factor in the persistence and spread of Ascariasis in family groups. Soil contamination can cause the spread of intestinal parasitosis of the hookworm type among this population. The installation of disposable latrines in the fields could do much to improve the control of this condition.

Diseases of the Nervous System and Sense Organs. The most common diseases of the nervous system and sense organs were eye disease such as conjunctivitis and foreign bodies. Otitis externa and otitis media were also reported, but no mastoid infections. Because of their importance in reference to the vision and hearing senses of the children, prompt treatment is essential. It is to be observed that in this group there were no cerebrovascular accidents reported. This negative finding is of importance in view of the type of patients we are dealing with and the many Negroes working as migrants. In Dade County, cerebral strokes secondary to hypertension are common among the Negro population. There were, however, three cases of convulsive seizures, possibly epilepsy.

Accidents, Poisoning, and Violence. About 5 percent of all the total cases were classified as accidents, poisoning, or violence. Poisoning with pesticides was not reported. Gunshot wounds, lacerations, abrasions, and burns were reported.

Diseases of the Circulatory System. Diseases of the circulatory system formed about 4.5 percent of the total number of diagnostic findings, with hypertension and sequelae forming almost 90 percent of the conditions reported. These cases of hypertension occurred mostly in the older population group. Cases of congenital heart disease, congestive heart failure, and rheumatic fever were reported.

Allergic, Endocrine, Metabolical, and Nutritional Disease. Of allergic, endocrine, metabolical, and nutritional disease, diabetes was the leading diagnostic finding, but of a low incidence. Clinical malnutrition, not severe enough to be meaningful in terms of overall health of the individuals, was found in about 53 patients.

Diseases of Bones and Organs of Movement. Diseases of bones and organs of movement made up about 3.4 percent and were not of any great importance. It is to be observed that bending and squatting positions are constantly assumed in the migrants' work. It is possible to conjecture that the constant use of the joints and organs of locomotion may cause them to preserve greater elasticity and better functional capacity of these joints than is possible in persons who are less physically active.

Diseases of the Genito-Urinary System. Diseases of the genito-urinary system (excluding sex-related diseases) accounted for about 3.4 percent of the cases. Urinary bladder infection was found in the males, and vaginal moniliasis and gynecologic problems in the female.

Diseases of the Blood and Blood-forming Organs. Diseases of the blood-forming organs had an incidence of about 3.4 percent, mostly cases of anemia. This incidence of anemia is lower than one would expect and reflects only cases seen in the clinics. Anemia is a meaningful diagnosis since the level of hemoglobin can be used as a crude index of the health status of a person. Anemia in the preschooler and school age child must be rapidly corrected for optimal learning capability. Anemia means a lower quantity of oxygen carrying hemoglobin in the blood of the person, and in the anemic child the brain is deprived of the proper amount of oxygen it requires to function properly and effectively. His learning capabilities can, therefore, be impaired.

Mental, Psychoneurotic, and Personality Disorders. Mental, psychoneurotic, and personality disorders had an incidence of only 2 percent. This low incidence may indicate a greater degree of maturity, a sense of responsibility with acceptance of and adaption to the migrant way of life.

Symptoms and Ill-defined Conditions. Ill-defined conditions of different categories, mostly backaches, headaches, nose bleeds, and senility complaints, were found in 1.4 percent of cases.

Neoplasms. Only about five benign and unspecified neoplasms were found within this group for an incidence of 0.1 percent.

As can be seen by the preceding description of the health conditions found in these 3,172 patients out of the total peak occupancy of 5,780 persons, roughly two-thirds of these migrants requested some type of medical or dental consultation. The number of referrals to hospitals were so minimal as to further emphasize the need for this type of outpatient service and its effectiveness in keeping the migrant healthy while working. It also reduces the cost of medical care at hospitals. The other observation to be made is in reference to the type of illnesses which have as a common denominator poor nutrition, not only as to quantity, but as to the quality of nutrients used by these migrants. The lack of refrigeration prevents an adequate utilization of dairy products and the meats so necessary to build up body tissues and to keep in good health. Migrants are a fairly healthy group with the same range of minor ailments that would affect any other low income group. The provision of health services is definitely a need in any community that depends on migrant labor.

Health Conditions Found among Migrant Head Start Children

The medical findings among migrant Head Start children attending three schools in south Dade County, Florida, were reviewed during the school year 1967-1968. Even though the sample is small, the data give an idea of the health status of these migrant children. Of thirty-six children evaluated, 32 or 88 percent had medical conditions that required follow-up care. The children averaged 1.8 conditions per child, which compares evenly with 1.88 conditions per child for the total Head Start enrollment. Medical conditions found according to order of frequency were:

Anemia, as demonstrated by hemoglobin levels under 11.0 grams per 100 ml. of blood, was the most common and most significant finding. There was one case of sickle cell trait found. Since this condition is an inherited recessive characteristic defect of the black race, one must be on the lookout for children with the trait (8 percent incidence in the black race) and the disease (0.3 percent incidence in the black race). Both conditions can produce anemia but the disease is much more severe than the trait. Phimosis, or a very tight prepuce, was the commonest condition found in the genito-urinary classification. Although large tonsils are characteristic of this age group, only one case was found with diseased tonsils requiring tonsillectomy. Dermatologic conditions have great significance as has already been explained. Four cases of impetigo and one of ringworm of the scalp were reported. Both conditions are contagious and required prompt treatment. Enlarged lymph glands were found in six children, possibly indicative of underlying infectious processes elsewhere. Under gastrointestinal system, one child had a right inguinal hernia requiring operative correction. Five children had umbilical hernias. This condition does not require operation unless it persists into childhood and there is evidence of possible complications. Traces of albumin and glucose were found in four cases, but without medical significance. Three children were found with significant heart murmurs. These children should have a yearly recheck, since these murmurs tend to disappear if they are not medically significant. Children with anemia will frequently have a physiologic heart murmur that tends to disappear as soon as the anemic state is corrected. Two children were found to have flat feet, but these were asymptomatic since the condition did not produce pain or discomfort to the child. Only those cases of painful flat feet need to be referred to the orthopedic surgeon for further treatment. Only one child was undersize for age, and one was underweight for age. Height is the most reliable indicator of growth during this age period, but the familial factor must be considered in evaluating a child's growth pattern. Only one child had bronchitis at the time of examination, but that child did not require hospitalization.

In general, one can say that the five-year-old migrant child is fairly healthy, active, and contented.

Analysis of Hospital Referrals

An analysis of hospital referrals describes the nature of severe illnesses among these migrant workers by age, race, and sex. Noteworthy is the relatively small number of cases that had to be referred to a hospital for emergency care. This further emphasizes the fact that the migrant family is not in such poor health as is commonly expressed. It also demonstrates the importance of providing for health care services easily accessible to the migrant and the effectiveness of prompt treatment for incipient disease conditions.

Of the 178 cases referred to the hospitals, 93 were white and 85 Negro; 98 were male and 80 female. By age, referred cases were grouped as follows: Under one year, one case; 1 to 2 years, two cases; 3 to 5 years, 16 cases; 6 to 18 years, 30 cases; 19 to 44 years, 71 cases, 45 to 65 years, 58 cases. Almost 77 percent of referrals were migrants over 19 years of age, 16.8 percent were school age children aged 6 to 18 years, and 6.2 percent were infants and preschoolers.

Seventy-eight patients were referred to Jackson Memorial Hospital and a similar number to South Dade Hospital, with nine children referred to Variety Children's Hospital. The more common causes for referral in the migrant group under 18 years of age were:

1. Diarrheas, particularly in the infant and preschool age group.
2. Skin infections, lacerations, trauma, abscesses. A one-year-old child with whooping cough had to be hospitalized, showing the need for intensification of childhood immunizations. Some of the lacerations were infected due to lack of proper care.

3. Hernias, inguinal and scrotal, were another important group, both types requiring operative correction.

4. Cardiac conditions requiring referral were: tachycardia, congestive heart failure (age 10 years), arrhythmias, congenital heart disease, and significant systolic murmurs.

5. Other important causes for referral were: convulsions, pneumonia, dental abscess, appendicitis, vaginitis, and conjunctivitis in a five-year-old girl, two cases of postpolio defects, and burns.

In the older age group over 19 years of age most of the conditions requiring hospitalization referrals were typical of the older individual. In the 19- to 30-year-old group of young adults, trauma seemed the chief cause, followed by lacerations, pregnancy and gynecologic conditions, and conditions of the gastrointestinal system. In the 31- to 40-year-old group, cardiovascular conditions were in first place, with trauma, lacerations, and fractures in second order of importance.

In the 41- to 50-year-old group cardiovascular conditions were also in first place, gastroenteric conditions second. Trauma, lacerations, and fractures were less frequent. Two cases each of arthritis, lipoma, and asthma were reported. Anemia, renal colic, diabetes mellitus, burns, and bilateral hernias were also diagnosed.

In those over 50 years of age cardiovascular and gastroenteric conditions prevailed. Trauma, lacerations, arthritis, diabetes, and hernias were reported. Two cases of tuberculosis were found in this age group.

There is nothing unusual in the range of conditions found, and they parallel those in similar low income, low educational groups. My personal impression is that the migrant family, in spite of its unusual way of life and limited resources, is much healthier, has greater stamina, and is better adjusted emotionally than the ghetto or slum dwellers in our metropolitan cities.

Summary and Recommendations

The migrant worker and his family live a nomadic type of life of their own choice. There are advantages and disadvantages inherent in such mobile existence. Health problems found are characteristic of such a culture and its low income category. These do not differ too much from those found among other low income, poorly educated minority groups in our nation.

Local communities fear the migrant for the contagious illnesses he may bring into the community. They distrust migrants as they would any other unknown, atypical, nonconforming group. They do not understand the migrants' way of life and culture, and they fail to provide for the migrants' health, education, and welfare needs.

Local communities must be adequately helped by federal supplemental funds to provide for the health, educational, and welfare needs. At the same time, an intensive educational program must be established for the resident population of local communities, to orient them on the role, life, and cultural characteristics, as well as the health, educational, and welfare needs of these nonresident citizens.

There is need to develop the "Migrant Health Aide" concept. This specially selected, trained health aide would accompany traveling groups and remain in their camps on full time assignment the year round. He would have to identify with and be accepted by the migrant workers as their resource person on matters pertaining to health and welfare. He would be trained in first aid and in medical recording and reporting. He would be responsible for continuity of medical care for specific cases under treatment as the migrant group moves from one area to another. He would immunize, vaccinate, and contact hospitals and health and welfare departments along the way. He would supervise camp sanitation, facilities for personal hygiene, and housing conditions, and intercede for suitable facilities. His other very important sphere of action would be health education and good living practices among the migrants.

Continuity of medical care must be thought of particularly in reference to children with handicapping conditions, chronic medical conditions under care (e.g., diabetes), pregnant females, and family planning services. These particular groups should have easy access to clinics, public and private, and services along their route of work where they could go for continued medical care and supervision.

Finally, but most important, there must be a greater involvement of federal agencies in the provision of medical supervision and welfare needs of the migrant population throughout the nation as they move from state to state. The referral services must be improved so that these patients get similar services wherever they go through a greater utilization of the Health Service Index already developed and in use (10).

References

1. Anderson, Otis L. "The Migrant and the Rest of Us." *Public Health Reports,* 72 (June 1957).

2. Bergstrom, W. H., and Devlin, L. B. "Pediatric Care for Migrant Workers: An Opportunity for Teaching and Investigation." *Pediatrics,* 30 (August 1962).

3. Browning, R. H., and Northcutt, T. J., Jr. "On the Season." *Florida State Board of Health, Monograph No. 2.* Bureau of Maternal and Child Health, Jacksonville, Florida, 1957.

4. "Children in Migrant Families." *Children's Bureau.* A Report to the Senate Appropriations Committee of the Eighty-Seventh Congress, United States Department of Health, Education, and Welfare, Social Security Administration, December 1960.

5. Crocker, E. C. "A Child Welfare Worker in a Program for Migrants." *Children,* 10 (May-June 1963).

6. Delgado, G., Brumbick, C. L., and Deaver, M. G. "Eating Patterns Among Migrant Families." *Public Health Reports,* 76 (April 1961).

7. "Education for Migratory Children." *The Harbinger,* Florida State Department of Education, 1 (April 1967).

8. *The Educational Problems of the Migrant Child.* National Committee on the Education of Migrant Children of the National Labor Committee, 145 East 32nd Street, 12th Floor, New York, New York 10016.

9. Gilbert, A., and Schloesser, P. "Health Needs of Migrant Children in a Kansas Day Care Program." *Public Health Reports,* 78 (November 1963).

10. "Health Service Index." *Florida State Board of Health,* Jacksonville (March 1964).

11. "Health Services and the Migrant." *Currents in Public Health,* 3 (February 1963).

12. Johnston, H. L., and Lindsay, J. R. "Meeting the Health Needs of the Migrant Worker." *Hospitals,* (July 1965).

13. Koos, Earl L. "They Follow the Sun." *Florida State Board of Health, Monograph No. 1.* Bureau of Maternal and Child Health, Jacksonville, Florida, 1957.

14. Leone, L. P., and Johnston, H. L. "Agricultural Migrants and Public Health." *Public Health Reports,* 69 (January 1954).

15. Lindsay, J. R., and Johnston, H. L. "The Health of the Migrant Worker." *Journal of Occupational Medicine,* 8 (January 1966).

16. Maddox, T. P. *Migrant Health Project Annual Progress Report,* June 1, 1967, through May 31, 1968, Dade County Department of Public Health, NSPHS Grant MG-34D.

17. Matta, E. L., Jr. "Planning of a Family with the Puerto Rican Migrants." Dade County Department of Public Health, Special Report (August 1966). Unpublished.

18. Northcutt, T. J., Browning, R. H., and Brumbach, C. L. "Agricultural Migration and Maternity Care." *Journal of Health and Human Behavior,* 4 (Fall 1963), pp. 173-178.

19. "Pediatric Teaching Clinic Aids Migrant Farm Workers." *The Pediatric Herald* (September 1963).

20. Rosetti, Michael A. *Sanitarian: Connecticut Health Bulletin* (July 1961).

21. "Rural Migrants to Urban Centers." *Currents in Public Health,* 4 (March 1964).

22. Shafer, J. K., et al. "Health Needs of Seasonal Farmworkers and Their Families." *Public Health Reports,* 76 (June 1961).

23. Sowder, Wilson T., and Lawrence, J. "A Migrant Labor Crisis in Immokalee." *Public Health Reports,* 74 (January 1959).

24. Stott, T. W. "Migrant Syphilis Casefinding Demonstration Project." Progress Report, Fiscal Year 1968. Unpublished.

25. "Health Service Index." Florida State Board of Health, Jacksonville (March 1964).

The Dade County Migrant Health Project was devised and organized and is directed by W. R. Stinger, M.D., M.P.H., acting county health officer of Dade County, Florida. Dr. L. Albornoz, attending physician, Mr. T. P. Maddox, sanitarian field director, and Mrs. Margaret Nichols, nursing supervisor, as well as many others, have helped Dr. Stinger develop in Dade County one of the best migrant health services in the nation. Almost all of the data discussed in this article was abstracted from the Migrant Health Project *Annual Progress Report,* 1967-1968.

CHAPTER **5**

Perspectives on Deprivation and Stimulation

DeFOREST L. STRUNK

Dr. Strunk presents a review of the literature in the area of extreme deprivation in childhood. His conclusion and charge to educators and others is that children should start formal learning as early as age one or even before in order to combat the effects of environmental deprivation.

Dr. DeForest L. Strunk was coordinator of special education and professor of education and pediatrics at the University of Miami before moving to the University of San Diego as director of special education. Mental retardation is his area of special competence, and he is a consultant to numerous private and governmental organizations. He received his Ed. D. from the University of Virginia.

A close associational relationship exists between cultural deprivation and mental retardation. Aside from the fact that there is a high rate of malnutrition and incidence of disease among the culturally disadvantaged, there is a concomitant lack of appropriate development in the learning sphere which could be attributed to experiential poverty. This experiential poverty produces a child who enters learning situations with decided inadequacies.

When one studies the debilitating effects of cultural deprivation on the developing child, these may be found to be so severe as to influence the incidence of mental retardation among such a group. This is supported by a report from the President's Committee on Mental Retardation (141) which contends that three-fourths of the nation's mentally retarded are to be found in isolated and impoverished urban and rural areas. It was also reported that "children of low income families often arrive at school age with neither the experience nor the skills necessary for systematic learning. Many are found to be functionally retarded in language and in the ability to do abstract thinking which is required in order to read, write and count" (141, p. 19). These same children continue to have difficulties in the school situation, falling further and further behind as they continue their school program. This report points out that the conditions of life in poverty—whether in the urban ghetto, the hollows of Appalachia, a prairie shacktown, or in an Indian reservation—cause and nurture mental retardation.

If children from culturally disadvantaged areas are to be helped, this help must come to them as early as possible while they are young enough to profit from it. If a child's learning is impaired by early deprivation together with a continuation of debilitating effects, it is necessary to examine whether stimulation can intervene in the process to change such action. If it is possible, then is there an optimal time for this intervention to occur? And, are there any effective models for such stimulation? One federally-sponsored educational attempt to remedy the inadequacy of early environment is Operation Head Start (65). Evidence from studies that have been carried out on children involved in Head Start programs indicates that perhaps the program is unable to compensate for the effects of early deprivation and, further, that appropriate programs should be started with boys and girls who are younger than the five- and six-year-olds for whom the programs are designed.

This chapter presents a review of the literature in the area of extreme deprivation in childhood, together with the impact of various stimulative approaches. It is provided in the hope of pointing out the necessity of reaching children at a very young age—younger than the age of four or five. While this age has been traditional for participation in early childhood developmental programs, the failure of many of these to achieve their goals has created a search for a new attack on this problem. There is an increasing body of literature that supports the view that children should start formal learning as early as age one or even before in order to combat the effects of environmental deprivation. These and other studies are reviewed for the reader to consider.

Basic to understanding the effects of deprivation and stimulation, it is necessary to recognize the role of the determinants of intelligence. In the 1920s, a disagreement raged over this question. This later came to be known as the nature-nurture controversy. Investigators such as Skeels and Dye (127), Goodenough (59), Rogers, Durling, and McBridge (123), and Davidson (29) were concerned with this question. While scientists now believe both nature and nurture to be important, this early area is still of interest historically and because some of these studies made valuable contributions to the understanding of the importance that environment does play.

It is popular to now call the nature-nurture question passé and to state that it is no longer a controversy, as each has come to be appreciated as important in the development of the child. There are many signs, however, that this is still a hot issue in the minds of some researchers. Arthur Jensen, in the Winter 1969 issue of the *Harvard Educational Review* (74), argues that a new look should be given at the detriments of intelligence. He suggests that the genetic determinants are more, if not as, important as environmental influences. Jensen further argues that the failure of the current programs of compensatory education may be due to the fact that too much emphasis has been given to the role of environment and not enough to the differential learning patterns that may be attributable to genetic influences.

Other writers take issue with this line of thinking. Jensen is answered in a later issue of this journal by a prominent group of psychologists. These gentlemen argue for a more "environmentalist" consideration of the issue of nature-nurture and its implications for compensatory education. Among this group is Jerome Kagan (79), who questions the logic used by Jensen in examining his data. Another of this group, J. M. Hunt (68), refutes Jensen's arguments as being unsubstantiated. He further offers results in animal research that suggest that the physical development of the brain is directly influenced by activities dealing with the processing of information.

Studies in several different areas, which will be discussed in this chapter, were performed during the 20s and 30s and formed the background for many studies in the 50s and 60s. The broad subsections relative to the question of the importance of early environmental effects are grouped as follows: (1) Effects of change to a stimulating environment; (2) Effects of extreme deprivation; (3)

Effects of institutionalization; (4) Nursery and preschool studies; (5) Early teaching of reading; (6) Animal studies; and (7) Effects of language stimulation. Additional information relative to Jensen, et al, is presented later in this chapter.

Change to a More Stimulating Environment

This area is one which, as will be noted below, has interested psychologists involved in the nature-nurture controversy. One early study was conducted by McGraw (95) in 1939. This study involved anecdotal reports on the development of Johnny and Jimmy, identical twins within the normal range of general endowment. One twin, Jimmy, was given a minimum of stimulation and the other twin, Johnny, was taught many motor skills, including swimming. One purpose of this clinical study was to contradict the stress on the role of maturation in infant behavior as emphasized by Gesell and Thompson (55). McGraw concluded:

> There is no reason to believe that exercise in special activities will accelerate mental functions as measured on standardized scales. There seems to be a superiority of general muscular coordinations on the part of Johnny, who received the longer and more intensive practice in motor activities. (95, p. 19)

It was also concluded from the Rorschach test and psychiatric interviews that Johnny was the more "complex" of the twins. It must be noted, however, that many of the findings of this study were analyzed rather subjectively. It must also be noted that the degree to which these findings could be generalized to the area of cognitive stimulation is extremely limited as the emphasis of this study was on motor rather than cognitive stimulation.

Skeels and Harms (128) and Skodak and Skeels (129) have also conducted research relevant to the area of change to a more stimulating environment. Skeels and Harms (128) studied three groups of children selected from an orphans' home. In one group were children whose alleged fathers were in unskilled or slightly-skilled occupations. Another group contained children whose mothers had tested IQs of 75 or less. The investigators found that: (1) the children with fathers of low status and/or mothers with low IQ scored equal or higher on intelligence tests than the general population, after having been placed in adoptive homes of higher socioeconomic status at infancy; and (2) there were no more mentally retarded children, and a greater frequency of superior children (in terms of their tested IQs), than might be expected from a random sample of the population. This study was one of the first to point up the importance of environment for the young child's mental development.

Several years later, Rheingold (118) studied institutionalized infants to determine if their social responsiveness could be modified. She alone provided daily care for groups of four six-month-old infants for five days a week for eight weeks. The control groups in the two parallel experiments received the usual institutional care from many "mothers." At the conclusion of the study, it was indicated that the experimental infants were more socially responsive than the control groups. Their social behavior apparently had been modified by their enriched environment, or care by a single "mother." However, it was also noted that the children in the control group did not suffer significantly from the lack of one mother figure. This left Rheingold with the impression that the damage suffered by children as a result of institutionalization was not alone the result of mothering by multiple attendants but rather was due to the lack of attention and experiential stimulation that characterizes many institutional settings.

Moss and Kagan (100), contrary to the studies mentioned above, studied a mainly middle-class group from the Fels Research Institute. They hypothesized that maternal concern with the child's early achievements would correlate positively with the child's IQ test performance. Their findings in two studies indicated that this maternal concern facilitated the performance of boys at age three, but not of the girls, and there was no significant correlation in either study between the child's IQ at age six and maternal acceleration. In this study, sex differences apparently were important with different variables having differential effects on the boys' and on the girls' IQ scores. This indicated that the cohesive pattern of interaction between mother and child varied with the sex of the child. It should be remembered that this was a predominantly middle-class group of children. It seems unlikely that these findings could be generalized to lower-class children, in which case maternal attention and concern in an impoverished environment might produce quite different results.

Casler (20) tried another method of environmental enrichment —that of extra tactile stimulation. The experimental group of sixteen babies was given twenty minutes per day of extra tactile stimulation over a ten-week period. The baby's skin was stroked, with the exception of the hands, mouth, and genitals. The "handler," while gazing at the infant's midsection, would say, "Hello, baby," every sixty seconds. In the control group there was no extra tactile stimulation administered, but the handler would say, "Hello, baby," to each infant in this group twice a day, every sixty seconds for ten minutes. The results of this experiment were as Casler hypothesized: On the Gesell Developmental Schedule, the experimental group had higher total developmental quotients, and on scores in the language, adaptive, and personal-social subtests. Only in the case of the motor subtests were the differences not significant although the small differences shown were again in favor of the experimental group. Casler noted, interestingly, that both groups showed a general decline in scores during the following ten weeks in the institution after the conclusion of the experimental situation.

Studies on Deprivation

Several studies have been concerned with the area of deprivation of stimulus, how it affects the cognition of the young child, and the reversibility or irreversibility of its effects. Most studies concerning deprivation of stimulus have employed animals as subjects, due to ethical limits involved in studying deprivation in children. Those involving children have for the most part been concerned with children from very deprived home backgrounds. The first study to be discussed, however, used a different approach.

Dennis (35, 36), in an early study, raised twin babies under conditions of very limited stimulation for their first seven months, and under conditions described as slightly more stimulating near the completion of their first year. The author and his wife attempted to prove that stimulus deprivation during the early stages of development did not have a dysgenic effect on the infant. Their final general conclusions were that (1) behavioral development will take its normal course if the well-being of the infant is assured during the first year of life, and (2) learning plays an important part in the development of autogenous responses of the first year with maturation in and of itself seldom producing new developmental items. The findings of this study have to be regarded as inconclusive, for it was found that one of the twins had an intracranial birth injury which contaminated observation. It must also be noted that while it is true that the investigators did not observe any marked retardation in the remaining twin, what they provided as a "minimally stimulating" environment was by far richer than that of many institutions and deprived homes.

Davis (30, 31) studied a case of extreme deprivation in Anna, a child of more than five years found in a highly neglected state in an upstairs room. Although the progress made by this child after placement in a richer environment was rather limited (learning to drink from a cup and taking a few steps), she never achieved normality before her death approximately five-and-one-half years later. The new environment, however, also left much to be desired. Anna was taken first to a county home for the aged, then to a foster home, and finally to a school for defective children. This in itself was not the kind of environment that would foster optimal development. By comparison with another case, Davis concluded that, at least for some individuals, extreme isolation up to age six does not permanently impair socialization.

Pasamanick (107) studied a group of fifty-three Negro infants (twenty-eight males and twenty-five females). He compared them with a group of white infants from various backgrounds including low socioeconomic and superior backgrounds. In testing the infants, Pasamanick found that the Negro infants performed slightly better than the normative group of white infants, although the differences were not significant. Pasamanick concluded that for the children in this study, the average Negro infant was equal to the average white infant. For two reasons this study was of special note. First, it helped vanquish the racist idea of white superiority which was prevalent at the time; also, it helped point up the importance of environment for the infant. Pasamanick states that one important variable was the fact that at the time of the study the diet of the average Negro in New Haven, Connecticut, approached that of the New Haven white, as these infants were born during World War II when the food distribution had reached more of the Negroes. Considering development at each half-year of life,

Pasamanick concluded that "the onset of the depressing influence of exegenous factors upon Negro development might be construed as beginning during this third half-year of life" (107, p. 42).

Dennis and Najarian (37) studied the effects of deprivation on children of two age groups institutionalized in Lebanon. The infants were from two to twelve months of age, and the older children were from four-and-one-half to six years of age. The poor conditions under which the infants in the institution were raised included a ratio of ten infants to each attendant, swaddling of infants, and propping of the infants' bottles. The older children, from ages one to three, were put in groups for play, with one supervisor and one assistant for twenty children; from three to four, they were placed in a nursery situation in which they were taught skills such as object-naming, reading, writing, French and Arabic. On the Cattell Infant Scale, Dennis and Najarian found that the mean developmental quotient (DQ) at the age of two months was 100; children under one year showed retardation beginning at three months, scoring a mean DQ of 63. A control group of children from the well-baby clinic of the American University scored in the normal range. For the institutionalized children from four-and-one-half to six years, the mean score was 90, tested with the Goodenough Draw-a-Man Test, the Knox Cube Test, and the Porteus Maze Test. Dennis and Najarian concluded that a mean DQ of 65 and retardation in the last nine months of the first year does not result in a generally poor performance at four-and-one-half to six years, and that "this study therefore does not support the doctrine of the permanency of early environmental effects" (37, p. 12).

Many early studies, however, have explored the possibility that early deprivation is most harmful in the area of language development, and language ability was not tested by Dennis and Najarian. Further, the program for the children they tested that began at age four (even learning of two languages) sounds far superior to many compensatory programs for the young deprived in which children are not subjected to training in as many different areas.

Effects of Institutionalization—Maternal Deprivation

Related to the area of sensory deprivation is that of maternal deprivation. Much research on the topic of maternal deprivation has employed institutionalized infants and children as subjects.

One very early report in the area of maternal deprivation was by Lowrey (91). In this study, Lowrey discussed a syndrome which he felt was common among children who had undergone an isolated type of experience. He included in this syndrome personality characteristics such as unsocial behavior, hostile aggression, inability to receive and give affection or to understand and accept limitations, insecurity in adapting to environment, and other personality traits which he felt combined to produce a style of behavior characteristic of children raised in an institution from infancy. Lowrey concluded that the raising of children in an institution should be avoided; if this is unavoidable, provision should be made for planned adult contact and participation in a home-type schedule.

Orgel (104) took issue with Lowrey's article, stating that of sixteen comparable institutionalized cases he had observed, he saw only two children having those characteristics mentioned by Lowrey. He did not describe in detail, however, the type of care these children had received. Agreeing that young children should not be placed in institutions, Orgel felt that personality distortion may be limited to the individual child rather than specific for all children in early institutional care.

A study in this area has been done by Spitz (131), who described in detail the detrimental effect that maternal deprivation through continuous institutional care can have on children. He observed the behavior of young children where care was inadequate and inconsistent. Spitz noted that many of these children suffered from what he terms "anaclitic depression" or a reaction characterized by motionless withdrawal and detachment from the environment. The lack of the mother-child relationship in the first care carried over into the child's lack of future development.

Bowlby (13) discussed the psychodynamic problem of the stress of separation for the child under four or five. Personality development may be affected in a negative manner with hostile and violent behavior becoming a pattern in later life, due to the special characteristics of the initial learning of immature organisms, and the powerful emotional forces generated by the early separation of the child from his mother.

Casler (21), in an extensive review of the literature in the area of maternal deprivation, takes issue with what he terms the hypothesis that the lack of a single caretaker is the cause of the many ill effects of institutionalization. Casler offers several arguments as support: Present research in institutionalization is neither conclusive nor particularly instructive because of possible failure to take into account certain critical variables in the research. "The first of these concerns is the age at which the separation occurred. . . . A second variable is the nature of the institution. . . . A third crucial matter . . . is the reason for the separation" (21, pp. 3-4). Furthermore, Casler summarized that there is increasing evidence that the ill effects in children often assumed to be caused by maternal deprivation can have other causes. These might be the absence of tactile and other sorts of stimulation, rather than the lack of one maternal figure as proposed by others. Casler further proposes a neuroanatomical hypothesis which implies that as the muscles need a minimum of stimulation to preserve "muscle tone," so do the receptive systems of the organism need a minimum of stimulation to preserve their "tone." This hypothesis, proposes Casler, is substantiated by the work done by neurophysiologists into the nature and functions of the ascending reticular activating system.

Gelinier-Ortigues (54) described a child who had suffered severe maternal deprivation. The child manifested several symptoms, including "pseudo-deafness" and psychomotor retardation. Discussion following the case presentation at the International Institute of Child Psychiatry (Toronto, 1954) concluded that "findings in cases such as this help us to realize the importance of motivational factors as well as the factor of the stimulation of a young child by his social milieu in regard to the physical aspects of his growth and development" (54, p. 243). The discussants felt that too often children had been labeled retarded and put in institutions when they perhaps could have been helped by treatment, as was the boy described.

Nursery Studies

One group of studies was concerned with the problem of education of the young child—specifically, the effect of kindergarten and nursery education on cognition of the young child. These studies, over several decades, have followed a rather parallel format.

One of the earliest studies was by Goodenough (59). Twenty-eight children of two, three, and four years of age were tested before and after a year of nursery school attendance. Their paired controls were tested with no nursery school experience. In the experimental group, the younger children (CA 1.0-2.5) made an IQ gain of 9.9 points, and the older group (CA 3.3-4.2) made a gain of 12.5 points. Goodenough did note that irregular standardization of the instrument for the early ages could have contaminated results of actual increase in intelligence. An increase in score was also found in the control group. The IQ gain in the experimental group was too small to be reliable. Greatest gains, however, were made by the nursery school children.

Barrett and Koch (2) also studied children to determine the effect of an enriched environment upon their mental development. In this study, twenty-seven orphanage children, aging from thirty-five months to five years, were placed in a special nursery school regime for six to nine months. A matched control group was selected from other institutions and deprived of such experiences. It was found that 77 percent of the nursery school group raised their IQ 15 or more points when tested after the special regime. In comparison, only 11.8 percent of the control group performed as well on the "crude" method of analysis.

Lamson (87), in comparing a group of children in the second, third, and fourth grades who had attended nursery schools for two years with a group of children in the same grades who had not, found no significant differences between the two groups in IQ or reading achievement, or in social development. For these children, the nursery school experiences seemed to neither increase nor decrease intelligence quotients.

Peters and McElwee (110) undertook an interesting experiment—first, to analyze the components of intelligent behavior, or "functioning intelligence"; then to train a group of nursery school children, incorporating into their training the types of experiences that would help them manifest this type of behavior. The experiment involved six environmentally deprived children who had IQs lower than 100 and low teacher ratings in initiative and "quickness to learn." The children ranged in age from two years, nine months to four years, two months. A specially trained teaching assistant spent two hours, three days a week with these children for a period of eight months. She also made home visits and conferred with the mothers. Special activities included those judged best to develop functioning intelligence. The children all gained in intelligence and social quotients, and tested sociability. It was concluded that this program was beneficial in fostering techniques to improve the functioning intelligence of the children involved.

More recently Jensen (75) effected a review of the literature on the nature of early learning and the factors affecting concept formation and problem solving in young children. He proposed that during the preschool years the child acquires a series of verbal mediations and verbal associations which will facilitate future learning and verbal control of behavior. Furthermore, he concludes:

> Some of the research we have carried out so far has led us to believe that in certain segments of our society a large proportion of children who appear to be mentally retarded or slow learners in school may not be defective in any basic neurological sense. They are handicapped by the failure of their particular environment to inculcate a sufficiently complex system of verbal mediation to enable the child to profit from school learning or to engage in the complex symbolic behavior known as human thinking. (75, p. 138)

In the early 1960s, several researchers turned their attention to the questions of the effectiveness of early education and the best methods of teaching young children.

Feldman (45) reported on the first year of a three-year demonstration and research program for four-year-old culturally deprived children, part of the work under the Institute for Developmental Studies, New York Medical College. This nursery program was designed to explore the value of an enriched curriculum that stressed particular areas of intellectual function (language, concept, and perceptual development), and of a program that would involve the parents. Goals were helping the children attain a positive self-image and, later, school orientation and motivation. The teachers were given increased training, and workshops were held with the parents to teach them how to encourage and add to what the child learned in school. Limited evaluation gave positive signs that increased school achievement would be the result from the program's activities.

Caldwell and Richmond (19) described a day care program recently initiated at the State University of New York in Syracuse for children of low-income employed mothers. It was planned that the center be operated twelve hours a day, five days a week for eleven months of the year. Children between the ages of six months to three years were to be included. One of the goals of the program was to engender in these children awareness, a feeling of mastery and personal accomplishment. The setting was to provide care in an appropriate environment programmed to offset any developmental detriment associated with maternal separation. This environment might also be richer than usually found in the homes of these children. Behind the rationale for this program was a recognition of the importance of the first three years of life on subsequent cognitive, social, and emotional functioning. The project's background information noted that an increasing number of studies have been unable to indicate harmful consequences of "short-term, intermittent maternal deprivation" (19, pp. 482-483).

Hunt (68) in a recent review discussed the changes that have occurred in attitudes toward the IQ and preschool programs. Many scientists have come to accept the idea that the early years are very important for learning in many areas, especially language. Hunt suggests that the deprived infant may develop well the first year, show some retardation during the second, and increasing retardation during the third, fourth, and fifth years. While Hunt felt that retardation occurring during the second and even third years could be reversed in the preschool at age four or five, he felt it would be preferable to start with such training at the age three.

One very interesting study was reported by Triplett (139). In this longitudinal study, the Pine School Project, one goal was the study of children with endogenous or familial retardation, and the families of these children. The children in this project, aged three to six, were admitted to the school and given various types of stimulation, including a variety of new social experiences. A multidisciplinary team, including a pediatrician, social worker, public health nurse, special educator, psychologist, and home economist, gave direct services to the children and their families. The socially isolated, culturally deprived mothers were offered a mother's club that met twice monthly over a five-year period. The group approach was used to help the mothers improve their self-concept, develop skills, and gain self-confidence and concern for others. Many topics were discussed at the meetings, including homemaking and child-rearing principles. While there were no specific quantitative measures taken, Triplett felt that the mothers both improved their self-concepts and became less lonely. Such changes, increased motivation, plus learning how to be better mothers, would seem to be an important step in helping to effect positive images in their children.

Spicker, Hodges, and McCandless (130) reported on partial results of a longitudinal study aimed at identification, development, and evaluation of a diagnostically-based curriculum for retarded, psychosocially deprived children. Children selected for the three-year experimental preschool project were five-year-olds who had scored between 50 and 85 on the 1960 Stanford Binet L-M Intelligence Scale, who were from families of the lowest socioeconomic class in Appalachia, and who did not display gross organic or emotional problems. Four groups of thirteen children were compared on kindergarten pretests and posttests, and followed up for the first grade. The experimental preschool class was exposed to a curriculum designed to stress work in such areas as language deficiencies and perceptual problems. Indicated gains will have to be followed through the first three grades in school to determine effectiveness of this diagnostic curriculum with young children. One criteria of program success will be how well the children can compete with others in the public schools.

Reading Stimulation

Closely related to the area of preschool enrichment in the very early years is the idea of teaching reading at a young age. Several experimenters have proposed that this could be quite important in mentally stimulating the young child.

Davidson's study (29) is particularly interesting because the research question involved whether or not children with a mental age of four years could learn to read. A second question was whether bright, average, and dull children, all of this mental age, could learn to read equally well under the same conditions. Davidson felt, from studies in the area, that children would have to have at least this mental age in order to learn to read. Conclusions were that some children with a mental age of four years could learn to read with the success of the average first grader. Individual and environmental differences were suggested as affecting the results. The bright, average, and dull children were found to also have differences in learning to read.

One experimenter, Fowler, has written extensively on this subject (50, 51) and demonstrated that a two-year-old could be taught to read. He also undertook a very complete review of the literature in the area of early stimulation (49) and, more specifically, early stimulation in areas such as music, reading, motor learning, knowledge, and creativity. After reviewing the available literature in these areas, Fowler stated that:

> The first years are unquestionably important as the foundation for subsequent development and the epoch when cognitive sets and personality-cognitive styles may get launched. But how many experiences for any individual are critical enough to establish forms and modes so unalterable or fixed in direction as to remain untouched by the myriad of ensuing experiences every individual encounters? Our ultimate course might better be defined as, not only to discover the techniques which can establish rational and creative orientations in the early years, but to relate these efforts to a study of how we can foster the continuance of such courses throughout the span of development and adulthood. (49, p. 35)

Animal Studies

Animal Studies have also, at times, involved early deprivation and/ or stimulation. Because these studies were controlled in a way that is impossible in dealing with human infants, due to ethical concerns, their results are of special interest.

Harlow's work with infant monkeys is of particular relevance to the area of early deprivation. He selected infant macaques in part because of their apparent similarity to behavioral responses of human infants. In one series of studies designed to test affectional development (62), infant monkeys were placed with surrogate mothers. For some infants, feeding came from a bottle attached to the "chest" of a plain wire mesh cylinder. Others were fed by an artificial "mother" of a wood cylinder covered with terry cloth. When given a choice, the infants consistently preferred being fed from the terry cloth mother, and spent significantly more time clinging to it than to the plain wire mesh mother. Even while fed from the plain wire mesh mother only, the infants returned to the terry cloth mother after feeding. Further, when an object designed to produce fear was introduced into the cage, the infants with the terry cloth mother were able to gradually overcome their initial anxiety and were more prone to investigate the fear-producing object.

As part of these studies, Harlow and Harlow (61) raised infant monkeys in isolation. The infants so raised developed a series of symptoms of abnormal behavior. They avoided all social contact, appeared very fearful, clutched at themselves, and crouched. It was noted that if the period of isolation was longer than six months, the ill effects of isolation were irreversible. Harlow's findings on the abnormal behavior exhibited by the monkeys raised in isolation are described in similar terms as the behavior noted by Spitz (131) in his observations of institutionalized children. Furthermore, even the monkeys raised with terry cloth surrogate mothers showed impairment in social interactions during adulthood.

A number of studies in the area of early environmental stimulation and/or deprivation have been carried out with rats as subjects. Although the amount of results from this type of study that can be generalized to human beings is rather limited, nevertheless some findings are very interesting.

Bingham and Griffiths (11) manipulated the early environment of rats to determine the effect of differential early environments on their behavior. After raising the rats in this experiment in restricted or enriched environments, the results indicated that the rats raised in the enriched environment were superior in maze-learning activity. Other behavior and temperament in adulthood showed no differences that could be traced to differential early environments. These experimenters concluded that:

In the rat, early environments, characterized as wide, have an influence on certain forms of adult behavior, such as maze learning, but that the particular factors constituting the richness of the wide environments did not seem related to the superior maze performance of experimentals over controls. It was evident that all forms of adult behavior were not measurably affected by the differential early environments utilized in this study. (11, p. 30)

A review of the literature on animal studies by Beach and Jaynes (4) caused them to conclude that much of the presently available evidence is equivocal and of undetermined reliability. However, three broad ways were suggested in which later behavior is affected by early experiences:

1. Persistence in adult behavior of habits formed in early life.
2. Early perceptual learning affecting adult behavior.
3. Critical periods of development in which brief stages in the life of the animal may have strong effect on later behavior.

Cooper and Zubek (26), in testing forty-three rats of the McGill bright and dull strains, divided the rats into four groups and exposed both the bright and the dull strains to either an enriched or deprived environment. The enriched environment was two cages containing balls, swings, and other stimulating devices, facing a brightly colored partition. The deprived environment contained two fairly barren cages facing a gray partition. The results of this study indicated that the dull rats in the enriched environment were so aided by this environment that they became equal in ability on the Hebb-Williams maze test to the bright control group of rats. There was, however, little increase of learning ability among the bright experimental rats in the enriched environment. Conversely, in the restricted environment, the bright experimental rats were retarded to the extent that there was no difference in performance of the bright experimental rats and the dull control group rats. The dull animals suffered no impairment.

Language Studies

Much of the recent interest in cultural deprivation has centered around the question of language development. Many researchers seem involved with the question of the relative importance of early language.

Pringle and Tanner (112) studied eighteen pairs of nursery school and institutionalized children for the purpose of determining qualitative and quantitative differences. Although tested intelligence was at least average, the present or former homes of these children were all considered impoverished. It was concluded that while there was overlap in the achievements of the two groups, the language skills of the preschool children in residential care were somewhat retarded.

Rheingold, Gewirtz, and Ross (119) studied the effects of a social reinforcer upon the vocalization behavior of a group of institutionalized infants. Two groups of eleven infants were studied to determine the similarity between experiments. Results were almost identical, which led the experimenters to conclude that some fairly stable characteristics of these infants were being explored. The infants' social vocalizations were found to increase significantly during a conditioning period in which positive reinforcement, such as clucking, patting, and smiling, was used. A lack of adult response lowered the rate of vocalizing to the baseline level.

Irwin (72) tested the hypothesis that reading to very young infants would increase their phonetic production. Thirty-four infants between thirteen and thirty months from working families were studied for a period of a year and a half. The parents of the children in the experimental group were told to read a book (supplied to them) to their child each day. In the control group, there was no such procedure. Upon testing every two months, little difference was found between the experimental and control groups until the seventeenth month. From then on, differences increased consistently in favor of the experimental group.

John (76) was interested in studying linguistic and cognitive behavior in Negro children from various social classes. Consistent class differences in language skills were found between groups of children of different socioeconomic classes, even though they were from the same subculture. The middle-class children appeared to have a larger vocabulary and higher nonverbal IQ than the lower-class children. At the relational level of language, however, group differences were less striking.

Weisberg (147) studied institutionalized physically healthy three-month-old infants to determine if their vocal behavior could be modified by manipulating the physical and social environment. Over eight consecutive days, he found that the infants' behavior could be conditioned by the experimenter's touching, smiling, and talking to the subject, but conditions other than social reinforcement did not seem to change the infants' vocal behavior.

Blank and Solomon (12) propose an alternative to the "philosophy of total enrichment" in working with the young deprived child, as this does not diagnose the key deficits. Instead, they developed a specialized language program which, they felt, would help in the abstract thinking processes of these young children. They hypothesized that such language intervention would aid not only language but also other aspects of thinking. In their experiment they used twenty-two children from three years, three months to four years, seven months from a nursery school in a deprived area of New York City. They were divided into four groups. The first group, a tutored group, received individual teaching five times a week for fifteen-to-twenty minutes. The second tutored group received such teaching only three times a week. In the third group, which was untutored, there were individual daily sessions with the teacher, with no individual tutoring involved. The fourth group, which was also untutored, received no individual attention. In the results it was found that significant improvements in performance may be directly correlated to the amount of tutoring each week, a verbally rich environment. Use of the language was felt more important than numbers of words. The authors reported that the most striking gains, not shown statistically in IQ testing, were the apparent joy in learning and the feeling of mastery displayed by the tutored children as the tutoring progressed. The untutored children showed none of these attitudes. Thus active involvement in the learning process is a requirement for learning in addition to exposure to materials, a schoollike atmosphere, and interested adults.

Cazden (22) reviewed some of the literature on language development, and his first few words say much about the knowledge that has so far been attained concerning this area:

> Our understanding of the role of environmental assistance in language development is tentative and incomplete. We have a growing set of descriptive analyses of the course of language development, and a large body of correlational data on the relation between measures of language and measures of gross features of the child's environment. While these data make group predictions possible, they do not provide a fine-grained analysis of the processes involved. Only a few manipulative experiments exist. (22, p. 131)

Current Status of Early Environmental Deprivation and Its Implication for Compensatory Education

The topic of compensatory education provides the axis around which the issue of early environmental deprivation currently revolves. The disadvantaged and their plight in American society today has been the theme of many controversies. As Kirk says in an "Editor's Introduction," "there is no doubt today that American society has at long last recognized the problems of its impoverished and underdeveloped members—those referred to variously as 'the disadvantaged,' 'the deprived,' or 'the culturally disadvantaged' or 'culturally deprived' " (115, ix). Educational changes, however, are being delayed. The delay may come from a fundamental ideological conflict as to why children of lower socioeconomic families perform poorly in school. The ensuing debate continues to embroil psychologists, sociologists, educators, and parents alike.

One point of view, subscribed to by many educators, apportions the major blame to the family, home, and community, maintaining that they have failed to provide the motivational forces, the varied experiences, the language background, and the aspiration level necessary to succeed in acquiring the requisite socialization for the student role.

A second point of view proposes that the failure of the disadvantaged to succeed is an academic situation as a result of differential learning patterns that may be due to a difference inherent in the genetic makeup.

A third point of view, voiced primarily by sociologists and lower class parents, apportions the major, if not the sole, blame to the teachers and schools for their inefficiency and ineffectiveness in teaching lower class children. Classroom teachers, administrators, and entire school systems have been accused of perpetuating the "self-fulfilling prophecy" of nonlearning. This is the situation in which the disadvantaged student senses the teacher's and administrator's lack of faith in his character and abilities. This is accompanied by a consequent disrespect and lower expectations for him. The student internalizes these expectations and then proceeds to act out the prophecy of failure.

Evidence presented thus far in this chapter contributes to all points of view. Studies that were reviewed and the evidence presented in the areas discussed strongly tend to suggest that the effects of stimulation or deprivation operating in the early environment of the organism under study, whether human or animal, were definite and lasting into subsequent stages of development.

As mentioned earlier in this chapter, Arthur Jensen (74) has recently published a rather controversial article on the nature and characteristics of the disadvantaged and the effectiveness of compensatory education. Jensen begins his article by pointing out the failure of the current programs of compensatory education. After taking the reader through a series of scholarly and well-elaborated arguments, Jensen concludes that this failure is due to the fact that genetically attributable differential learning patterns have not been taken into consideration in the development of these programs. These differential learning patterns, argues Jensen, have resulted from the fact that the disadvantaged constitute a genetic population unto their own. This population as a whole has a lower mean of intelligence, which in turn provides a regression to a lower mean. Jensen further argues that this population possesses a different learning style from the "normal" middle-class population. On this basis Jensen proposes that social classes as well as races may profitably be construed as Mendelian populations or relatively isolated groups in terms of reproduction, whose variations may be associated with genetic sources.

I feel that the reader must keep in mind that Jensen does not really wish to do away with the concepts of compensatory education, but that he feels compensatory education as practiced today is of questionable value to the disadvantaged, whom he feels constitute a different type of organism. It must also be noted that in other writings (75), Jensen has emphasized the importance of early childhood verbal stimulation as a factor in future intellectual development.

Jensen's article has motivated responses by a number of psychologists who sponsor a more "environmentalist" position. J. M. Hunt responded:

> Although I have found many points in Jensen's paper with which I can heartily agree, I have also found others with which I can just as heartily disagree. These are, first, several matters concerned with the measurement, the distribution, the development, and the nature of intelligence; second, the nature of his emphasis on biological versus psychological and social factors in behavioral development and the implications he draws for the relatively fixed nature of the existing norms for "intelligence." Third is Jensen's implicitly limited view of the learning process, coupled with his apparent lack of appreciation of the cumulative and dynamic implications of existing evidence of plasticity in the rate of behavioral development. Fourth are the implications which he draws for class and race differences from the measures of heritability of the IQ in European and American Caucasians. Finally, comes a disagreement about the wisdom of his opening sentence that "compensatory education has been tried and it apparently has failed" in the light of his avowed predilection for keeping all hypotheses open to investigation (and hopefully to technological development) as well as debate. (68, p. 282)

Hunt proposes that compensatory education has not really been tried, as Jensen states. He feels that Jensen is only dwelling on the obvious as education has a great component of individualization anyway. Hunt further states that Jensen's concept of intelligence is not as solid as Jensen proposes and concludes his argument by offering evidence from animal research that suggests that the physical development of the brain is directly influenced by activities dealing with the processing of information.

Lee J. Cronbach (28) is another member of this group of selected "environmentalists" who reacted to Jensen's work. With a background in educational psychology, Cronbach challenges Jensen's recommendations for a program of compensatory education on the grounds that the changing nature of our society requires less and less the type of "intelligence" that Jensen proposed to develop in the disadvantaged. Cronbach argues that associative or memoristic learning ability will not suffice in the near future but will have to be accompanied by a fairly high degree of problem-solving, conceptual, abstract learning ability.

Jerome Kagan (79) is critical of the logic of Jensen's arguments and offers evidence from intraracial studies that supports the notion that the quality of mother-child interaction has an effect on mental growth and test scores.

The views presented thus far have in common the presentation of evidence to suggest that the disadvantaged child is inadequately prepared for an academic environment and is bereft of the skills and habits necessary for meeting the school's expectations. Another viewpoint has evolved in relation to the issue of compensatory education. This position holds that since these children are not really culturally disadvantaged but are only educationally disadvantaged, the most meaningful way to contribute to the academic advancement of the disadvantaged child is to become an accepting, enthusiastic, and creative teacher. It is not always easy, however, to be this kind of teacher in depressed urban schools. Tiedt (138) reveals that many teachers from middle-class backgrounds are dismayed at the disadvantaged child's impulsive acts and lack of self-control. This undisciplined behavior and the use of language not considered appropriate for a middle-class child are only two manifestations of the acute differences in teacher-child experiential backgrounds and values. The resultant for the teacher or pupil often is a phenomenon known as "culture shock." Moore points out in the introduction to his *Realities of the Urban Classroom* (98, pp. 3-4), a report of observations in "slum" elementary schools, that this culture shock can be a great force for creativity and innovation, or that it can cause withdrawal and apathy. To assist teachers in turning this culture shock into a creative force is one principal reason that most comprehensive compensatory education programs provide some type of orientation and in-service training for instructional and administrative personnel.

Many educators concur that the educationally disadvantaged

should be educated in terms of their own experiences, interests, and needs; and that the teacher must learn to perceive anew in order to insure reasonably objective reactions to child, family, and community, and to kindle mutual respect. The power of profit from experience is normally distributed in all social groups. Thus observed differences in behavior can be accounted for as a function of the quality of individual experience.

Bruner (16) makes the point that ability to construct rules, models, and strategies for inference ("a formidable factor" in perceiving) develops as a result of a normally rich perceptual environment. Deprivation prevents this cognitive activity and later ability to adapt to a shifting environment.

Barbe (1) agrees with other researchers when he states that functional intelligence is not rigidly fixed. Many well-intentioned teachers, however, seem to unconsciously discount this reality and point to low intelligence and achievement test scores, "poor heredity," and "cultural deprivation" as basis for the belief that low socioeconomic status students just cannot learn.

To overcome these kinds of feelings and to provide some guideline for programs of teacher training for service in schools in urban disadvantaged areas, a task force approach has been used (23, pp. 318-319). This task force comes from a current cooperative project of the "Great Cities" schools and cooperating colleges and universities, under a developmental contract between the United States Office of Education and Northwestern University. The teacher behavior required for satisfactory performance in disadvantaged urban areas has been described in detail. Through preservice and in-service programs focused on the attainment of these behaviors, teachers working with the disadvantaged can be helped to become more efficient.

Some of the proponents of this point of view are less positive and appear to reject the theory that cultural deprivation leads to major cognitive deficit. They seem to support the theory that the learning difficulties of the student from a low socioeconomic status family are a result of nothing more complex than poor teaching, and nothing more mysterious than bigotry and fear—which in the last analysis reflects not only educational but societal inadequacy.

There are others like Taba who recognize ". . . that the lack of success in school for certain groups of children suggests a two-way cause: the factors residing in the backgrounds of the children and the factors residing in the school program" (134, p. 156); and like Deutsch who ". . . can accept that some of this cumulative deficiency is associated with inadequate early preparation because of corresponding environmental deficiencies" but who also points out that ". . . the inadequacy of the school environment must be questioned: in a model system, one should expect linearity in cognitive growth" (42, p. 80). These two authors, as many others, perceive the vital interrelation between the two realities.

Summary

The research indicates a close relationship between cultural deprivation and mental retardation. In terms of the determinants of intelligence, research is still in progress. The concern continues in the nature-nurture or environmental-hereditary controversy. The evidence presented in this chapter suggests that the effects of stimulation or deprivation operating in the early environment of the organism, whether human or animal, are definite and lasting into subsequent stages of development. In effect, the earlier help is given in the life of the individual, the better the chances for more complete development.

References

1. Barbe, W. B. "Identification and Diagnosis of the Needs of the Educationally Retarded and Disadvantaged." *The Educationally Retarded and Disadvantaged.* Sixty-sixth Yearbook of the NATIONAL Society for the Study of Education, Part I. Chicago: National Society for the Study of Education, 1967.

2. Barrett, H. E., and Koch, H. L. "The Effect of Nursery-School Training Upon the Mental-Test Performance of a Group of Orphanage Children." *Pedagogical Seminary and Journal of Genetic Psychology,* 37 (1930), 102-122.

3. Bayley, N., and Jones, H. E. "Environmental Correlates of Mental and

Motor Development: A Cumulative Study from Infancy to Six Years." *Child Development,* 8 (1937), 329-341.

4. Beach, F. A., and Jaynes, J. "Effects of Early Experience upon the Behavior of Animals." *Psychological Bulletin,* 51 (1954), 239-263.

5. Bennett, E. L., Diamond, M. C., Krech, D., and Rosenzweig, M. R. "Chemical and Anatomical Plasticity of Brain." *Science,* 146 (1964), 610-619.

6. Bereiter, C. "A Nonpsychological Approach to Early Compensatory Education." *Social Class, Race, and Psychological Development.* Edited by M. Deutsch, I. Katz, and A. R. Jensen. New York: Holt, Rinehart, 1968.

7. Bereiter, C. and Engelmann, S. *Teaching Disadvantaged Children in the Preschool.* New York: Prentice-Hall, 1966.

8. Bernstein, B. "Language and Social Class." *British Journal of Sociology,* 11 (1960), 271-276.

9. Bexton, W. H., Heron, W., and Scott, T. H. "Effects of Decreased Variation in the Sensory Environment." *Canadian Journal of Psychology,* 8 (1954), 70-76.

10. Bijou, S. W. "Theory and Research in Mental (Developmental) Retardation." *Psychological Record,* 13 (1963), 95-110.

11. Bingham, W. E., and Griffiths, W. J., Jr. "The Effect of Different Environments during Infancy on Adult Behavior in the Rat." *Journal of Comparative and Physiological Psychology,* 45 (1952), 307-312.

12. Blank, M., and Solomon, F. "A Tutorial Language Program to Develop Abstract Thinking in Socially Disadvantaged Preschool Children." *Child Development,* 39 (1968), 379-389.

13. Bowlby, J. "Some Pathological Processes Set in Train by Early Mother-Child Separation." *Journal of Mental Science,* 99 (1953), 265-272.

14. Brodbeck, A. J., and Irwin, O. C. "The Speech Behaviour of Infants Without Families." *Child Development,* 17 (1946), 145-156.

15. Brownfield, C. A. "Deterioration and Facilitation Hypotheses in Sensory-Deprivation Research." *Psychological Bulletin,* 61 (1964), 304-413.

16. Bruner, J. S. "The Cognitive Consequences of Early Sensory Deprivation." *Sensory Deprivation.* Edited by P. Solomon, et al. Cambridge, Mass.: Harvard University Press, 1961.

17. Bruner, C. "Preschool Experiences for the Disadvantaged." *The Educationally Retarded and Disadvantaged.* Sixty-sixth Yearbook of the National Society for the Study of Education, Part I. Chicago: National Society for the Study of Education, 1967.

18. Caldwell, B. M. "What Is the Optimal Learning Environment for the Young Child?" *American Journal of Orthopsychiatry,* 37 (1967), 8-20.

19. Caldwell, B. M., and Richmond, J. B. "Programmed Day Care for the Very Young Child–A Preliminary Report." *Journal of Marriage and the Family,* 26 (1964), 481-488.

20. Casler, L. "The Study of the Effects of Extra Tactile Stimulation on a Group of Institutionalized Infants." *Genetic Psychology Monographs,* 71 (1965), 137-175.

21. Casler, L. "Maternal Deprivation: A Critical Review of the Literature." *Monographs of the Society for Research in Child Development,* 26, No. 2 (1961), 1-64.

22. Cazden, C. B. "Some Implications of Research on Language Development for Pre-School Education." *Early Education: Current Theory, Research, and Action.* Edited by R. D. Hess and R. M. Bear. Chicago: Aldine Publishing Co., 1968.

23. Chandler, B. J., and Bertolaet, F. "Administrative Problems and Procedures in Compensatory Education." *The Educationally Retarded and Disadvantaged.* Sixty-sixth Yearbook of the National Society for the Study of Education, Part I. Chicago: National Society for the Study of Education, 1967.

24. Cheyney, A. B. *Teaching Culturally Disadvantaged in the Elementary School.* Columbus, Ohio: Charles E. Merrill, 1967.

25. Coleman, R. W., and Provence, S. "Environmental Retardation (Hospitalism) in Infants Living in Families." *Pediatrics,* 19 (1957), 285-292.

26. Cooper, R. M., and Zubek, J. P. "Effects of Enriched and Restricted Early Environments on the Learning Ability of Bright and Dull Rats." *Canadian Journal of Psychology,* 12 (1958), 159-164.

27. Craviote, J., DeLicarie, E. R., and Birth, H. G. "Nutrition, Growth, and Neuro-Integrative Development: An Experimental and Ecologic Study." *Pediatrics Supplement,* 38, pt. 2 (1966).

28. Cronbach, L. J. "Heredity, Environment, and Educational Policy." *Harvard Educational Review,* 39 (1969), 338-347.

29. Davidson, H. P. "An Experimental Study of Bright, Average, and Dull Children at the Four-Year Mental Level." *Genetic Psychology Monographs,* 9 (1931), 119-289.

30. Davis, K. "Extreme Social Isolation of a Child." *American Journal of Sociology,* 45 (1940), 554-565.

31. Davis, K. "Final Note on a Case of Extreme Isolation." *American Journal of Sociology,* 52 (1947), 432-437.

32. Dawe, H. C. "A Study of the Effect of an Educational Program upon Language Development and Related Mental Functions in Young Children." *Journal of Experimental Education,* 11 (1942), 200-209.

33. Dember, W. N. "Response by the Rat to Environmental Change." *Journal of Comparative and Physiological Psychology,* 49 (1956), 93-95.

34. Denenberg, V. H. "The Effects of Early Experience." *The Behavior of Domestic Animals.* Edited by E. S. E. Hafez. London: Balliere, Tindall, and Koch, 1962.

35. Dennis, W. "Infant Development under Conditions of Restricted Practice and of Minimum Social Stimulation: A Preliminary Report." *Journal of Genetic Psychology,* 53 (1938), 149-157.

36. Dennis, W. "Infant Development under Conditions of Restricted Practice and of Minimum Stimulation." *Genetic Psychology Monographs,* 23 (1941), 143-189.

37. Dennis, W., and Najarian, P. "Infant Development under Environmental Handicap." *Psychological Monographs,* 7, No. 436 (1957).

38. Dennis, W., and Najarian, P. "Causes of Retardation among Institutional Children: Iran." *Journal of Genetic Psychology,* 96 (1960), 47-59.

39. Deutsch, C. P. "Environment and Perception." *Social Class, Race, and Psychological Development.* Edited by M. Deutsch, I. Katz, and A. R. Jensen. New York: Holt, Rinehart, 1968.

40. Deutsch, M. "Facilitating Development in the Pre-School Child: Social and Psychological Perspectives." *Merrill-Palmer Quarterly of Behavior and Development,* 10 (1964), 249-263.

41. Deutsch, M. P. "The Disadvantaged Child and the Learning Process." *Education in Depressed Areas.* Edited by A. H. Passow. New York: Teachers College, Columbia University, 1963.

42. Deutsch, M. P. "The Role of Social Class in Language Development and Cognition." *American Journal of Orthopsychiatry,* 35 (1965), 78-88.

43. Doman, G., Stevens, G. L., and Orem, R. C. "You Can Teach Your Baby to Read." *Ladies Home Journal* (May 1963), 62-63.

44. Ebbs, J. H., Tisdall, F. F., and Scott, W. A. "The Influence of Prenatal Diet on the Mother and Child." *Journal of Nutrition,* 22 (1941), 515-526.

45. Feldman, S. "A Preschool Enrichment Program for Disadvantaged Children." *New Era,* 45 (1964), 79-82.

46. Ferguson, G. A. "On Learning and Human Ability." *Canadian Journal of Psychology,* 8 (1954), 95-112.

47. Foss, B. M., ed. *Determinants of Infant Behaviour. II.* Proceedings of the Second Tavistock Seminar on Mother-Infant Interaction, London, September, 1961. New York: Wiley, 1963.

48. Fowler, W. "Cognitive Learning in Infancy and Early Childhood." *Psychological Bulletin,* 59 (1962), 116-152.

49. Fowler, W. "The Effect of Early Stimulation in the Emergence of Cognitive Processes." *Early Education: Current Theory, Research, and Action.* Edited by R. D. Hess and R. M. Bear. Chicago: Aldine Publishing Co., 1968.

50. Fowler W. "Structural Dimensions of the Learning Process in Early Reading." *Child Development,* 35 (1964), 1093-1104.

51. Fowler, W. "Teaching a Two-Year-Old to Read: An Experiment in Early Childhood Learning." *Genetic Psychology Monographs,* 66 (1962), 181-283.

52. Frost, J. L., and Hawkes, G. R., eds. *The Disadvantaged Child: Issues and Innovations.* New York: Houghton Mifflin, 1966.

53. Buschillo, J. C. "Enriching the Preschool Experience of Children from Age 3. Part II. The Evaluation." *Children,* 15 (1968), 140-143.

54. Gelinier-Ortigues, M., and Aubrey, J. "Maternal Deprivation, Psychogenic Deafness and Pseudo-Retardation." *Emotional Problems of Early Childhood.* Edited by G. Caplan. New York: Basic Books, 1955.

55. Gesell, A., and Thompson, H. "Learning and Growth in Identical Infant Twins." *Genetic Psychology Monographs,* 6 (1929), 1-124.

56. Gewirtz, H. B., and Gewirtz, J. L. Visiting and Caretaking Patterns for Kibbutz Infants: Age and Sex Trends." *American Journal of Orthopsychiatry,* 38 (1968), 427-443.

57. Goldfarb, W. "Effects of Psychological Deprivation in Infancy and Subsequent Stimulation." *American Journal of Psychiatry,* 102 (1945), 18-33.

58. Goldfarb, W. "Emotional and Intellectual Consequences of Psychologic Deprivation in Infancy: A Revaluation." *Psychopathology of Childhood.* Edited by P. H. Hoch and J. Zubin. Proceedings of the Forty-Fourth Annual Meeting of the American Psychopathological Association, New York City, June, 1954. New York: Grune and Stratton, 1955.

59. Goodenough, F. L. "A Preliminary Report on the Effect of Nursery-School Training upon the Intelligence Test Scores of Young Children." *Nature and Nurture.* Twenty-seventh Yearbook of the National Society for the Study of Education, Part II. Edited by G. M. Whipple. Bloomington, Illinois: Public School Publishing Co., 1928.

60. Gordon, I. J. "Stimulation Via Parent Education." *Children,* 16 (1969), 57-59.

61. Harlow, H. F., and Harlow, M. "Learning to Love." *American Scientist,* 54 (1966), 244-272.

62. Harlow, H. F., and Zimmerman, R. R. "Affectional Responses in the Infant Monkey." *Science,* 130 (1959), 421-432.

63. Hechinger, F. M., ed. *Pre-School Education Today; New Approaches to Teaching Three, Four, and Five-Year-Olds.* Garden City, New York: Doubleday, 1966.

64. Hellmuth, J., ed. *Disadvantaged Child.* Vol. 1. New York: Brunner/ Mazel, 1967.

65. Hellmuth, J., ed. *Disadvantaged Child.* Vol. 2. *Head Start and Early Intervention.* New York: Brunner/Mazel, 1968.

66. Hess, R. D., and Bear, R. M., eds. *Early Education: Current Theory, Research, and Action.* Chicago: Aldine Publishing Co., 1968.

67. Hilgard, J. R. "The Effect of Early and Delayed Practice on Memory and Motor Performances Studied by the Method of Co-Twin Control." *Genetic Psychology Monographs,* 14 (1933), 493-657.

68. Hunt, J. McV. "Has Compensatory Education Failed? Has It Been Attempted?" *Harvard Educational Review,* 39 (1969), 278-300.

69. Hunt, J. McV. "How Children Develop Intellectually." *Children,* 11 (1964), 83-91.

70. Hunt, J. McV. *"Intelligence and Experience.* New York: Ronald Press, 1961.

71. Hunt, J. McV. "The Psychological Basis for Using Pre-School Enrichment as an Antidote for Cultural Deprivation." *Merrill-Palmer Quarterly of Behavior and Development,* 10 (1964), 209-248.

72. Irwin, O. C. "Infant Speech: Effect of Systematic Reading of Stories." *Journal of Speech and Hearing Research,* 3 (1960), 187-190.

73. Jackson, R. L. *Effects of Malnutrition on Growth of the Preschool Child.* Washington, D.C.: National Research Council, National Academy of Sciences, 1966.

74. Jensen, A. R. "How Much Can We Boost IQ and Scholastic Achievement?" *Harvard Educational Review,* 39 (1969), 1-123.

75. Jensen, A. R. "Learning in the Preschool Years." *Journal of Nursery Education,* 18 (1963), 133-139.

76. John, V. P. "The Intellectual Development of Slum Children: Some Preliminary Findings." *American Journal of Orthopsychiatry,* 33 (1963), 813-822.

77. John, V. P., and Goldstein, L. S "The Social Context of Language Acquisition." *Merrill-Palmer Quarterly of Behavior and Development,* 10 (1964), 265-275.

78. Jones, H. E. "The Environment and Mental Development." *Manual of Child Psychology.* 2nd ed. Edited by L. Carmichael. New York: Wiley and Sons, 1954.

79. Kagan, J. S. "Inadequate Evidence and Illogical Conclusions." *Harvard Educational Review,* 39 (1969), 274-277.

80. Katan, A. "Some Thoughts about the Role of Verbalization in Early

Childhood." *Psychoanalytic Study of the Child,* 16 (1961), 184-188.

81. Kephart, N. C. "Influencing the Rate of Mental Growth in Retarded Children through Environmental Stimulation." *Intelligence: Its Nature and Nurture.* Thirty-ninth Yearbook of the National Society for the Study of Education, Part II. Edited by G. M. Whipple. Bloomington, Illinois: Public School Publishing Co., 1940.

82. Kirk, S. A. *Early Education of the Mentally Retarded; An Experimental Study.* Urbana, Illinois: University of Illinois Press, 1958.

83. Kittrell, F. P. "Enriching the Preschool Experience of Children from Age 3. Part I. The Program." *Children,* 15 (1968), 135-139.

84. Klackenberg, G. "Studies in Maternal Deprivation in Infants' Homes." *Acta Paediatrica,* 45 (1956), 1-12.

85. Knobloch, H., and Pasamanick, B. "Environmental Factors Affecting Human Development, Before and After Birth." *Pediatrics,* 26 (1960), 210-218.

86. Kulka, A., Fry, C., and Goldstein, L. S. "Kinesthetic Needs in Infancy." *American Journal of Orthopsychiatry,* 30 (1960), 562-571.

87. Lamson, E. E. "A Follow-Up Study of a Group of Nursery-School Children." *Intelligence: Its Nature and Nurture.* Thirty-ninth Yearbook of the National Society for the Study of Education, Part II. Edited by G. M. Whipple. Bloomington, Illinois: Public School Publishing Co., 1940.

88. Levy, R. J. "Effects of Institutional vs Boarding Home Care on a Group of Infants." *Journal of Personality,* 15 (1947), 233-241.

89. Lewis, H. *Deprived Children: The Mersham Experiment; A Social and Clinical Study.* London: Oxford University Press, 1954.

90. Loevinger, J. "Intelligence as Related to Socio-Economic Factors." *Intelligence: Its Nature and Nurture.* Thirty-ninth Yearbook of the National Society for the Study of Education, Part I. Edited by G. M. Whipple. Bloomington, Illinois: Public School Publishing Co., 1940.

91. Lowrey, L. B. "Personality Distortion and Early Institutional Care." *American Journal of Orthopsychiatry,* 10 (1940), 576-585.

92. Lynch, E. I., and Mertz, A. E. "Adoptive Placement of Infants Directly from the Hospital." *Social Casework,* 36 (1955), 451-457.

93. McCandless, B. R. "Environment and Intelligence." *American Journal of Mental Deficiency,* 56 (1952), 674-691.

94. McGehee, W., and Lewis, W. D. "The Socio-Economic Status of the Homes of Mentally Superior and Retarded Children and the Occupational Rank of Their Parents." *The Pedagogical Seminary and Journal of Genetic Psychology,* 60 (1942), 375-380.

95. McGraw, M. B. "Later Development of Children Specially Trained during Infancy; Johnny and Jimmy at School Age." *Child Development,* 10 (1939), 1-19.

96. Miller, H. L., ed. *Education for the Disadvantaged: Current Issues and Research.* New York: Free Press, 1967.

97. Milner, E. "A Study of the Relationship between Reading Readiness in Grade One School Children and Patterns of Parent-Child Interaction." *Child Development,* 22 (1951), 95-112.

98. Moore, G. A., Jr. *Realities of the Urban Classroom; Observations in Elementary Schools.* New York: Frederick A. Praeger, 1967.

99. Moore, J. K. "Speech Content of Selected Groups of Orphanage and Non-orphanage Preschool Children." *Journal of Experimental Education,* 16 (1947), 122-133.

100. Moss, H. A., and Kagan, J. "Maternal Influences on Early IQ Scores." *Psychological Reports,* 4 (1958), 655-661.

101. Mundy, L. "Environmental Influence on Intellectual Function as Measured by Intelligence Tests." *British Journal of Medical Psychology,* 30 ('1957), 194-201.

102. Murphy, L. B. "Preventive Implications of Development in the Preschool Years." *Prevention of Mental Disorders in Children: Initial Explorations.* Edited by G. Caplan. New York: Basic Books, 1961.

103. Norris, A. S. "Prenatal Factors in Intellectual and Emotional Development." *Journal of the American Medical Association,* 172 (1960), 413-416.

104. Orgel, S. Z. "Personality Distortion and Early Institutional Care." *American Journal of Orthopsychiatry,* 11 (1941), 371-373.

105. Palmer, F. H. "Learning at Two." *Children,* 16 (1969), 55-57.

106. Parsons, M. H. "A Home Economist in Service to Families with Mental Retardation." *Children,* 7 (1960), 184-189.

107. Pasamanick, B. "A Comparative Study of the Behavioral Development of Negro Infants." *Journal of Genetic Psychology,* 69 (1946), 3-44.

108. Passow, A. H., Goldbert, M., and Tannenbaum. A. J., eds. *Education of the Disadvantaged.* New York: Holt, Rinehart, 1967.

109. Pavenstedt, E. "A Comparison of the Child-Rearing Environment of Upper-Lower and Very-Lower-Lower Class Families." *American Journal of Orthopsychiatry,* 35 (1965), 89-98.

110. Peters, C. C., and McElwee, A. R. "Improving Functioning Intelligence by Analytical Training in a Nursery School." *Elementary School Journal,* 45 (1944), 213-219.

111. Pinneau, S. R., and Jones, H. E. "Mental Development in Infancy and Childhood and Mental Abilities in Adult Life." *Review of Educational Research,* 25 (1955), 415-437.

112. Pringle, M. L. K., and Tanner, M. "The Effects of Early Deprivation on Speech Development: A Comparative Study of 4 Year Olds in a Nursery School and in Residential Nurseries." *Language and Speech,* 1 (1958), 269-287.

113. Provence, S., and Lipton, R. C. *Infants in Institutions: A Comparison of Their Development with Family-Reared Infants During the First Year of Life.* New York: International Universities Press, 1962.

114. Provence, S., and Ritvo, S. "Effects of Deprivation on Institutionalized Infants: Disturbances in Development of Relationship to Inanimate Objects." *The Psychoanalytic Study of the Child,* 16 (1961), 189-205.

115. Rees, H. E. *Deprivation and Compensatory Education: A Consideration.* Boston: Houghton Mifflin, 1968.

116. Reymert, M. L., and Hinton, R. T., Jr. "The Effect of a Change to a Relatively Superior Environment upon the IQ's of One Hundred Children." *Intelligence: Its Nature and Nurture.* Thirty-ninth Yearbook of the National Society for the Study of Education, Part II. Edited by G. M. Whipple. Bloomington, Illinois: Public School Publishing Co., 1940.

117. Rheingold, H. L. "Controlling the Infant's Exploratory Behaviour." *Determinants of Infant Behavior.* Edited by B. M. Foss. New York: Wiley, 1961.

118. Rheingold, H. L. "The Modification of Social Responsiveness in Institutional Babies." *Monographs of the Society for Research in Child Development,* 21, No. 63 (1956).

119. Rheingold, H. L., Gewirtz, J. L., and Ross, H. W. "Social Conditioning of Vocalizations in the Infant." *Journal of Comparative and Physiological Psychology,* 52 (1959), 68-73.

120. Richardson, H. M. "The Growth of Adaptive Behavior in Infants: An Experimental Study at Seven Age Levels." *Genetic Psychology Monographs,* 12 (1932), 195-359.

121. Reissman, F. *The Culturally Deprived Child.* New York: Harper & Row, 1962.

122. Roberts, J. I., ed. *School Children in the Urban Slum.* New York: Free Press, 1967.

123. Rogers, A. L., Durling, D., and McBridge, K. "The Effect on the Intelligence Quotient of Change from a Poor to a Good Environment." *Nature and Nurture.* Twenty-seventh Yearbook of the National Society for the Study of Education, Part I. Edited by G. M. Whipple. Bloomington, Illinois: Public School Publishing Company, 1928.

124. Schaefer, E. A. "A Home Tutoring Program." *Children* 16 (1969), 59-61.

125. Schoggen, M. "An Ecological Study of Three-Year-Olds at Home, Final Report." *DARCEE Papers and Reports,* 3, No. 7 (1969). Nashville, Tennessee: George Peabody College for Teachers, 1969.

126. Scrimshaw, N. S., and Gordon, J. E., eds. *Malnutrition, Learning and Behavior.* Cambridge, Massachusetts: M.I.T. Press, 1968.

127. Skeels, H. M., and Dye, H. G. "A Study of the Effects of Differential Stimulation on Mentally Retarded Children." *Proceedings of the American Association on Mental Deficiency,* 44 (1939), 114-136.

128. Skeels, H. M., and Harms, I. "Children with Inferior Social Histories; Their Mental Development in Adoptive Homes." *Journal of Genetic Psychology,* 72 (1948), 283-294.

129. Skodak, M., and Skeels, H. M. "A Final Follow-Up Study of One Hundred Adopted Children." *Journal of Genetic Psychology,* 75 (1949), 85-125.

130. Spicker, H. H., Hodges, W. I., and McCandless, B. R. "A Diagnostically Based Curriculum for Psychosocially Deprived, Preschool, Mentally Retarded Children: Interim Report." *Exceptional Children,* 33 (1966), 215-220.

131. Spitz, R. A. "Hospitalism: An Inquiry into the Genesis of Psychiatric Conditions in Early Childhood." *Psychoanalytic Study of the Child,* 1 (1945), 53-74.

132. Stendler-Levatelli, C. B. "Environmental Intervention in Infancy and Early Childhood." *Social Class, Race, and Psychological Development.* Edited by M. Deutsch, I. Katz, and A. R. Jensen. New York: Holt, Rinehart, 1968.

133. Stippich, M. E. "The Mental Development of Children of Feeble-Minded Mothers: A Preliminary Report." *Intelligence: Its Nature and Nurture.* Thirty-ninth Yearbook of the National Society for the Study of Education, Part II. Edited by G. M. Whipple. Bloomington, Illinois: Public School Publishing Co., 1940.

134. Taba, H. "Cultural Deprivation as a Factor in School Learning." *Merrill-Palmer Quarterly of Behavior and Development,* 10 (1964), 147-159.

135. Taylor, A. "Deprived Infants: Potential for Affective Adjustment." *American Journal of Orthopsychiatry,* 38 (1968), 835-845.

136. Thomas, H. "Visual-Fixation Responses of Infants to Stimuli of Varying Complexity." *Child Development,* 36 (1965), 629-638.

137. Thompson, W. F. "Early Environment—Its Importance for Later Behavior." *Psychopathology of Childhood.* Edited by P. H. Hoch and J. Zubin. Proceedings of the Forty-Fourth Annual Meeting of the American Psychopathological Association, New York City, June, 1954. New York; Grune and Stratton, 1955.

138. Tiedt, S. W., ed. *Teaching the Disadvantaged Child.* New York and London: Oxford University Press, 1968.

139. Triplett, J. L. "A Women's Club for Deprived Mothers." *Nursing Outlook,* 13 (1965), 33-35.

140. U.S. Department of Health, Education, and Welfare. National Institutes of Health. *Perspectives on Human Deprivation: Biological, Psychological, Sociological.* Washington, D.C.: Government Printing Office, 1969.

141. U.S. President's Committee on Mental Retardation. *MR 68: The Edge of Change.* A Report to the President on Mental Retardation Program Trends and Innovations, with Recommendations on Residential Care, Manpower, and Deprivation. Washington, D.C.: Government Printing Office, 1968.

142. U.S. President's Panel on Mental Retardation. *A Proposed Program for National Action to Combat Mental Retardation.* Washington, D.C.: Government Printing Office, 1962.

143. Vincent, C. E. "Trends in Infant Care Ideas." *Child Development,* 22 (1951), 199-209.

144. Walters, R. H., and Karal, P. "Social Deprivation and Verbal Behavior." *Journal of Personality,* 28 (1960), 89-107.

145. Warkany, J. "Congenital Malformations Induced by Maternal Nutrition Deficiency." *Journal of Pediatrics,* 25 (1944), 476-480.

146. Waters, E., and Crandall, V. J. "Social Class and Observed Maternal Behavior from 1940-1960." *Child Development,* 35 (1964), 1021-1032.

147. Weisberg, P. "Social and Nonsocial Conditioning of Infant Vocalizations." *Child Development,* 34 (1963), 377-388.

148. Werkman, S. L., Shifman, L., and Skelley, T. "Psychosocial Correlates of Iron Deficiency Anemia in Early Childhood." *Psychosomatic Medicine,* 26 (1964), 125-134.

149. Whitman, M., and Deutsch, M. "Social Disadvantage as Related to Intellective and Language Development." *Social Class, Race, and Psychological Development.* Edited by M. Deutsch, I. Katz, and A. R. Jensen. New York, Holt, Rinehart, 1968.

150. Wortis, H., Bardach, J. L., Cutler, R., Rue, R., and Freedman, A. "Child-Rearing Practices in a Low Socioeconomic Group." *Pediatrics,* 32 (1963), 298-307.

PART II

Curricular Considerations

CHAPTER 6

Working More Effectively
with Migrants in Our Schools

ELIZABETH SUTTON

Dr. Sutton develops a theoretical rationale upon which to discuss practical methods that can be used by classroom teachers. The central theme running through the chapter is that teachers must build upon the experiences of children. The experiences that can be used are numerous and allow for a wide variety of instruction.

Dr. Elizabeth Sutton has been a teacher at all levels of education and did a particularly interesting original study of the migrants of the East Coast stream with whom she worked closely for three years. From this research came her book *Knowing and Teaching the Migrant Child.* She received her Ed.D. from Florida State University. Dr. Sutton is employed by the U.S. Office of Education in the Division of State Agency Cooperation.

AGRICULTURAL MIGRATORY CHILDREN constitute one of the most disadvantaged groups of children in America. Their mobile way of life places limitations on stability. They live as "outsiders," segregated from the life of the community. Economic and social factors contrive to make situations that are detrimental to physical health, to emotional and social well-being, and to educational development. Migrant children are usually retarded academically because of irregular school attendance and the inadequacies of their backgrounds; and the schools fail to identify and adapt to the unique experiences of migrant children.

Throughout our country increasing attention is being directed to extend and improve educational opportunities for migrant children. There must be continuous exploration for more effective ways of working with these children in our schools. Educators face a real challenge.

The purpose of this chapter is to offer ideas drawn directly from my observations and experiences and from selected research projects that point toward successful ways of working with migrant children. The following statements are given as the theoretical rationale for the practical teaching suggestions which follow.

1. The migrant child, like all children, grows and matures physically, socially, mentally, and emotionally, in terms of characteristic patterns of growth and development. Differences found are likely to be differences of degree resulting from his cultural pattern of living.

2. Like all children, as the migrant child grows he forms a picture of himself, of the kind of person he is, of the things he can and cannot do, of the kind of person he can eventually hope to become. This picture—his self-concept—the way he sees himself and others—will determine greatly his success or failure in school or in life.

3. The migrant child, like all children, has special strengths, abilities, and experiences which must be identified and taken into account when teaching him.

4. Because of his pattern of living and of his mobile way of life, the migrant child has had unique work and travel experiences which we may capitalize upon when teaching him. He has picked up scattered bits of information about places he has lived, about the country through which he has traveled, and about the growth and processing of various food and fiber crops.

5. The migrant child needs to develop the same kinds of skills, understandings, appreciations, and attitudes as do all American children; however, because of his irregular schooling and the inadequacies of his background, he has distinctive and unique needs to which immediate attention should be directed. Schools, therefore, must give priority to certain skills. Along with the fundamental skills of literacy, migrant children need educational experiences that give them direction toward improving their lives immediately as well as in the future.

6. Migrant children, like all children, differ in their needs, abilities, interests, motivations, and backgrounds. Hence, we must not stereotype the migrant child; instead, we must hold fast to the theory of individual differences to which we have subscribed for many years.

7. If schools today are to meet the needs of migrant children, it seems imperative that some consideration be given to the modification of curriculum content, to the modification of instructional patterns, and to the modification and development of materials.

8. Finally, the basic principles of good teaching are the same for the migrant child as they are for all children.

What are the priorities that should be given first attention when teaching migrant children? What are the kinds of experiences that migrant children need to improve their lives now and that may open vistas to them for continuous learning and for successful living in the future? Of primary importance are the following.

A More Adequate Self-image

The migrant child needs experiences that will help him develop a more adequate self-concept and dispel his feelings of insecurity. He needs to feel that he is accepted, that he is wanted, that he is needed, and that he can make important contributions to the living and learning experiences at school. Even on his first day in the school it is important that the migrant child be given a special responsibility. He needs daily tasks that he can complete successfully: tasks that are within the range of his immediate competencies but of sufficient difficulty to challenge him.

The process of developing a more adequate self-concept applies to all areas of study and to all his school experiences. A daily challenge for each teacher is: Have I provided a learning experience that caused this migrant child to feel good about himself?

Basic Concepts and Habits of Good Health and of Healthful Living

It is imperative that teachers provide daily experiences that will help the migrant child to develop understandings of and appreciations for good health. We must provide a school environment that is not only conducive to good physical health but promotes desirable mental and social health. The migrant child needs to practice basic health habits at school: washing hands; brushing teeth; taking a shower (if there are no shower facilities, a water hose may be used); eating proper foods at regular periods, participating in a balanced day of work, rest, and relaxation; standing, walking and sitting properly; using all laboratory and school facilities properly and safely; noting classroom temperatures and ventilation; and covering his nose and mouth when sneezing or coughing.

Schools may need to modify their health curriculum so that

migrant children acquire knowledge and understanding of the health problems that are most common to migrant people. Therefore, the teacher will need to understand the home conditions of the migrants in order to help these children make practical adaptations as circumstances allow. Health topics such as the following are of importance to migrant children.

1. Food and Nutrition
    Foods needed daily
    Preparation of foods
    Practices of cleanliness in handling food
    Foods to use in traveling
    Inexpensive, nutritious one-dish meals that can be prepared with minimum cooking facilities
2. Personal Cleanliness and Grooming
    Proper care of hair, teeth, eyes, ears, and nails
    Regular bathing habits
    Suitable clothing
    Proper care of clothing
3. Rest, Relaxation, and Play
    Sleep and rest needed
    Developing of hobbies
    Team games that may be played in camps
    Games to play and songs to sing while traveling
4. Living Happily with Family and Friends
    Responsibility of the child as a worthy family member
    Good manners
    How to make new friends
    How to be a good friend
    Ways of keeping in contact with friends while traveling
5. Sanitation
    Sanitation at home (general sanitary precautions needed)
    Sanitation at school (general sanitary practices needed for healthful living, such as light, heating, ventilation, water, and toilet)
    Special "clean-up" projects at home, in the camp, and in the neighborhood
6. Communicable Diseases

Symptoms of common diseases
Home remedies and preventive measures
Innoculations necessary
Unsanitary conditions that cause disease
Care of bed patients in the home
7. Safety and First Aid
Practical safety measures at home, school, and on highways
Use of the first aid kit at home and while traveling
Importance of calling a doctor when accidents occur
Care of patient before arrival of doctor
8. Community Health Services
Local health department
Immunization programs
How to make contacts with appropriate health services
Importance of regular health checkups and of visits to dentist
Importance of keeping health records

Competencies in Performing Home Tasks

The migrant child needs experiences that will help him to perform his home tasks more competently. He grows up early and assumes family responsibilities at an early age. Even at the ages of six and seven he is likely to be responsible for the care of younger children, for making meals, for doing laundry, and for other household chores. Can we not include some experiences that will help him to care for younger brothers and sisters? What about appropriate songs to sing? Games to play? Pictures? Magazines? Picture books? Toys? Books and stories to read to smaller children? Can we not provide real purpose for audience reading of instructional materials since the migrant child can read orally stories or books at home?

What about meals? Snacks? Cannot the migrant child learn about those foods that are nutritious and which he may prepare easily and safely for snacks and meals at home for his younger brothers and sisters? Certainly, raw fruits, dry cereal, and milk make a better supper for children than the fried foods or cold snacks so frequently used. What about general housecleaning? Laundry? Are there not practical kinds of simple homemaking experiences we can provide for migrant children that will not only help them to perform these home tasks more effectively but also give status and dignity to the performance of these home responsibilities? The answers are, of course, a patent "yes."

A migrant child may begin to develop a more positive self-image when he sees that the teacher attaches importance to the competent performance of these home tasks.

Knowledge of Public Agencies, Organizations, and Institutions

The migrant child needs knowledge of and appreciation for the programs and services of public agencies, organizations, and institutions. It is imperative that schools provide experiences that will help the migrant child to know, to understand, and to develop desirable attitudes for the kinds of programs and services offered by various public and voluntary agencies.

Because of his transient way of life and because his life has not been related to community living in the usual ways, he needs many kinds of experiences that provide direct contact with people from such agencies and institutions as the health department, social security office, the chamber of commerce, the police department, highway patrol offices, local government, public libraries, parks, community recreational programs, banks, industrial plants, food processing plants, and museums. We need to arrange carefully many field trips to such public agencies and places.

Teacher-pupil planning for such trips is most important: Where are we going? Why are we going? Whom and what shall we see? What do they do? Why? What are the kinds of questions we may ask? How do we arrange an appointment? What are the polite ways to behave while we are there? How do we write a letter of thanks? This kind of planning will help the migrant child to assume responsibility for his own learning. These field trips and visits planned with a purpose may become short experiential teaching units that integrate learning experiences in the areas of language arts, arithmetic, social studies (emphasizing economics, geography, and history), science, art, music, health, safety, dramatics, and speech. Also, other short experiential units may be initiated as a result of such trips. A short unit on the purposes and values of the social security program is appropriate as is the study of the advantages and procedures of obtaining and using a public library card. Such experiences should cause the migrant child to be curious about and make appropriate inquiries about such agencies in each community in which he lives.

Basic Economic Concepts

The migrant child needs experiences that help him to develop basic economic concepts, particularly those related to budgeting and to the wise use of his earnings. At an early age, most migrant children work and supplement the family income. Many of these children, early in life, actually make their own decisions in spending their own money for clothing, for recreation, and for school supplies. How can we help the migrant child to learn how to manage his money more economically.

We can encourage "piggy banks" into which he places money for school supplies and for other needed expenditures in the future. We can encourage him to open a real bank account. We can provide actual experiences in selecting and buying needed commodities. One school developed a short teaching unit entitled "How to Prepare an Order from a Catalog." Older migrant children can become involved in making a weekly or monthly budget for a family of six, eight, or ten. They can set up and operate a make-believe store, service station, or a dry cleaning business. What would happen if high school migrant youth became actually involved in establishing a school bank? A stock company? Truly, this is a challenging area for exploration.

Appreciation of Educational Values Coincident to Travel

The migrant child needs experiences that will help him to know, to understand, and to appreciate the educational values coincident to travel. From his travels he has an unusual learning opportunity, but he is not likely to have the educational values in this travel pointed out to him. We should not only capitalize on the travel experiences that the migrant child has had but we should continually explore ways in which to guide and extend the migrant child's education while he travels. He can study about the places of historical interest and scenic beauty that are adjacent to his traveling routes. We can plan with crew leaders and parents to make such stops en route. The following successful experience of a teacher is indicative of what can happen.

> I talked to a crew leader about the school travel project explaining what the children had studied and what they had learned about interesting places to see along Route 17 from Virginia to Florida. Immediately, he responded, "That's a good idea, you just let me know those places and we will stop. I'd like to see them myself." Later, in Florida, I learned that he had made the stops and that the children had interesting information and pictures to share with their classmates about things they had learned from these visits en route.

Providing an experiential teaching unit entitled "A-Traveling We Will Go" can produce many relevant activities. For example:

> 1. Locating and reading about places to visit or to notice en route: historical shrines and landmarks, states, cities, counties, mountains, rivers, streams, lakes expressways, bridges, and tunnels;
> 2. Developing study guides or lists of questions to ask in order to learn more about these selected areas and places of interest;
> 3. Assembling appropriate maps to use. Children may plot or record such things as travel routes, places they stopped, places and things they observed, the temperature, climatic conditions, kinds of soil, physical terrain of the country, crops grown, and industries;
> 4. Devising forms for keeping records of expenses incurred en route for gasoline, oil, bus repairs, and food;
> 5. Learning appropriate songs and games to sing and play while riding along the highway;
> 6. Planning inexpensive, nutritious foods to take for preparing meals at picnic areas;
> 7. Conferring with and soliciting cooperation of crew leaders and parents to share in the travel project.

There are unlimited possibilities for extending and improving the education of the migrant child through careful guidance of things for him to see, to do, and to learn as he moves from one place to another. Travel offers a natural laboratory for placing more responsibility on the migrant child to learn from his transient way of life, to develop self-confidence, self-direction, and to "open doors" to him for continuous learning in each school that he attends. Many stimulating and educational experiences would happen if schools developed special travel-type projects that necessitated the gathering of information en route and the interviewing of people from various agencies and institutions in those communities in which the migrant child lives while on the trek. Such projects could be completed in another school under the supervision of a different teacher who in turn would begin another project.

Basic Concepts of Privileges and Responsibilities of American Citizenship

The migrant child needs experiences that will help him to develop more adequate concepts of his privileges and responsibilities as a responsible, contributing citizen in a democratic society. For the most part migrant children are drawn from the lower socioeconomic strata of our society. In many cases, migrant parents are nonvoters who have not established residency in any one state.

Since the life of the migrant child is lived apart from the main stream of the community, he has had little, if any, opportunity to participate in social, civic, and community affairs. He needs to become involved with regular community groups. Membership might be arranged for the child in Girl Scouts, Camp Fire Girls, Boy Scouts, or in other such clubs and community groups. We can provide learning experiences from which he finds that America is made up of many different ethnic groups and nationalities and that each has made its special contributions. Experiential units of work can be developed around such real life problems as:

1. What does it mean to be a responsible, contributing citizen of this community? (state? country?)
2. What is my heritage as an American Negro? (Anglo-American? American Indian? Mexican-American?)

These experiental units are relevant for children in today's world. If all children in classrooms, representing several ethnic groups, were involved in such studies, each contributing in terms of his ethnic background, much of the racial and general unrest we now experience might be alleviated.

Knowledge of the "World of Work"

The migrant child needs experiences that will help him to become familiar with the world of work and with the different ways in which people may earn a living. Since the migrant child is likely to drop out of school to go to work, he needs experiences early in his school life that will cause him to consider and to investigate different vocations, professions, and service positions. More importantly, he needs to be motivated to continue his education and to understand its advantages for him. We need to help him to plan his life in terms of these extended goals.

It is our responsibility to "open the doors" to him for an alternative way of life. He must understand that automation is replacing the need for agricultural workers. In this regard there are many kinds of experiences that an elementary school may provide to give guidance and understanding to the migrant child in the area of work possibilities. For instance there may be trips to and visits from various people in the community for the purpose of learning about their work, the education and training necessary, and the advantages and disadvantages of their work as they see it. The school can, through cooperative planning and teaching, provide special interest projects. Such projects carefully planned by the teachers may open the door to migrant children for potential future work. Projects such as the following have been found to be successful.

1. A school newspaper. As the project developed children visited the local paper; they learned to use the typewriter, to take and develop their own pictures for the paper, to conduct interviews with appropriate people for special columns, and to prepare different sections found in a regular daily paper.

2. Sewing project. This included the selection of patterns, materials, and even designing patterns for head coverings, dresses, and useful articles to use in the home.

3. Cooking projects. Included here were planning, buying, or obtaining foods, cooking and serving meals to which a guest was invited. (Migrant parents were frequent guests.)

4. Furnishing a model kitchen. Some boys renovated a "tin shelter," did repair work and put up a ceiling. They made kitchen cabinets; selected, purchased, and installed a refrigerator, sink, and an electric stove.

5. A nursery project. Children selected and planted seeds and bulbs, cared for the plants, and nurtured their growth, and transplanted the flowering shrubs, vines, and garden flowers to the school grounds. Some children planted flowers around their homes in the migrant camp.

6. Industrial arts shop. Migrant children made various articles for their parents and homes, and under the supervision of the teacher made simple repairs to the school building and grounds.

7. Auto mechanic project. An old car was acquired and those boys who were interested had many experiences in tearing it down and getting the engine operating again. (Fortunately, the sixth grade teacher was a natural mechanic who could give guidance and direction to this project.)

The migrant child needs prevocational types of experiences at the elementary school level. Former Commissioner of Education Howe, in an address before the Sixth Annual International Manpower Seminar, stated: "We can no longer wait until pupils reach high school before encouraging them to begin to plan their occupational future. We must stimulate interest in the world of work early in the child's life."

Fundamental Skills of Literacy

The migrant child needs experiences through which he acquires the basic skills of literacy. It is imperative that he develop competencies in communication and in basic computation. The fundamental skills of literacy are so important that all teachers receiving a migrant child at any grade level should direct special attention to the development of basic reading competencies, to fundamental number concepts, and to speaking and writing proficiencies that are comparable to his level of attainment at that time.

The migrant child, like all children, needs to learn to see (observe details), to listen (various listening skills), to talk (speak distinctly and express ideas coherently and meaningfully), to read (reading skills appropriate for different reading purposes and the habit of reading independently for information and for pleasure), and to write (including both manuscript and cursive writing skills, spelling, and creative writing to communicate ideas). He needs the basic concept of numbers; he needs to know how to figure the amount of earnings due him, how to keep records and accounts and expenditures, how to write a check, how to prepare legal forms, and many other practical skills involving numbers. These skills become an integral part of all the learning experiences provided. Learning experiences are much more meaningful to the migrant child when he talks, reads, writes, and figures about his own experiences and about the kinds of problems that he faces in his daily living.

These basic skills need to be taught as an integral part of school experiences which have meaning for the migrant child and which are relevant to improving his life now, as well as holding "open doors" for an alternative life tomorrow. We need to explore more fully the language-experience approach to reading as we teach communication skills. Indeed, such an approach provides unlimited possibilities for observing, listening, talking, reading, and for writing, all of which have real purpose and meaning for the migrant child. Such teaching strategies are exciting, challenging, and rewarding.

The utilization of the foregoing school experiences can give direction to the selection, modification, and development of more appropriate instructional materials. As migrant children talk, ask questions, explore, and recount what they have learned, both in oral and in written expression, teachers can find unlimited possibilities for developing special materials as well as identifying more appropriate published materials. This, too, is an area that needs much exploration and research.

Research indicates that as we develop more effective ways of working with migrant children in our schools, we discover more effective ways of working with all children in our schools. Hence, we improve the quality of education for all children. Although the task is formidable, the goal is worth every effort.

CHAPTER 7

Teaching the Linguistically Dispossessed: A Dialect Approach

J. A. REYNOLDS

Dr. Reynolds develops his discussion of dialect by presenting two perspectives: moralistic and scientific. Using these terms as a point of departure he then develops illustrations about the dialects that migrants might bring to school. He stresses that teachers must realize that there are several forms of English and that it is not too much to expect, in terms of fuller communication, that teachers understand the dialects of the children.

Dr. J. A. Reynolds is a philologist and student of medieval languages and literatures at the University of Miami. His chief linguistic interests are the dialects and the dialect variants in the standard speech in the Americas. In 1967, as chairman of the American Dialects Section of the Southern Speech Association, he conducted a colloquium in the theoretical and practical aspects of English as a secondary language for culturally disadvantaged groups. He studied at Tulane, the National University of Mexico, and received his Ph.D. from Louisiana State University.

MOST OF US, and it is unfortunate that those of us who teach languages are among the many, regard such terms as "language" and "dialect" as always and by nature mutually distinct. The truth is, of course, that such terms have meaning only within certain clearly defined frames of reference. As an example, we should not hesitate to say, with perfect accuracy, that English, Dutch, German, and Swedish are "languages." They are, in fact, historic entities as languages; moreover, each is both an "official" and "national" language; and, finally, each is the proper and proud carrier of a distinguished body of literature.

Having so established these as languages, we may now with

equal propriety speak of them collectively as Germanic "dialects," which, in the historic sense, they are. We may go still further, designating the first three as West Germanic dialects and the fourth as a North Germanic dialect. We may go still further and refer to the first two as "Low German" dialects (i.e., modern languages that developed from the dialects spoken in the geographic lowlands of the extensive West Germanic area) and the third as "High German" (i.e., a language that developed in the geographic highlands of that area).

But of course we have been speaking of historic developments; and, one readily assumes, every teacher knows that "English" is, certainly in modern times, a "language." And this language is one that is well defined in all manner of grammar books and well exemplified in print, from the daily newspaper to the most abstruse learned journal. But the uneasy truth is that modern English, like all other modern languages, is an overlapping series of related dialects. And the chances are very good that each of us, actively or passively, has command of several.

If we limit modern English just to usage in the United States and, accordingly, speak as Mencken does of an American language, we are still faced with quite a number of interrelated dialects that compose this American English. If we are to be understood by our students and, perhaps even more important, if we are to understand them, we might profitably become familiar, first, with the existence of such dialects and, second, with the nature, provenance, and basic characteristics of those most relevant to our individual work.

Most of our American dialects are historic. Basically, our dialects are geographic. We speak of Eastern, Southern, Midwestern, and Far Western American English; frequently, we combine the last two into a generalized area that we refer to as General American. Each of these broad areas is subject to considerable subdivision. Fortunately, the history of the United States and especially the history of the broadly based and increasingly "universal" educational system in our country has assured a mutual understandability among our regional dialects far superior to that in most other large countries that profess to speak a "single" language.

Furthermore, in addition to our broad historic dialect areas, we have within each one marked dialect differences between speakers from urban areas and those from rural areas.*

In addition, there is something to which we properly refer as our "literary" dialect. This last, sometimes called Standard (American) English is only slightly different (though still different enough to require some careful attention, both semantically and lexically and even to some extent grammatically) from the standard literary dialects of England, Scotland, Ireland, Wales (all of these almost but not quite identical with each other), Canada, Australia, New Zealand, and South Africa.

Quite categorically, it is within the framework of this standard or literary dialect that the concept of English as a single and worldwide language exists.

And it is at this point that we (especially as teachers) must examine rather objectively our attitudes towards dialects, both generally and specifically. The vast majority of us have inherited the attitude that anything to which the term "dialect" might be applied is somehow substandard and, in the interest of "good" English, should be avoided.

It is for this reason that I began by identifying such highly respected world languages, such literary vehicles and carriers of culture and technology as English and German as "Germanic dialects." And I might with equal propriety refer to such other great languages as French and Spanish as neo-Latin dialects, to Great Russian, Polish, and Czechish as Balto-Slavic dialects; in short, I wanted at the very outset to disavow a necessarily pejorative meaning for the term "dialect."

There are two perfectly legitimate attitudes toward language study; but, to avoid confusion, we should keep them clearly separated in our minds. These two attitudes, each fully justifiable in itself, may be called the scientific and the moralistic. In the scien-

---

*A still further complication is that I, for one, recognize an already emergent "coastal city dialect" that crosses the lines of the historic geographic dialects. Though the dialect of each such "big city" is ultimately rooted in that of its own geographic area, it has developed common characteristics with the speech of other large coastal cities that tend to supersede the regional characteristics. Thus at both educated and uneducated levels, there is a strong community of speech characteristics among such cities as Boston, New York, Philadelphia, Baltimore, New Orleans, Houston, and San Francisco. More detailed study might indicate peripheral relationship with such cities as Atlanta, Chicago, Detroit, and Saint Louis.

tific approach, we regard all linguistic phenomena from a purely objective point of view; accordingly, everything and anything that occurs or may occur in linguistic usage is grist for our mill and worthy of being studied. Here there is no "right" or "wrong," no "good" or bad"; here we are dealing with linguistic experience without rendering judgments of a moral nature. We study these phenomena as though they were laboratory cultures under the lens of a microscope. The medical researcher may not like or approve of certain germs or viruses, but he studies them all objectively.

In the moral approach, we are concerned with aesthetics, desirabilities of usage, highly refined accuracy, flexibility, and stylistic judgments. Sometimes there is an overlap in these two attitudes; but, if we are to understand language ourselves, if we are to teach it to others, if we are to use it as an instrument for teaching other subjects, especially to people who do not share our own particular dialect preferences, we must keep these attitudes separate in our thinking and in our techniques of communication.

Where American dialects are concerned, my own view is that all the historic geographical dialects enjoy equal status and equal respect. From a moralistic point of view, all enjoy high aesthetic potentials and demonstrated capabilities at colloquial and literary levels. Within each such dialect, I regard the standard form as that of its cultivated speakers. At this level of usage, there is rarely the chance of interdialect difficulty in communication.

But what of our less standard, less acceptable dialects? These I must regard primarily from the viewpoint of the scientist. And functioning as a scientist, I hold the belief that any dialect capable of reasonably accurate communication within its own areas of interest is a legitimate subject of study; as such, it is entitled to the same considerations of analysis in historic depth, of study in its functional achievements as any other (and more acceptable) dialect of the language.

Though I make this statement in the obvious role of scientist, I am equally aware that in the long and increasingly demanding process of education certain dialects cannot stand the pressure demanded by today's complex academic levels. It should be noted, therefore, that when a student's natural environment leaves him functioning within a dialect that cannot, either actively or passively, carry him successfully through the demands made upon him in the classroom, we may anticipate one of several possible consequences. One possibility is that to a lesser or greater extent the academic procedures of the classroom may proceed beyond his level of comprehension. If this happens he then becomes, regardless of where his body may be, a partial or nearly complete school dropout. I need not belabor his frustrations, resentments, and complex emotional attitudes, directed at first against the small world of the classroom, a world embracing the academic discipline, the teacher, and his more successful classmates; still later, most unfortunately, it may become a generalized complex of antisocial attitudes and behavior. Another possible consequence is that under the ministrations of an observing and linguistically skilled teacher, the student's inadequate dialect may well be expanded so as to permit, within reasonable or increasing levels, comprehension on the student's part of classroom activities.

Under these conditions, the student may be, at one level, led into a viable dialect that, although adequate for academic communication at the passive level, may be inadequate at the active level, that is, the level of his own expression. A still further step may lead him into an expanded dialect area that is adequate for reasonably accurate academic expression at the active level but which, by still retaining certain "dialect" characteristics, is of such nature as to be unacceptable at various "social" levels, levels to which the student might reasonably aspire in view of his academic achievement.

Because this is a highly complex and generalized statement, I believe that I should illustrate this point. For the last, or "social" level, is an aspect of socio-linguistic behavior that I call the "Emily Post" area. For instance, within the framework of modern, acceptable, literate English, the double negative is frowned upon and generally regarded as a mark of illiteracy at worst or semiliteracy at best. Yet it does not interfere with communication. Very clearly the nonacceptable statement, "That boy ain't got no money," is an affirmation of financial competency only in the minds of pedants committed, not to reality, but to an artificial system of language that I refer to as "Freshman English." In Old English, in Middle English, and in every other language with which I am famil-

iar as a popular speech used by real people the double or even
multiple negative is an acceptable device frequently used for emphasis, that is, the more negatives, the greater the negation.

"The crying child who says, "We'uns ain't got no candy no-
how" or "Him hit us and us is hurt(ed)," is committing more
solecisms than mere multiple negation. By all our modern standards, this is speech on an illiterate level, and in our role as moral-
ists we do not willingly tolerate it. Yet as scientists we should be
aware of the fact that this is well within the framework of a once
established historic dialect of English and that the statement, however socially unacceptable, conveys the child's meaning as he
speaks for himself and one or more companions.*

A more advanced stage and one more closely approaching the
acceptable English usage of school and college might be exemplified by such statements as, "We shouldn't do nothing in the face
of such circumstances" and "He did not know the name of the
man whom they thought was guilty." Both the double negation in
the first and the solecistic accusative in the second example lie
outside the confines of cultivated speech and would generally be
regarded as semiliterate; yet I suggest that despite all the rules in
our grammar books to the contrary, the student's meaning is quite
clear in each case. We have, in these instances, come within the
Emily Post area of usage, that is, an area of conventional acceptance or rejection of certain patterns not in terms of their capacity
to communicate, but because they violate certain conventional
standards of acceptance.

And in entering this area, we are faced with a more subtle and
possibly more dangerous situation so far as the emotional frustration of the student is concerned. Here we have a student just on
the threshold of highly sophisticated speech. Passively, he may be
fully capable of understanding the most intricate and precise academic English; actively, he has not yet mastered the nuances of
that level. In communicating with those who have achieved this
mastery, he may find himself rejected on "conventional" grounds.
And it is precisely at this point that the teacher meets the most

*It will well repay the seriously oriented teacher to review G. P. Krapp's *The English
Language in America* (New York, 1925), for early examples, by highly trained and
sophisticated writers, of English usage that would not meet the test of acceptance today.

critical period, that of simultaneously protecting the student from discouragement and a sense of rejection and leading him into greater mastery of the conventions without his suffering loss of linguistic initiative and self-confidence. It is not necessary to abandon either standards of accuracy or standards of traditional convention; it is necessary constantly to review the applicability of these standards to the given student. I feel that he should be helped to achieve these "conventional" standards when he is ready for them, that is, when he has developed or is in process of developing high standards of accuracy. Frustration can be avoided if the teacher is constantly aware that it is more important for the student to learn to express himself with accuracy first and subsequently to master the "conventions" as he proceeds.

It becomes increasingly evident that the successful teaching of students who have lived (and are likely for some time to continue to live) in a milieu in which the normal communication patterns of the community lie within what is generally regarded as substandard dialect places the following double burden on the teacher:* first, a knowledge of the substandard dialect(s) that the students use in homes and neighborhoods; second, a willingness and capacity to (a) lead the individual student into a complete change of dialect or (b) train him to use a secondary (or schoolroom) dialect of standard level but otherwise neutral.

The first obligation above, a basically diagnostic one in the teacher-student relationship, is as important as the second (the therapeutic) responsibility. To put it another way, the teacher must learn to accept the fact that the student who comes from such a dialect community is not merely speaking "bad" English; he is speaking a dialect that among its own speakers is capable of a high degree of linguistic accuracy within the (often, it is true, limited) interests of its speakers. This dialect may be at slight or considerable divergence from standard American English. If the young and academically inexperienced student is expected to adjust to and understand the standard dialect of the teacher, it is not asking too much in the interest of fuller communication that the teacher be expected to understand the dialect of the student.

*The responsibility lies not only with the teacher of "English" but rather with all teachers. After all, in American schools, every subject is taught in English.

What are these substandard dialects that American students are likely to bring into the classroom? Some come readily to mind: the English spoken by the native French-speaking Acadians (Cajuns) in southern Louisiana, the English spoken by the Pennsylvania Dutch, and that spoken by the Mexican-Americans in the Southwest. All of these dialects are for the most part rural. In the large cities of the East, teachers must reckon with ghetto dialects of concentrated non-English speaking immigrants: Italian, Polish, Yiddish, Puerto Rican-Spanish, and others. To pick a single example of the responsibility on the teacher in assuming his or her share of the burden of accurate communication, the Latin American child (though several generations removed from Latin America itself) will speak of a couple as "escaping" where we would refer to their act as "eloping." This is one of the basic and legitimate meanings of the Spanish verb *escapar* and, in the particular ghetto area in which these children reside the English cognate preserves that meaning in the dialect of that group.

The variants from standard American English that I have cited are readily recognized by the teacher, who needs little encouragement in meeting the demands that they impose. There is still another dialect that poses a much more subtle problem, if only because it is not easily recognized as a dialect. It is more likely to be seen merely as "bad" English. Yet it is in reality an historic dialect, though the form in which we meet it is far from cultivated.*

 Currently this dialect, where it is recognized at all as a separate speech pattern rather than merely as "bad English," is called by such terms as "Negro Speech," or by such euphemisms as "Urban Ghetto English" or "the language of the disadvantaged," or "Inner City Speech." In each of these (and similar) designations, the identification is primarily with the Negro.

The fact remains, however, that many whites speak essentially the same dialect; furthermore, this is a dialect whose historic provenance is not the city at all.

At this point some attempt should be made to trace broadly the history of this dialect and to establish some of its more obvious

---

*Again the serious student is referred to Krapp's *The English Language in America* as well as to any edition of H. L. Mencken's *The American Language,* but preferably, *The American Language: The Fourth Edition and the Two Supplements,* edited by Raven I. McDavid, Jr., New York, 1963.

characteristics. To do so we must revert to some consideration of the Middle English dialects in the British Isles.

Roughly the years A.D. 1100 to A.D. 1500 cover the Middle English period. The four main dialect areas, corresponding to similar areas in the Old English period, are generally referred to as Northern (that part of England north of the Humber River and the English-speaking regions of Scotland, later extending to Ulster in Ireland), Midland (the extensive area between the Humber and the Thames), Kentish (primarily limited to the county of Kent and certain adjacent areas), and Southern (the area south of Thames, excluding the Kentish area).* Two of these dialects should occupy our particular interest, the Northern and the Midland. Beginning about the middle of the fourteenth century, the Midland dialect (specifically, the southeastern part, including London and the two universities, Cambridge and Oxford) began to emerge as the standard literary dialect of England.† The Northern dialect, as a literary language, centered about Edinburgh. It is important to note that in the continued Reformation, although the evangelical and dissenting movement was not confined to any one part of the British Isles, it was particularly active in the areas where the Northern dialect prevailed. This assumes considerable significance when we consider the original settlements in the American colonies, especially during the period from 1607 to about 1725, when this Northern dialect was probably the predominant English speech on the American continent. Again the reader is referred to Krapp's extensive study for specific examples. Furthermore, as Cleanth Brooks showed in his detailed monograph, with the possible exception of one term (*turkle* for *turtle*), every variant linguistic form in the Uncle Remus stories derives from the English dialects, and predominantly from the Northern dialect (1).

Early colonial education was as homespun as the cloth from which the colonists' garments were made. The preacher was also the teacher; in fact, the vast majority, including those who were

*These are primary areas, each of which is subject to considerable subdivision. For instance, even as late as the twentieth century, when many of the dialects were rapidly disappearing, Professor Skeat designates nine in just that part of the Northern dialect area north of the Scottish border. See W. W. Skeat, *English Dialects From the Eighth Century to the Present Day*. Cambridge: Cambridge University Press, 1911.

† Because this is the dialect area in which the kings of England were born and reared, and whose dialect they spoke, this dialect came to be known additionally as "the King's English," a term that did not necessarily refer to its linguistic superiority.

technically ordained priests of the Anglican Church, preferred the title teacher to preacher. What was taught was, of course, the dialect of the speakers themselves, though increasingly modified by the language of the English Bible.* This predominantly Northern British dialect with some admixture of the other provincial dialects, which I generally call the Jamestown-Mayflower dialect, was the language of the home, of business, government, and religious discussion, including sermons. Throughout the colonies, only in the actual biblical readings was the Midland dialect undiluted.

The language of the whites was also the language of the Negro slaves and, eventually, of the freedmen among them.† Some physiological, social, and cultural differences may well have produced divergences; but for all practical purposes, both whites and Negroes spoke the same dialect.

With the beginning of the eighteenth century, increased affluence and broadening interests soon resulted in less homespun and more formal education in the colonies. The newly imported books (textbooks and others), as well as the newly arrived teacher-preachers were linguistically oriented to the now dominant Midland speech of England. By the mid-eighteenth century, the linguistic change among the educated and cultivated classes was significant in every colony, more so, of course, in areas that were urban or semiurban. By the time of our War of Independence, the linguistic change was complete: as a nation we now spoke, studied, and read a Midland dialect—except for those people living in rather isolated areas (as in Appalachia) or under cultural interdict. What had once been a reasonably common language in early colonial times now ceased to be that; we reeducated most of our white children into speaking a new dialect, but we forgot to educate our

---

*Though our now familiar authorized (or King James) version was not unknown, the most popular version, both at home and in the colonies, was the Geneva Bible. But this, like the King James Version, was in the Southeast Midland dialect, whose formal influence on the speech of Americans was thus established very early.

†An important distinction here is that between Negro speech in the continental colonies and that in the British island colonies of the Gulf and Caribbean. In these latter, the Negroes developed (as they did in the French- and Spanish-speaking nearby colonies) a form of "creolized" speech, which, in the English islands, tended to become predominantly English in vocabulary and Sudanese in structure. Apparently, in the continental colonies, too few slaves spoke mutually understood African languages; even to communicate with each other, they were forced to do so in English.

black children and many of our isolated whites. But these "dispossessed" in the new linguistic dispensation continued to learn their English on a parents-to-children basis; the speech patterns persist to this day. They are still heard in isolated rural areas among the whites; the migrating rural Negroes have carried them to the new ghettos of the most complex and sophisticated of our modern cities. These patterns are not, in and of themselves, "bad" English, except as we view "good" and "bad" English from the viewpoint of our accepted standards; they are rather survivals of a once popular speech.

It will repay us to review some of the characteristics of this earlier American dialect in terms of its origins in the provincial Middle English dialects, most especially the Northern dialect.

Two closely related characteristics are (1) the reduction of case forms in the personal pronouns and (2) the extension of the final -*s* in the third person singular to all forms of the verb in the present indicative. Note also that in a verb of multiple forms in the present indicative (such as the verb *to be*) only one form (in this case *is*) might survive. Thus, under (1), there was a tendency to substitute *me* for *I* and *thee* for *thou*. Though both *thou* and *thee* have disappeared from standard speech, the substitution of *thee* as a nominative form is still current in the closed speech of the Quakers. Similarly, *us* tended to replace *we*, etc. Hence, in terms of (1) and (2) above, we have the old ballad, *Us Wants to Go to Widdicomb Fair* and we have the survival of such forms as *I eats, him sleeps, we* (or *us*) *knows*, etc.

Another characteristic (3) is in the free position of adjectives and adverbs. Consider in this regard the long (and quite futile) teacher-student struggle over the position of the adverb *only*. (4) Similarly, the possessive flexion (commonly written -*'s*) attached itself, not to the possessor, but to the beginning of the designation of the possessed. Thus, we justify in modern accepted English the expression, "the Queen of England's throne," on the appeal to the concept of Queen-of-England as a single compound expression. We do not even attempt to explain "anyone else's book" for the simple reason that most of us are completely unaware that this is a variant of "anyone's else." And one still hears such unconscious creations of syntactical contortions as "the man I saw yesterday's hat." This last form is completely without sanction in cultivated speech, but I suggest that the reader listen carefully and identify the source of the next example that he hears.

There are still other variants in this older dialect, many of which are not unknown historically in the Midland itself. Double negation has already been discussed; the reduction of personal pronouns is not unknown (though with a preference for the nominative) even in the Midland; compare Shakespeare's "you have seen Cassio and she together" (*Othello, iv, 2*). The Northern dialect showed a preference for the accusative absolute, as in "Him being sick, we waited"; our now standard English prefers the nominative absolute. An old Northern form is *I'se,* serving variously for *I is* (i.e., *am*), *I shall,* and *I has* (i.e., *have*). There is a tendency to use a singular verb with a compound subject whose elements are singular. But this was once characteristic of all the English dialects; a sense of "logic" and the weight of remembered Latin grammar have suppressed it in our present standard usage. But note how often even educated speakers ask, "How is your mother and father?"

In short, teaching the student to bridge the dialect gap is difficult enough even when we are aware that he is functioning within another dialect; it becomes impossible when we are unaware of it or unaware of the characteristics of his native dialect. The student does have a task and a responsibility, but so does the teacher. And the teacher's basic responsibility is, first, to know that there are several forms of historic English; second, to know the relevant forms themselves. As Professor Skeat said some eighty years ago:

> It is not the first time that I have called attention to the fact that the English language is the *sole* subject which is treated of by those who have never properly studied it. If botany or chemistry were so treated it would be considered very strange; but when the subject happens to be the English language, a want of scientific knowledge seems to be considered as being absolutely meritorious. (2)

References

1. Brooks, Cleanth. *The Relation of the Alabama-Georgia Dialect to the Provincial Dialects of Great Britain: LSU Studies, No. 20.* Baton Rouge: Louisiana State University Press, 1935.

2. Skeat, Walter W. "Knowledge for the People," *Notes and Queries,* 7th series, vol. 63(1888).

CHAPTER 8

Developing
Expressive Powers

ALEXANDER FRAZIER

Dr. Frazier describes the strengths of migrant children such as experiences with people and places, socializing, funning and fooling around, aggressing, and narrating. Upon this framework he then outlines a program of varied expressive activities which build on and extend these strengths.

Dr. Alexander Frazier has had wide experience in the field of education as a curriculum and instructional specialist in public school systems of Arizona, California, Texas, and Ohio. He is now professor of early and middle childhood education at The Ohio State University. Active in numerous groups, he was president of the Association for Supervision and Curriculum Development during 1969-1970. As an editor for ASCD and the National Council of Teachers of English he has made valuable contributions in organization, instructional procedures, and in the English curriculum. He received his Ed.D. from Teachers College, Columbia University.

THE CHILDREN of those whom we have variously identified in recent years as the disadvantaged, the deprived, or the dispossessed have been perceived by us for the most part as victims of the surrounding society. In relating to them, we have thought of our efforts as a kind of rescue mission. How can we protect children, we have said to ourselves and one another, from the impact of a subculture or set of circumstances that progressively disables those who grow up in it for full participation in the wider culture? When we have been honest with ourselves, we have wished that we could tear out the inner city and resettle its inhabitants; we would like to be able to close the mines and rip up the vineyards and orchards and plow up the lettuce fields and disperse their tenders to the suburbs and small towns of America where most of us are rearing our children. That would really take care of the problem as we have perceived it.

But now the new leaders of some of the poor, the leaders of the black and brown communities in particular, are asking us another question: Do you know what you have been doing to our children by addressing them and us in these terms?

In consequence, we are beginning to try to think in a different vocabulary. If our purpose ought to be something other than the "rescue" of those we have seen as victimized by a way of life and values of which we have frankly disapproved, what does our purpose become? What do we tie onto? What bases for action may there be that we have overlooked?

The present treatment of the development of expressive skills in the children of migrant workers attempts to exercise the newer and more respectful vocabulary for dealing with the educational needs of the poor. First, an effort will be made to review some of the strengths in such children. Then a program of expressive education will be proposed to build on and extend these strengths in a somewhat broader context of ultimate intentions.

The Strengths of Migrant Children

From a bulletin describing a state program for the education of migrant children comes this partial list of what are called the "Characteristics of the Migrant Child":

He has the ability to achieve satisfactorily when his special needs are met.

He is often shy and may feel unaccepted.

He is subject to a marked increase in fears as he starts to school.

He comes from a patriarchal culture.

He is absent frequently, often because of lack of proper food and clothing.

His readiness for reading will come only after he has the oral vocabulary.

His concepts will be limited because his learning experiences at home have been restricted.

He has experienced little success.

He may be two or more years educationally retarded, due to his limited knowledge of English and/or to absence from classes.

He may be mature in the areas of travel and adult association but lack other experiences necessary for success in the classroom.

His concept of sex and sex roles are governed by his cultural values and may differ from middle class values.

His parents often receive aid from welfare agencies. (8)

This characterization of the migrant child is typical of many such statements in its highly judgmental and heavily negative assessment. A child thought of in these terms would seem indeed very unlikely to learn much in the schools waiting to receive him.

There are, however, other frameworks in which to think of this child. Let us try for the development of one that will make the most of what may be some of the uniquenesses and some of the differences in his life.

Experiences with People and Places

"Most Americans see America at 30,000 feet and 600 mph." This statement commands our attention in a current car rental advertisement (5). It capsulizes a truism of our traveling society: we have been everywhere, some of us have, and seen nothing.

This fact was brought home to me again on a recent weekend when I met with a group of twenty persons who had flown in from all over the United States to attend a meeting at a guest ranch outside of Tucson, Arizona. In the three days we were there, newcomers to the Southwest did learn something about the flora and fauna of the desert. A dozen varieties of cacti lined the walks from cottages to dining hall. Birds of many kinds exchanged warnings or sang their songs of welcome as we passed by. In the early morning, we were awakened by the howling of coyotes up in the hills.

But after the meeting was over, as the others climbed into station wagons to head for the airport, my wife and I, who are wintering in Phoenix, drove on down to Nogales by way of Patagonia, where along the highway in the high country we saw herds of cattle, fat from the rich grasses of the region, and enjoyed the ever-changing views of even higher mountains beyond, where patches of snow and exposed red rock contrasted with the cedars that suddenly show up at that elevation. In Nogales, we went across into Mexico for an hour of looking and shopping and were then ready to drive back to Phoenix along the Santa Cruz River to Tucson and up Route 10, a completed throughway, into the irrigated valleys of central Arizona. While our friends were in the air en route to Tallahassee and Detroit and Seattle, strapped into their seats and doubtless half-asleep, we were gathering, on our roundabout 270-mile return trip to Phoenix, many impressions and ideas denied those who chose a faster trip home. They missed the kind of learning that comes from contact by eye and ear (and, remembering our quick trip across the line, by nose) for those who are lucky enough to be able to take their time as they go.

Children who belong to families who travel from one work situation to another have chances to learn that are not open to most children. They have a greater range of experiences with people and places upon which to draw for insights and understandings about the nature of the world.

About People

People differ from one area of the country to the next. They speak other languages than English or other dialects than one's own. They vary in color and customs. They may dress differently in terms of climate as well as season.

"We have almost every kind of person there is in here except Chinese and Eskimo." This conclusion of a boy in a Michigan classroom of migrant children (10) reflects the richness children may find in meeting and going to school with children from many parts of the country.

Teachers differ, too. So do filling station operators and storekeepers, bosses and weighers-in and paymasters, and public officials encountered at rest stations and in camps or when trouble comes and help has to be asked for or the law dealt with.

A sociologist has pointed out that a century ago a person would have done well to meet in a lifetime the number of persons to look at and listen to and learn about and from that today's child may come into contact with in a month's time. Trips to the shopping center, Sunday drives, visits to cousins across town bring under a child's scrutiny great numbers of others. Television, the three hours a day spent before it, contributes, too; a child knows scores of other persons through that medium by sight and style if not by name. The modern child has much more knowledge about people than the child of earlier eras.

The child who travels the year around buttresses such common knowledge with the data of more direct contact. He learns people the way other children may learn books.

Places

The child who travels also learns the landscape.

He learns that in places with cloudless skies and little vegetation, it may be a long ride from one restroom to another.

He learns that in some places it rains nearly every day, and the floor of the tenthouse has to be built high off the ground, and days in the field are often missed, and the house gets crowded. He learns that in some places it never seems to rain and cooking can be done outside most of the time.

He learns what it means when the family gets some place before the peaches or cantaloupes are ripe. Or what it means when the heat holds and the crops become overripe and work has to go on all night.

He learns there are slim pickings when the season has been dry. He learns about canneries shut down for one reason or another while the produce rots in the field. He learns about freezes and dry rot.

He learns about escaping north when the desert heat has become too much. And about thinking of the south when the chill begins to hang on in the morning air.

He learns about radiators that boil over between Yuma and Blythe—and also in mountain passes. He learns to measure distance in terms of travel time. "We could be in Orlando day after tomorrow if we drove straight through."

He learns to like best some of the places they go to—where there is water to swim and fish in, where there are trees to climb and squirrels and chipmunks to chase, perhaps where it's warm enough to sleep outside.

The child who travels a lot and lives in many places has experiences with people and places from which he learns much that other children do not have a chance to learn firsthand. Some of

these learnings may be available at secondhand for sedentary learners but many and possibly most of them are not. They are the
lessons of one kind of life to be learned by those who live it.

Competencies from an Oral Culture

As a people, some students of communications are telling us, we
have moved through a long period of print-mindedness, the Gutenberg era, into a new era that is sometimes called postliterate (7).
We have before us, they say, the task of trying to learn how to
learn from nonprint media—films, recordings, television, new
graphic media, combinations of many media. We are already in the
midst of this effort to understand and revalue the oral as well as
the pictorial aspects of contemporary culture.

The child of migrant families is often an heir to what may be
called a preliterate and more purely oral culture. Much of what we
are thinking about analyzing and understanding he grows into
without choice. He learns many of the skills and much of the
substance of his way of life by listening and speaking as well as by
watching and witnessing.

The competencies developed out of this oral culture are perhaps
no different in kind, most of them, from those of preliterates who
stay on the farm or who come to town and are sequestered in the
shabbiest section of the city with their own cafes and bars and
storefront churches. Indeed, many of the competencies, as we
shall categorize them here, are common to all human beings. But
what we hope to do is to appreciate that children of the sort with
which we are concerned bring to school many language and nonverbal expressive competencies on which we can build. Let us
review the range of such competencies.

Socializing. On the move for a good part of the time and
thrown together at each pause and stopover with new faces, the
migrant child learns how to get to know others in short order.

He learns to feel others out and size up the social situation, the
uses of shyness and showing off, how to catch an eye, how to
invite further interest, and how to cover retreat if it becomes plain
that a possible new playmate is in no mood for making friends.

He learns to run the risk of being rejected if he goes too fast in
trying to get acquainted. He realizes, too, that a possible friend in

a new location may not want to play today but might tomorrow. The other child may be tired out or cross about something or suffering from a runny nose, or he may be the kind that has to make the approach on his own terms. So waiting is all right. And there are so many other children, so many who will, most of them, welcome another kid to play with, at least for a while.

Established in a new setting, the migrant child learns many ways to invite the interest of subsequent newcomers. There are secrets to share—the closest sluice box big enough to swim in, a tree house or a cave to hide out in, a gopher hole to be dug out, a mulberry tree on which the fruit is ready to eat. There is so much else to share—new games to learn, new tests of courage to propose, new kids to meet, new adults to steer clear of.

Squatting at midday in the dust under a tamarisk tree, the migrant child learns to trade news and gossip and confidences that make the time pass and build a bond that will cause friends who may soon be parted to rejoice at reunion months later in another state to which their family wanderings have taken them. He has the model before him and all around him of how to socialize in a rich and ever-changing human environment.

Funning and fooling around. The play element in an oral culture looms large. The migrant child learns how to make his own fun and how to fool around with and fox and outfox those with whom he must live so closely and transiently.

He soon gains a fund of rhymes, riddles, jokes, and humorous or pithy epithets and sayings that is always being perfected and added to from interchange with new acquaintances.

He learns to kid as well as to be kidded.

He learns miming and mimicking and dramatizing as means of highlighting a point or a posture.

He learns to play language games with both children and adults. Like other children, he learns how to cajole and persuade. Because he encounters more adults than most other children, he may learn to play a broader repertoire of roles. A child with a certain talent for self-dramatizing may become a con artist at an early age.

As far as play is concerned, the main resource of the migrant child is other children. Thus he learns all the old group games, the chasing and hiding games and turnabout and toss-the-ball games, and teaches them in turn to others. He makes up games that use bottle caps or soft drink cans or other found objects.

He expresses his high spirits in push and tag games. He cavorts and capers and roams and runs wild to exhaust his spirits, often in pairs or packs that range farther and sound noisier than more closely supervised play gangs or groups.

In some subcultures, he learns to dance to express his joy in being alive and with others. Or he learns party games much like dancing. He learns the words as well as the music and may make up his own songs to tell the world how he feels.

He learns early about the differences between boys and girls and what these mean in adding to the joy of being alive. And he may develop a vocabulary for sharing and sharpening what he learns and feels that is richer or at least earthier than our own.

Aggressing. Some of the skills developed in an oral culture for expressing aggression may have been about bred out of the quieter segments of our society. But for those for whom withdrawing behind the hedge or the high fence, visiting a psychiatrist, moving to a new neighborhood, or complaining to the police are not viable options, these skills are certainly still learned. The child who grows up in the rural regions, the city slums, and the work camps of America learns how to express his feelings of aggression in many ways that seem to him to work out all right.

Teasing and tormenting are familiar in every subadult culture as ways of teaching age and sex roles but assume more importance when supervision is lessened. The migrant child has to learn to take it as well as dish it out.

He learns to talk out his feelings, too, when he feels hurt, neglected, or put upon. He learns that it takes time and persistence to get others to listen and respond. He learns to talk up and to talk back. He learns to tell it like it is or seems to him to be.

"She done had her turn!" a child of five may exclaim as he jumps up and elbows some other overchosen child out of the ring in a crowded classroom where the teacher is trying to provide turns in prancing like ponies.

The migrant child finds many models around him for perfecting his skills in disputing and arguing. In his culture there is not time to write it all down. Time passes fast. Camps close. Everybody is on the move again. Grievances and complaints about living and working conditions or against those supposed to speak for one have to be aired directly and fully if anything is to come of them. Confrontation is a matter of here and now.

He learns, too, how to cut loose and cuss out.

He may learn to throw a temper fit or go on a rampage. There may come a time when nothing else seems to be left, he may have learned, and dishes get broken and sometimes heads.

He knows that at such times he may kick and bite and hit harder than he would if he were himself.

He learns in time that there are limits within which he and others must confine themselves or they may be booted out of school or a job or locked up someplace; or in a hospital with a bad cut or a concussion; or all by themselves, minus family or friends who couldn't take it any longer.

When he simmers down and assesses the situation after the air has been cleared, he learns how to go about making amends on the basis of a new understanding by all concerned of the feelings that have been expressed.

Narrating. An oral culture puts a high value on the skills of storytelling. The child who grows up in such a culture learns the stories and develops as he can the skills he comes to rely on and value.

He learns from his elders stories about how it was when they were young.

He listens again and again to heightened versions of incidents that occurred on the road or in previous work situations—the freeway pile-up in Southern California last year, the forest fire or the big flood, the Colorado strike three summers ago, the history of the grape boycott.

He hears the plots of favorite movies remembered from earlier days or one seen last night by an older child who stayed up and went down to the camp "rec" room to watch television.

He hears and learns ballads that celebrate the exploits of men who were shot down or cut up—and of women who remained true while their men were away at war or serving time in the pen.

He learns to chime in on familiar stories and to remind the narrator when something has been left out. He learns to make the most of reports of his own experiences, fixing them up a little so his companions listen more closely.

He likes to tell tales he has learned in school. "Then Papa Bear said, 'Somebody done been in my porridge!'" He makes up stories for younger children he may have to entertain—scary stories and funny and improbable tales.

Like any other child deep in an oral culture, the migrant child values and practices the art of narration as an important part of his way of life.

Getting serious. No realm of an oral culture is more highly formalized than that devoted to celebration of the truly crucial events of human existence. On serious occasions, the oral culture comes into its own.

The migrant child learns how to lament the misfortunes to which all are subject but which are less protected against among the poor. The range of such misfortunes, from the burning out or final breakdown of the family car to the collapse in the field and hospitalization of the family head, is wider than for others. The modes of lamentation, learned in and for such times, vary from one subculture to another but are always loud and mounting in their duration, not subject to being lessened by conventional overtures of sympathy. Only a willingness to share in the suffering is welcomed.

The migrant child learns to express his grief fully at the time of ultimate human tragedy, the death of another member of the family. The "funeralizing" of the dead exhausts the energies of the living.

He learns, too, the function of prayer in focusing thought on goods and goals as yet beyond achievement or at least in doubt.

He may learn to pray aloud with a fervor and facility surprising in the young.

He learns to respond to preaching styles in a way lost to most of us. The rhetoric of his preachers belongs to another era when congregations could give themselves over to being taken out of themselves. This child may learn to sway and clap hands and "amen" with his elders and perhaps to talk in tongues.

He plays at preaching as some children play at teaching. He learns to sing songs of faith with the same vigor and sometimes the same beat that he applies to the songs he learns from the jukebox.

The migrant child brings with him to school a lifetime of learning how to celebrate the serious side of life, as well as a lifetime of learning how to socialize, to have fun and fool around, to express aggression, and to tell stories. Heir of an oral culture, he is skillful in ways that may have been lost to many of us and are possibly undervalued by most or all of his teachers.

Contributions of Ethnic Subcultures

In this country in the early years of this century, the problem of what to do with the diversity of cultures represented by the influx of immigrants from middle and Southern Europe was viewed from several perspectives, as Cremin reminds us (2). Some persons were all for anglicizing the newcomers to insure their full Americanization. Others, like Zangwill, proposed that we trust in the melting pot of cultural interaction to produce a more vital common culture, enriched by new ingredients. Somewhat apart from these more competitive viewpoints was the idea that we ought to value in the United States a kind of cultural pluralism that would welcome and support the maintenance of separate cultures that could prove sources of unique contributions that might enliven the national life.

Today, as we listen to those who are proposing to reconstitute pride in the racial and ethnic heritage of Negroes, Mexican-Americans and other Spanish-speakers, and Indians in terms of cultural pluralism, we are turning our attention to a better understanding of what such contributions may be. Many of us are undertaking a revision of history as we have taught it to find a fairer place in it for minority groups and are otherwise engaged in redressing the balance. Therefore, it may seem less urgent to deal fully with the nature of what children learn from their ethnic subcultures and what they may have to draw on when they come to us. We may, however, wish to review briefly the variety of such learnings.

We understand, of course, that not all migrant children come from easily differentiated ethnic backgrounds, but we know that many do. Our question is: What special learnings do such children bring to school?

Language. California and Texas are states in which there is much sentiment for requiring that all children be educated in both English and Spanish. Children who grow up with some degree of proficiency in both languages would seem to have a head start on others. Children who develop adequacy in three languages, as is true among some of the Indian tribes of the Southwest, would seem particularly blessed.

The bilingual or trilingual child of a migrant family is able to communicate more certainly with the diversity of persons he meets on the road or in changing work settings. Such a child has more language resources for dealing with all his experience. If he exhausts the resources of one language for naming or describing, he can call upon those of another. He serves as a resource to monolingual children in learning another language.

He finds it easier to understand the nature of language when he has a chance to study with a teacher capable of making comparisons between languages.

He finds it easier to learn another language when he already knows two or three (1).

As a kind of postscript, something should be said about the resources represented in a classroom by children who may be monolingual in our native tongue but have pronounced regional dialects. Teachers who can resist trying to alter these dialects to conform to standard English (this is, cleaning up the roughest grammatical differences and altering the vowel sounds to those of the local dialect) may find that study of vocabulary, idiomatic expressions, and intonation patterns can be pursued much further and with more excitement than in classrooms where recordings have to be used to demonstrate to pupils samples of dialects other than their own.

Music and dances. Ethnic groups may have songs in their language or from their subculture that are unique to them, music with accents and patterns that differ from the music of the majority culture, and dances familiar to members of the ethnic group but not to others.

A child from such a group learns to sing the songs and dance the dances valued by the dominant culture in the community. He may learn how to go about teaching the dances of his group to younger members and to others.

He may learn to accompany songs or perform music on a variety of instruments available in his group—guitar, harmonica, drums and percussion instruments of one kind or another. He may know variant versions of songs that have been adopted by the majority culture. He may have become skillful in improvising beyond or around the music and dances of his group.

Customs and traditions. Subcultures are characterized by differences in the customs and traditions preserved by the elders and taught to their young. A child growing up in such a group may learn to celebrate holidays common to the broader culture in ways distinctive with his smaller community. He may also learn to celebrate holidays not generally found outside his group.

He may learn to like some kinds of holiday foods and other foods, too, that are unique to his subculture. He may learn to wear certain kinds of clothing traditional among his people, at least on holidays and other formal occasions. He may learn church rituals or practices that differ from those of other professors of the same faith.

He may grow up with a knowledge of heroes and villains that carries meaning only in his group. He may learn ways of behaving to his elders and to members of the opposite sex that are at variance with those of the majority culture.

In short, the migrant child who comes from an ethnic group brings unique learnings of many kinds with him when he comes to school—language and dialect differences learned from his subculture, music and dances, and a great range of customs and traditions, some of which are merely suggested here.

Knowledge of the strengths of migrant children should provide us with a better base for planning school programs. As reviewed here, these strengths include learnings from the breadth of experience they have had and are having with people and places, the competencies derived from growing up in a highly oral culture, and the special contributions that ethnic subcultures have made and are making to the lives of some of these children.

The Development of Expressive Powers

The children of migrant workers, like other children, need help in learning the rudiments of the basic fields of study in the elementary school—reading and handwriting and spelling, mathematical processes, and the like. We are agreed, it would seem to me, that where mastery is the goal, we now know how to define in very precise terms the bits and pieces of such learning and to lay them out in most carefully arranged sequences in the form of scientifically prepared study materials. We are rapidly increasing our know-how for combining in such materials the devices of diagnosis and evaluation that will insure the placement of learners on the right step and encourage continuous progress. Individuals are able to move through such materials in terms of their special needs and at their own rate. We seem to be almost at the point where we can insure success for every learner, given time enough, in completing the learning needed by everybody in the simpler basics.

We must grant, too, that much of what we have in the past tried to teach in the elementary school has belonged to this level of basic facts and skills. We appear to face the pleasing prospect that in a few years we may be able to teach most of this level of content in half the time and possibly twice as effectively.

But here we wish to turn our attention to a higher level of learning. In the realm of expression we are concerned with a second rank of skills. These skills or powers as I would prefer to call them, draw upon the lesser learnings but go far beyond them. Powers of expression are developed rather than mastered or perfected. Growth, not mastery, is the goal (3).

Against this background a framework for developing the expressive powers of children from migrant families can be created.

Creation as Expression

The highest form of personal expression comes through the creation of something that has never existed before. The powers of creative expression can be exercised in an arena wider than the arts as we usually think of them or the crafts narrowly conceived. Rather than enumerate these dimensions in subject field terms, it may be more rewarding to try for a way of thinking about creation in general terms. One such way is to list the steps of creation with sample activities for each step:

Steps	Sample activities
Imagining	Fantasizing
	Improvising
	Inventing
	Problem setting
	Thinking up
Planning	Analyzing
	Designing
	Forming
	Laying out
	Outlining
	Thinking out
Making	Composing
	Constructing
	Drawing
	Modeling
	Painting
	Problem solving
	Sewing
	Shaping
	Writing

If we recognize that the steps often merge (inventing may involve trying out various designs and writing may find its form as it goes), such an analysis may have its uses.

Supporting conditions. We may need a set of guidelines to assist us in planning for building into our program continuous attention to the development of the expressive power to create. After some fifteen years of close study of the nature of creativity, we should find that such guidelines come easily to mind (4).

Creative behavior is learned and thus can be deliberately taught. It is not enough merely to provide opportunities for occasional creative experiences, as we have sometimes been satisfied to do in our busy classrooms. It is obvious that the easel or two available to children who have finished ahead of others can hardly be considered an adequate program of art instruction. Encouraging children thought to be talented or specially adept to share poems they may have written or sing songs they may have made up, while to the good, does not go far enough. We believe that the teacher should give deliberate, planned attention to developing the creative power of all children.

Creative behavior needs to be experienced in the full range of school studies. The exercise of creative behavior and the consequent development of power to create can be provided in most fields of study. Children should be helped to learn how to frame new problems in mathematics and how to seek unique solutions to open questions or unresolved problems in the social studies. Valuing creative behavior leads a teacher to set up many situations in a day's time, from the reading group to the handling of crises in living and working together in the classroom and the school, where divergent rather than convergent thinking is to be expected and supported. We believe that learning creative expression should be an all-day concern of the teacher.

Creative behavior involves the use of varied tools and materials which need to be amply provided without cost to the children. If children are to be taught how to create, they need saws and brushes; they need wood and paint and paper. They may also need on occasion specialized work spaces and facilities—clay areas and a kiln, a sink, a place to set up experiments. The power to create is hard to exercise in a vacuum. The teacher has a right to demand what is needed to do the job right.

Creative behavior rests on but goes beyond the past experience of the learner. Children imagine first out of the context of what they know. The migrant child knows the road better than the city. An assignment to plan an ideal highway over a terrain charted in terms of the swamps and piney woods and bayous he knows will make more sense to him immediately than to plan an ideal new town for a prospective population of 50,000. Once some planning principles have been learned and a map of the new terrain tied in with symbols he now knows, he should be guided to apply his power to create in that other world. The teacher necessarily begins where the child is and should push for development of the ability to deal with the new or relatively unfamiliar.

Specific activities. Against this rather elaborate background, I will point out the kinds of specific activities that may seem to be appropriate in helping migrant children strengthen and extend their powers of creative expression. These activities are offered only as examples; the variety of possible activities may be suggested by the lists to follow, but teachers will be easily able to broaden the range and improve upon the quality of the suggestions. Moreover, the effort here is tied particularly to trying to build directly on the strengths of migrant children as defined earlier and thus excludes many appropriate extensions of classroom study.

Primary Level Activities

Setting up and solving problems
     How to organize the class into groups of three pupils, with a good "teacher" of English and one of Spanish in each group
     How to make newcomers to the class feel most welcome and quickly at home

Thinking up jokes and tricks
     On boys who think they have been everywhere
     On girls who think they know the words to all the songs
     On somebody who is always trying to be bossy

Making up stories
     How the jackrabbit got long ears
     How the rattlesnake got his rattles
     Why the flamingo blushes all the time

Making up plays
     Last day in the work camp before moving on
     Fiesta to welcome an uncle home from the war

Composing dances
     To perform when the principal visits the class
     To move from pairs to fours to eights
     To represent joy at arrival of a new baby in the family

Designing and making costumes
     For the fiesta
     For one of the dances

Modeling in clay
     Animals of the desert

Constructing
     Storage rack, using milk cartons
     Counting frame for home use with bottle caps as counters

Inventing

New kinds of concrete materials for manipulation in mathematics lessons

Making up songs or chants
  My saint's day celebration
  My favorite friend who is far away
  Before I came to school
  People who have made me laugh or cry

Intermediate Level Activities

Setting up and solving problems
  A day with the same number of minutes but fewer or more hours—new time schedule for getting up, going to work, etc.
  Preferred location and facilities of stop-and-sleep stations for traveling families from El Paso to Orlando
  Selection of twenty best terms from English and Spanish to describe range of weather from hot to cold

Making up stories
  What happened when it rained for a month in the desert
  When the snow on the mountains did not melt
  When the Everglades went dry

Designing or making plans
  Building a bridge from Puerto Rico to the mainland
  Harvesting kelp from the ocean—work sites, equipment for harvesters, etc.
  Damming the rivers of Texas to make lakes and provide water for irrigation

Constructing
  Model of an ideal work camp or trailer park
  Flats to use in growing and experimenting with plants under varied conditions of light and moisture
  Flour-and-salt map to show typical valley terrain with irrigation system

Writing songs or chants
  The day the trailer came unhitched
  A child who got left behind
  Curse on a mean old man who charged too much for soda pop and gasoline
  When the wind blows and the dust flies
  All kinds of people
  Saturday night

Drawing and painting
  Home life in the tenthouse or trailer
  Under the trees when the day is over

Where I wish we could have stayed longer
An accident on the highway
A happy occasion

Making masks
  For a dance about spooks and other such things
  For a play about animals in the Everglades

Again, these activities have been devised through reference to the preceding analysis of creative expression, the guidelines proposed under the treatment of supporting conditions, and the earlier effort to highlight the assets of migrant children. If the reader finds the activities to be repetitious and unimaginative, he is urged to view their deficiency as a result of the impoverished experience of the writer and not an inadequacy in the proposed approach.

Performance as Expression. Most children, including those of migrant families, come to school with developed powers to express themselves through what we call performance. The child can report on what happened last night at home, he can tell or retell simple stories, he knows some songs or jingles (maybe learned from television commercials), he can caper around to music, he knows how to bang on something handy to accentuate the beat or rhythm of music, he can mimic his companions or his elders, and he has his favorite games. The performance realm broadly conceived encompasses many kinds of skills which we value and can build on and extend in the school setting. To provide a framework for reference, we may think of these in terms of agents and activities.

Agents	*Sample activities*
Voice	Reading aloud
	Reciting
	Singing
	Speaking
	Telling stories
Body	Dancing
	Moving to music
	Pantomiming
	Playing games
	Playing music

Voice and body   Acting
                  Putting on a puppet show
                  Singing and dancing
                      at the same time

Our challenge is to provide many and varied school experiences
that call up and exercise and extend such powers of performance
as a base for more successful learning.

Supporting conditions. So much value is already attached to
forwarding some of the performance powers in school that formal
guidelines may not seem to be as necessary as they may have
seemed when we were dealing with creative expression. However,
here are several that may have some use.

*Performance powers are better developed in children than we
have sometimes thought.* The concept of language competence
that has been proposed by the new grammarians may be relevant
here. Normal children from all kinds of backgrounds are now
thought to come to school with the power to generate new sentences that employ most of the structures of their native language
(9). As we have tried to indicate in our analysis of learnings from
an oral culture, migrant children have a wide repertoire of performance powers in the use of language. Those with ethnic backgrounds have other performance powers on which the school may
build.

Performance powers develop as they are used. We may need to
note that in our busy day it takes planning to insure that time is
reserved for exercising the powers of performance. Sometimes we
have thought of "active" versus quiet activities and have seen the
former as needed relief from the latter. While relief from boredom
or sore bottoms may be one of the virtues of physical activity, this
virtue will scarcely serve as an adequate base for a planned program that has to do with the development of performance powers.
Moreover, the hardest part of the performance program to make
provision for is the least active in the physical sense—the set of
skills that is voice-related. Quiet in the room is so much a part of
our predisposition that time for purposeful talk requires real planning.

*Performance powers require materials, space, and equipment as
well as time and intention for their development.* If teachers are to

plan and implement a better program of the development of the performance powers, the school needs books, music, musical instruments, records, record players, game equipment, costume materials, materials out of which to make puppets, a stage, surfaced play areas outdoors, and indoor facilities for play and dancing.

Specific activities. Expression through performance defined in this chapter most often makes use of a vehicle already created by others—a story or song, a game, a dance, a piece of music. In proposing examples of performance activities here, however, some instances where young children are performing what they have created themselves may be included. Such opportunities for the exercise of expression carry a double value. We may note that with younger children most experiences in speaking and dramatizing will be examples of creating and performing at the same time. It seems unnecessary to repeat that the examples offered here are meant as illustrative rather than as exemplary in the sense of serving as models.

Primary Level Activities

Telling stories
A favorite animal story
Something that happened to my father when he was a boy
The family that moved in the night
A story I have heard a hundred times

Pantomiming
Waking up a sleepy brother so he can get off to work on time
Promenading around the square
A cat and dog fight, a cock fight

Moving to music
Like an alligator, roadrunner, toad, prairie dog, deer, hawk
Picking tomatoes, cotton, lettuce, apples, cherries, oranges
Trucks going up a steep hill

Speaking
How to travel light
Preparation of a favorite family food
A visit to relatives at home

Playing games
Old games adapted to school setting

A game taught by a newcomer

Singing
   Play songs from Puerto Rico
   Favorite songs, prepared by one or several children
      for sharing with the rest of the class (several times a week)
   A song learned from my mother
   Songs taught the class by one of the children

Intermediate Level Activities

Telling stories
   Favorite ghost story
   The life of my favorite saint
   A story told me that I don't believe ever really happened
   My version of "Little Red Riding Hood" or "Goldilocks and the Three
      Bears" (what really happened)

Reading aloud
   A letter from a faraway friend or one written to him
   A familiar tale already known to the reader but found in a book
   A new story that reminds the reader of a story he already knows or of
      something that happened to him in the past

Putting on a puppet show
   The boy that always made trouble in camp
   A boy learns to please the girls or a girl learns to please the boys
   A priest catches the mischievous altar boys

Acting
   A strike that paid off
   A preacher who caused a bad man to confess or to give himself up
   A girl who persuaded her father to accept new ways

Playing music
   Our own band with instruments from home
   Solo performance of favorite pieces
   Records brought in to share with the class
   Brother or father who comes to school to perform

Singing
   A ballad of a hero or villain
   A sad story of a girl who lost her sweetheart (in English or Spanish or
      both)

Dancing
   Calling a square dance
   Teaching a dance to a record brought from home

Improvising steps, solo or in pairs, to a popular dance record (Latin, soul, country)

Singing and dancing
Program for own entertainment
Fiesta for another class, parents, or assembly

Interaction as Expression. As a profession, teachers are newly concerned about broadening the base of verbal interaction in the classroom. One investigator reports that there is plenty of talk in most classrooms. About two-thirds of that talk comes from the teacher, however, and two-thirds of what the teacher does is to ask questions with a right answer. The goal of our new concern is to provide for pupils to develop their expressive power for interacting with the teacher and with one another. The proposals for how to go about reaching this goal are numerous (6). For our purposes we are assuming that the main need is for us to know more about the interactive aspect of expression and to attach more value to it. Perhaps a framework such as the following may help.

Processes	*Sample activities*
Offering	Asking questions
	Complaining
	Explaining
	Expressing pleasure
	Making a statement
	Offering information
Responding	Accepting
	Adding information
	Approving
	Denying
	Doubting
	Remaining silent
Interacting	Agreeing
	Arguing
	Clarifying
	Concluding
	Disputing
	Redefining
	Summarizing

What is hoped for is that the processes of offering and responding will be often enough and purposefully enough exercised under the teacher's guidance that the interactive powers the child has already developed, sometimes to a fairly high level in an oral culture, will be strengthened and extended.

Supporting conditions. Guidelines for planning opportunities for development of expression through interaction are appropriately varied in the kinds of concerns with which they deal. The range of opportunities for interaction in school as in the rest of life is endless and some sense of focus needs to be provided.

Interactive expression calls for an atmosphere in which there is adult acceptance and support for the full exploration or revelation of feelings and other personal data. This may be a somewhat cumbersome way of talking about the need for permissiveness. Children who are willing and able to say what they feel and think and know can be dried up in short order if some of what they have to offer is screened out as inappropriate or unacceptable. Children from an oral culture may have learned to vent their feelings freely, including negative feelings, and have learned, too, to hold their own in the disputes that may be seen by them as a step on the way to reaching agreement or at least attaining a new level of mutual understanding. Their skills need more than acceptance; they may deserve support as models to other less open children who have to have help in "giving themselves away," so to speak.

Interactive expression is exercised differently in groups of different sizes and composition. One hundred percent participation in discussion can be insured if a teacher sets children to work in twos or threes on tasks that require interaction. The dynamics of a group of two, however, differs in some important ways from what goes on in a group of three. Teachers need to be aware of the influence of size on interaction and on the kinds of roles that come to be assumed in groups of differing sizes. Selecting which children to put together for various kinds of tasks and knowing when to provide for free choice of work or play partners are also involved in setting up opportunities for the exercise and development of interactive powers.

Interactive expression includes a great range of competencies that require for their development many kinds of work and play tasks. Talk for the sake of talk may have something to be said for it. We do learn more about children whenever we listen to them and that doubtless holds true for the children who listen to one another. But we are after something more as well. The increase of opportunities for interaction can be valued because children learn to relate to one another more easily and effectively. Still, that is not quite enough. In brief, our focus must primarily be maintained on the growth of powers of interaction because such growth enables children to open themselves to the testing out of the information or ideas or skills they are learning in whatever is under study and discussion. As they succeed in putting their learning to the test in the social arena, they also put themselves to the test and learn more about themselves as well as others. But the focus remains on what they are getting out of what they are studying and what more they may need to know. For all of us, and particularly for children, the adequacy of much of our new learning is tested by reference to others.

Specific activities. Opportunities for children to talk about what they are learning are agreed to be important in almost every phase of the school program. Teachers are urged to prepare children for reading a new selection by drawing out an exchange of experiences pertinent to what is to be read. Many social studies concepts need full discussion if there is to be developed around them a freight of rich meanings. Yet, as we have indicated, the press of time tends to cut short the opportunities actually available for interactive expression in many classrooms. In the examples to follow, an effort will be made to refer back to our analysis of the migrant child's culturally developed competencies and at the same time relate the activities a little more closely than in the sections on creation and performance to what the child may be undergoing in school.

Primary Level Activities

Asking questions
Noting questions while a child makes a report to be asked afterwards
Framing questions together to use in making and adding to reports on: taming wild birds and animals, making a tree house

Explaining
   How a christening takes place
   Differences in ways various fruits and vegetables are packed and shipped
   What soul food is

Adding information
   After film on Everglades: what else could have been included?
   Library trip to find new information to report to class

Arguing
   How should a certain story have ended
   Best story in the reader that has just been completed
   Preference of languages: Spanish or English

Clarifying
   Cause of disagreement over how some incident that disrupted the class-
      room started
   Helping another child get the point: "Can someone help Lupe? "

Redefining
   Key terms in mathematics lesson with synonyms or short definition
   Using another language to add a meaning of a term
   Finding more acceptable way of expressing doubt or disagreement:
      "mistake" for "lie"

Intermediate Level Activities

Asking questions
   Listing questions to answer in work of committee (unit study)
   Preparing questions to cover in panel report

Expressing pleasure or support
   How to help other children contribute in group discussion: ask for ideas,
      smile approval of contribution, pick up and use contribution in further
      discussion
   Points to include in complimenting child who has made a report or
      shared an experience

Offering information
   What map colors really mean in terms of differences in terrain and
      climate
   Use of dictionary or encyclopedia to add needed information to discus-
      sion
   Experts appointed in class to keep track of news in various sections of
      country or world and make brief reports and answer questions

Doubting
   Why omission of some details in textbooks on parts of country pupil
      knows well

Identification of issues in current events on which more information is
needed

Examination of proposed solutions to problems in social studies or current events; discussion of other solutions.

Agreeing

Observer delegated to note points of agreement and disagreement from
time to time

Noting agreements and differences among television commentators in
reporting events

Rule for committees: review what you have agreed to do before meeting
ends

Disputing

Setting up rules for conducting debates

Listing key terms around which disagreement exists

Topics: Florida vs. Texas vs. California vs. Puerto Rico

Summarizing

Noting major points as discussion progresses

Pupil appointed to serve as summarizer

Summary and Conclusion

This chapter has approached the question of developing a program
of expression for migrant children in a framework that first of all
proposes a new kind of respect for the competencies such children
bring to school with them as travelers widely experienced with
people and places, as heirs to a vital oral culture, and possibly as
participants in a well-defined ethnic community.

On the basis of respect for these competencies, it has been here
proposed that expression be thought of in terms of powers to
create, perform, and interact and that the school see its obligation
for developing further the powers children bring with them by
relating school experiences to prior experiences and by taking
development of the expressive powers seriously enough to provide
both more time and more material support for this often neglected
portion of the school program.

References

1. Conant, James B. Various writings. Conant may serve as one advocate of
this point of view.

2. Cremin, Lawrence A. *The Transformation of the School.* New York: Alfred A. Knopf, 1961.

3. Frazier, Alexander. "Individualized Instruction." *Educational Leadership,* 25 (April 1968), pp. 616-624.

4. Guilford, J. P., Torrance, E. Paul, Getzels, J. W., and Jackson, Philip. See various works of these authors.

5. Hertz advertisement. *The American Way,* 1 (January-February 1969), back cover.

6. Hyman, Ronald, ed. *Teaching: Vantage Points for Study.* Philadelphia: J. B. Lippincott, 1968.

7. McLuhan, Marshall. *The Gutenberg Galaxy.* Toronto: University of Toronto Press, 1962.

8. *The Texas Project for Education of Migrant Children.* Austin, Texas: Texas Education Agency, January 1966, p. 7.

9. Thomas, Owen. "Competence and Performance in Language" in Alexander Frazier, ed., *New Directions in Elementary English.* Champaign, Illinois: National Council of Teachers of English, 1967, pp. 10-11.

10. Tomlinson, Ethel. "Language Arts Skills Needed by Lower Class Children." *Elementary English,* 33 (May 1956), pp. 279-283.

CHAPTER 9

The Social Studies:
Vehicle for Migrant Education

JOHN STRICKLER

Dr. Strickler sees the primary objective of migrant education as that of equipping migrant children with the skills necessary for induction into the mainstream of American society. He states that objectives for this induction can be accomplished by using teaching strategies relevant to and concerned with the migrant culture. The learning styles of migrant children can be utilized to effectively develop the teaching strategies. He ends with illustrations of how five successful teachers, using the philosophical structure he presents, have created stimulating social studies learning experiences for disadvantaged youngsters.

Dr. John Strickler has been a consultant to several organizations that deal primarily in migrant and inner-city educational problems. As a specialist in social studies he has taught at Ball State University, the University of Alabama at Birmingham, and the University of Miami where he is associate professor of education, and associate director of the Florida School Desegregation Consulting Center. He received his Ed.D. from Ball State University, Muncie, Indiana.

SOLUTIONS to the problems of migrant education are not easily found. Providing quality education has been extremely elusive because of the many difficult and complex problems concomitant to the social milieu of the migrant groups. Most experts agree that the most educationally deprived children in the United States today are those of migrant agricultural workers. School systems and individual teachers, however, have labored for too long under the illusion that easy solutions are readily available. Indeed, there are some who have concluded that the problem is one of human weakness rather than curricular inappropriateness.

A visit to a migrant farm labor camp and an awareness of the lack of success with school experienced by the typical migrant youngster will convince most observers that an integral part of the total problem is that the social malignancy sustains itself. One cannot be master of his destiny without the skills that permit him to gain control over his environment. It is extremely difficult for the migrant to learn these skills when it is necessary for him to remain mobile in order to secure the basics of life in the only manner he knows. The accumulative effect on the child of the migrant is that he is almost predestined to a life of ignorance and poverty and all that that encompasses. Caught in this trap, the young child usually becomes progressively more educationally retarded and falls further and further behind his less mobile counterpart. He will have sensed early in his life that most schools have not learned to accomodate him, resulting in his wholesale rejection of education. When large groups of migrant youngsters reject education as they find it, the seedbed is laid that perpetuates and sustains the impoverished conditions in which they are found.

Part of the blame for this problem can be placed on the public schools. They have failed to provide curriculum and instruction to which migrant children can adequately respond. For too long the curriculum has reflected a life that is not consistent with the one the migrant child knows. There appears to be a general lack of understanding of what the migrant's needs are and how to go about making the curriculum flexible enough that it accomodates him just as he is, rather than forcing him to adjust to the traditional curriculum. Little wonder that the migrant rejects education! And little wonder that there are identifiable potential dropouts in the early elementary grades—children who, early in their lives, have discovered they are in an "unfriendly" environment and, consequently, have removed themselves from it psychologically until they can do so physically and legally. Thus, the vicious cycle of educational deprivation, illiteracy, ignorance, helplessness, and impoverishment is begun all over again.

The educational system is indeed one reason why migrants have not acquired the skills necessary to overcome much of their culturally determined existence. Therefore, it must assume part of the responsibility for this undeveloped human potential. Paradoxically, the institution in the society whose primary responsibility should be to provide the vehicle by which the migrant could ascend beyond his plight is, many times, the migrant's barrier to progress. Educators and the general public must reassess their perceptions of what they consider quality education and redefine quality in relation to the needs of the migrants. This is not an easy task and, as H. L. Mencken observed, "There is always an easy solution to every human problem—neat, plausible, and wrong." Education for the migrant child has been inappropriate, and therefore wrong. The traditional curriculum has not worked.

The Mandate for Social Studies

There is ample evidence to suggest that the migrant's economic usefulness is diminishing because of the rapid advancements in agricultural mechanization. Technology will permit the farmer to be nearly 100 percent mechanized by 1979. This is frightening to those who know and understand the inadequate preparation the migrant has for such an event. It means:

1. The migrant will be forced to be physically immobile.
2. Most of the migrants will have to be assimilated by the urban society.

The education mandate seems clear. There must be education that prepares the migrant child for a social world that is dramatically different from what he knows. In order for education to be able to fulfill its obligation, drastic changes will have to be made in both subject content and the teaching process. This means the heart of teaching will have to be retooled. Inherent in this retooling is the task of choosing subject matter that will provide the knowledge needed by the migrant to cope with his future. It is my belief that the social studies can equip the migrant with many of these valuable skills. Joyce (5, p. 12) best explains the potentialities that this area of the curriculum holds. He states: "Insofar as we can find the best ideas about the social world in the social sciences, we need to expose children to them. The social sciences consist of models of the social world, models which have been developed by social scientists. As one learns these models, he comes to possess the most complete description of the social world in which he lives."

It is apparent that the above statement admonishes teachers to discard outdated social studies content (primarily prescribed by textbook companies) and traditional teaching methods (usually a textbook teaching approach, consisting of either reading or telling about the past). The creative teacher will ask herself, "What do my children need to know and what is the most efficient means for them to acquire this knowledge? " When the teacher allows herself to come to grips with this question, it will become apparent that much of what is taught as social studies to many youngsters is a waste of their intellectual time. When the migrant youngster is considered, this generalization is especially true.

What Do Children Need to Know?

When this question is asked about migrant children, the teacher will have to make choices about social studies content for his students. Many times teachers of migrant children make the mistake of assuming there is but one body of content in the social studies and that it is appropriate for her children.

It is particularly discouraging to visit classrooms in various parts of the United States from the most isolated rural school to one located in the heart of a metropolis and find the teachers teaching their youngsters the same content from the same textbooks. The obvious reason for this is the attitude that the basic guide of what is important to learn can be found in the textbook. Fenton (2, p. 69) points out: "A textbook should be the basic guide to what is taught only if the text can present materials for most objectives more effectively than any other material can." With disadvantaged migrant children, the text does not present subject matter commensurate with their needs. The inappropriateness of choosing content from textbooks was best illustrated by a Negro student teacher in a third grade classroom in an Indianapolis ghetto school. She informed the writer that her unit on community helpers was far from successful. Further probing revealed that she did not view the policeman as a community helper, nor did her third grade youngsters, but the regular teacher had prescribed the unit because "that's one thing you teach in the third grade." Such a judgment should not be taken as educationally sound, nor professional. A social studies topic is educationally sound only if the subject matter illustrates the objective to the learner better than any other content. Thus, the teacher must first start with the question, "What about this particular group of children?"

It is plausible for two groups of youngsters of different cultural and experiential backgrounds to start with the same objectives, study different content, and arrive at an understanding of the common objectives. Taba (10, p. 13) points out that the different levels of knowledge (basic concepts, main ideas, and specific facts) can help deal with the conflict between curricular rigidity and flexibility. For example, the teachers of the two groups may have decided that it is important for their youngsters to understand the concept: All groups of people are dependent on other groups for survival. The subject matter that the two teachers choose probably should be different because the youngsters' cultural and experiential backgrounds are different. The concept, since it focuses on human groups, is inherent within any human group regardless of whether it is a family group or a national group. Therefore, there is more than one subject matter content to teach the one concept. In fact, there are as many sets of subject matter data to test the concept as there are human groups.

Suppose teacher A has youngsters from an upper-middle-class suburban neighborhood and teacher B has youngsters from a migrant labor camp. Teacher A might have her youngsters pursue the concept from the way in which the occupations of the families represented in her classroom are examples of how men living in urban areas are dependent on one another. Teacher B might have her children study the economic processes that take place for them to enjoy a balanced breakfast at school. In this way the students gain a better understanding of nutrition and learn of many types of workers while they pursue the concept of the interdependence of man. Both teachers pursued the objective in a manner commensurate with the backgrounds and needs of their children. The content for one would not necessarily have been appropriate for the other, but both groups of children profited from the study. It would have been very easy for the two teachers to have chosen content on the basis of "that's what you teach this year."

Many teachers are faced with the problem of dealing with the seasonal influx of large numbers of migrant youngsters. This causes considerable consternation on the teacher's part, especially if she has had one group from the beginning of the school year and suddenly has to cope with an additional ten or twelve children in her classroom. In addition to the problems of classroom organization, adequate cumulative records seldom accompany the children to help the teacher determine what social studies experiences they may have had. This is especially frustrating if the teacher has chosen the social studies units from the textbook, for chances are the migrant will either not have an adequate background for the ongoing unit, or he will have had his social studies from another series, or both. Whatever the case, it is reasonable to assume the cumulative effect on the migrant youngster will be that he will never be able to "catch up" and in all probability he will lose most of his will to do so. In actuality, what the teacher is asking the youngster to do is to deal with foreign material that has no social relevancy to him and is beyond his comprehension level. Either causes the student to reject the social studies because he is asked to deal with materials at and beyond his frustration level. It is only natural for him to seek to be comfortable; he does this by "tuning out."

Just as the two teachers cited previously were able to choose different content for similar objectives, so can the individual teacher for the youngsters in her classroom. For those students whose reading, experience, and understanding levels are more advanced, the subject matter to be studied should be chosen to challenge their abilities. Similarly, for the less advanced the subject matter should be commensurate with the performance expectation. In this way the teacher literally "lowers the floor and raises the ceiling" of the curriculum and provides room for all, rather than a few. In the classroom of one creative teacher the children were pursuing the idea of how people in different cultures were alike and how they were unalike. This third grade had chosen four different groups to study—the American Indians, the Eskimos, the Japanese, and themselves. They were looking for information to help them compare how people in different parts of the world provide for the basic needs. Each of the youngsters in this class was excited about learning because each found materials and activities with which he could cope. The class was working in various small groups, with each person finding information about the culture of his choice. The more advanced students were helping others find and organize information. Each person contributed, felt worthy, and learned that all men have similar needs, regardless of outward appearance. The subject matter offered the children was varied and newcomers to the class were absorbed in the unit because all were able to find levels of content that accomodated their abilities. This unit opened up for the first time dimensions of self-awareness, understanding, and perspective that might have lain dormant if the teacher had been less creative. It is my opinion that all the youngsters in that class would be more able to cope with life as a result of that social studies unit.

The Fallacy of Coverage. Many teachers are conditioned to the fact that each year a child should be exposed to a certain prescribed body of knowledge. Apparently there is a tremendous psychological victory if, on the last day of school in June, the questions are answered at the end of the last chapter in the social studies book. It is doubtful if there is any particular thing one needs to know to be an effective citizen. The sixth grade youngster who has been dragged through unit after unit from prehistoric man to the present is likely to develop the attitude that anything of importance either happened a long time ago or a long way off. This kind of subject matter does not necessarily contain the knowledge one needs to analyze his environment and make desirable changes.

The gristmill for much of the social studies content selection should be the social lives of the children. For example, a youngster facing the upheaval of urban renewal finds few rewards in the worn-out community helpers unit as it is usually taught. But this immediate social problem can provide the teacher with an abundance of content to help the social studies come alive for her students.

Consider how one creative Dade County, Florida, teacher recently helped her fifth grade students obtain a better understanding and feeling for the times. There was urban unrest close to the school. A few racial incidents had taken place and the potentiali-

ties for an explosive situation existed. It was quite obvious her
children were anxious since many were directly involved in the
situation. The teacher found her children to be uneasy and rest-
less, with little interest in the social studies project dealing with
the early discovery of the United States. It suddenly dawned on
her that the real social studies was lying dormant within her students. The "discovery" unit was postponed and she led her class
into a discussion of the problems that existed in the community.
Such response! All were eager to contribute and each had a solution to offer. It was obvious to the teacher that many facts were
distorted and most students were reacting purely from emotions.
This was to be expected, but what else could be done? There was
another discussion of the class reaction and some questions raised
as to the real causes of the unrest. A list was made of the principal
participants in the troubled area. Students assumed these roles and
an extremely meaningful dialogue ensued. One student played the
role of a police officer, another a white store owner, another an
inhabitant of the neighborhood, and so on. Topics that were discussed and role-played included such things as civil rights, racial
problems, and education.

When the writer last spoke with the teacher the children had
decided they would like to explore the aspects of the society that
have contributed to the condition they were experiencing. There
were plans to interview black and white citizens, as well as to
explore the historical aspects of the development of the United
States. Indeed, the emphasis changed in this class from studying
about the early explorers to becoming explorers early.

Needless to say, the real issues of the times were being considered by this group of youngsters—issues which otherwise might
never have been pursued. The potentialities for learning appeared
to be almost limitless—interviewing, letter writing, decision making, understanding of others, language development, critical thinking, and many more. These are precisely the tools needed by
future adult citizens to be able to analyze the society and make
needed changes. These are also the tools needed to be able to have
a deep appreciation for those things inherent in the present society
that need to be preserved. What more can an area of the curriculum offer?

The society in which migrant children live abounds with opportunities similar to the one described above. Certainly these children should be afforded the opportunity to explore many of the issues that affect their lives. To do less deprives them of the few chances they may have.

When one views the process of content selection from the child's social perspective, coverage of prescribed textbook materials appears ludicrous. One might speculate, however, on the social weaknesses in the lives of migrant children and choose content based upon those weaknesses. When this is done, the teacher might conclude that the migrant's greatest social weakness comes from his inability to manage his economic life. Thus, units of work based upon actual production, consumption, and conservation of economic resources are extremely relevant to the needs of these youngsters. These ideas and concepts have transfer value to adult life and are too important not to be considered.

Whatever content the teacher decides is important for her students to study, she should remember that for the culturally disadvantaged quality of experience is much more important than quantity. In-depth studies of a few topics is much better than superficial studies of many. Therefore, content coverage is a fallacy. Jarolimek (4, pp. 149-150), in speaking of teaching culturally different youngsters, states: "The teacher needs to think of social studies learnings for these children. What do they need most to learn? . . . Should the contributions of the Greeks and Romans to western civilization receive priority over such social learnings as respect for public property, assuming responsibility, conservation, respecting rights of others, and consumer education?" These questions are the ones that a social studies teacher must ask when choosing content for migrant children.

What is the Best Way for Children to Learn Content?

Once the teacher decides on the content for her children, she must then choose what teaching process will best help them understand the subject matter. For example, a teaching strategy for developing the ability to think critically about issues would not use the method of rote memorization. In the core of critical thinking lies something with considerably more dimension than mere accumulation of information. To be sure, acquiring information is inherent in the problem-solving process, but one should be aware of the fact that he should not expect the subject matter to be the vehicle by which this knowledge is imparted to the learner. In other words, proper teaching methods are not inherent within content.

Many teachers have been lured into believing there is but one approach to teaching social studies content. This approach is to arrange events in the order in which they happened and have the students learn about them starting with the event that happened first and is thus the farthest from reality. This approach has proven to be disastrous when used with educationally disadvantaged youngsters. First, the only way one can learn about the past if it is beyond his own experience is to read about it. It is not unusual to find the migrant two, three, and even four years below grade level in reading ability. Most of the social studies information has a higher reading level than the grade level it purports. A child cannot handle successfully this great a disparity between his reading ability and that which he is asked to read.

Second, most of what the migrant child is asked to read and understand is based upon information demanding that the learner be equipped to assimilate a vast number of concepts. With youngsters whose cognitive and verbal developments have been arrested because of limited background experiences, these concepts require the child to deal with them in a highly abstract manner in order to bridge the gap between the word and the idea it represents. Time, geographical space, and chronology are abstractions that are difficult for most people, but to migrant youngsters the teaching efforts are pretty much wasted until there is a greater backlog of concrete experience from which they can draw.

Third, migrant children should be physically and actively involved in the learning. This means that other than passive avenues must be available for the assimilation of knowledge and the acquisition of skills. Social studies methods that deal with content removed from reality in time and space do not allow the migrant to become physically and actively involved. When this mistake is made he loses valuable learning channels that could allow educational experiences to be meaningful to him.

A teacher's strategy must be such that it translates the content into tasks that are within the learning realm of the student. This means that the teacher of migrant youngsters must consider the nature of the learner as she plans for his immersion into the selected content. A different principle should be applied to the selection of teaching methodologies than was suggested for content selection. When choosing content for the migrant, it was suggested that the decision be based on the voids or weaknesses found in his social environment. Conversely, when choosing the process for translating the content into learnable tasks, the decision should be based upon the strengths of the child. These two principles are compatible and may be used in all areas of the curriculum.

Strengths Useful For Teaching The Social Studies

The idea of using the strengths of youngsters as guidelines for teaching strategies and curriculum development for disadvantaged children is neither unique nor new. Riessman, writing of education for disadvantaged youngsters, proposes that the learning style of these youngsters be used and utilized to make educational experience more meaningful to them. Riessman (8, p. 332) states: "In everybody's style there are certain strengths and each of us has his own Achilles Heel. The issue in developing a powerful change in a person is related to what you are going to do with the Achilles Heel and how you are going to utilize the strengths."

Cheyney (1) also advocates an understanding of the learning styles of the disadvantaged to build a viable and meaningful curriculum. His book, *Teaching Culturally Disadvantaged in the Elementary School,* is based on the idea that disadvantaged youngsters have strengths around which teaching strategies should and can be built. He explains that it is not until teachers come to an intellectual and personal acknowledgment of this fact that good teaching can begin with the disadvantaged.

As a child grows he becomes a mirror of his social world. This means that most youngsters have learned to be socially competent in order for them to function in their particular environments.

The migrant youngster becomes disadvantaged when he is asked to function in an environment other than his own. The point is that he is capable of learning a culture and in the process certain styles of learning have been habituated as a result of the transmitting agencies inherent in the culture. The migrant learned his culture naturally, probably resulting from a will to learn or perhaps a competency drive that all human beings possess. What makes the migrant "different," however, is the fact that he was forced to learn something different because "that's what was there." All one has to do is to observe these youngsters to understand that they spend their time learning to cope with their environment. Teachers should be mindful that the skills the migrant learns naturally are not necessarily the skills needed to be competent in the school environment. But it should be remembered that the migrant child possesses the potentialities for acquiring them; he has already proven that.

What are these learning styles that the migrant possesses and brings to school with him? Cheyney (1, pp. 43-53) identified ten strengths which should play an integral role in curriculum development for disadvantaged youngsters. He describes the disadvantaged as being: physically oriented, fantasy prone, role players, inductive, problem oriented, expressive, spatially oriented, visual-artistic, perseverate, and verbally abstract.

What should this mean to the teacher of social studies? It suggests that an entirely different approach to content can be taken once there is an acknowledgment of the existence of these styles. It should also indicate that all children will not possess all the strengths with equal depth, just as we do not expect all children to have equal mental abilities. It means that all youngsters possess the facilities to assimilate the chosen content.

For example, a teacher who believes that the migrant needs concrete, firsthand experiences will provide for visits to places the child has never been to broaden his background of experiences. Realizing that they have other strengths to capitalize on, she can extend the learning experience beyond the actual visitation once the children have returned to the classroom. Taba (11, p. 83) points out there should be a rotation of intake and expression, and the youngsters should express information in a manner different from the way it was acquired. Therefore, a teacher who understands that her children are role players, resulting from a lifetime of learning their cultural roles, will be able to have her children reenact many of the things experienced on the field trip. They will have the experiences to talk about, as well as planning together for their parts in the role-playing situation. The teacher will have reason to use experience charts and other media. She will also be able to evaluate her teaching objectives more effectively. In this situation, the concomitant learnings of language development and positive self-concept reinforcement are probably as important as the primary objective of the social studies experience. However, the primary and secondary objectives of the teaching situation are supportive enough to each other so that one area of the curriculum (the social studies) acts as a vehicle for learning in others. It can be seen how a creative teacher could use this one experience as the motivation for further learning in all areas of curriculum.

There is more to say about the strengths and learning styles of migrants than could possibly be said in this chapter. It will be sufficient to say that I am convinced that a teacher who makes decisions about social studies teaching methods based on the positive learning styles of migrants will provide experiences more commensurate with their needs. That teacher will have chosen content based upon weaknesses and methodologies based upon strengths. Such instruction almost guarantees that the migrant will learn both skills and knowledge appropriate for his future.

Teaching Strategies For Teachers Of Migrants

Many times it is difficult to translate ideas to practical learning situations. Teachers have been heard to say, "Yes, it sounds fine, but what can I do in my class?" Several examples of how successful teachers have created stimulating and inspiring social studies learning experiences for disadvantaged youngsters follow. The examples are ones observed while working with teachers of disadvantaged children. It will be noted that the subject matter was chosen as a result of the recognition of the social needs of disadvantaged children, and it will be obvious that the youngsters' experiences had borrowed heavily on their strengths as learners.

"Significant Others" Project. One teacher was aware that many disadvantaged children never have the opportunity to meet the kind of persons who should become significant figures in their lives. This class launched on a social studies unit in which people who held jobs that were within the reach of the students were

introduced. Some occupations were: truck driver, mailman, carpenter, plumber, factory worker, seamstress, secretary, and beautician. The class visited each worker on the job and observed the kind of work he was doing. After the visit the worker was invited to come to the classroom and share his skills with the students. For example, the carpenter brought his tools and made the class two birdhouses while he was at school; the beautician talked about her trade and stressed points of grooming; the secretary demonstrated her typing skills but also stressed the need for promptness.

The interest shown by the students was amazing. Boys who had never displayed interest before were working hard to find information about trucks and the construction of birdhouses; girls developed interests in sewing. These youngsters were learning about things which could become a reality to them. They were also learning language, library, and social skills. When a person possesses these skills, he thinks more of himself and therefore can do more for himself.

The Community Project. A very creative teacher in Collier County, Florida, launched her class on a project that was designed to help the students gain a better understanding of how to plan and budget their money. Each student in the room assumed the role of a community worker. There were as many different kinds of workers as there were students and the children could change jobs every week if they wished. Stores were set up in the classroom to simulate different businesses found in the community. There was a bank, a grocery, a small loan company, a used car lot, a dime store, a gas station, and others. Each child was given a weekly paycheck with which he had to manage his weekly expenses, pay on money borrowed from a bank or loan company, and make weekly payments on such things as gasoline bought on credit or an automobile. The teacher had stipulated that each child had to save some money each week and invest it in some manner, even though he might have to give up something else in its place. It was the responsibility of these sixth grade children to operate the different stores. For example, the banker kept a record of the money deposited and also figured the interest rate on money invested in savings. Each child was responsible for his own economic affairs through the wise use he made of his money.

The testimony to the success of this project was a statement made by the teacher. She observed: "The children have a greater understanding that one has to plan for the future and that choices between luxuries and necessities have to be made."

Reenacting A Social Studies Event. One teacher found it almost impossible to get her students excited about special days throughout the year. She began using media that children are familiar with to help create a greater interest in what she thought was important for them to know. One day when I was visiting this classroom, the youngsters were presenting their version of a live telecast of the first Thanksgiving. Each person had a part to play; there were Indians, pilgrims, and television technicians, who were interviewing various persons. A mock television camera had been made by the youngsters, scripts had been prepared, and even commercials were used.

It was obvious that a great deal had been learned about the first Thanksgiving. Less obvious and less measurable was the amount of cooperation required in this project. The disadvantaged child needs projects that help him identify with group goals in which he can actually see things being accomplished. This teacher had all of her children physically and mentally involved. Learning was easy and rewarding, with few chances for failure.

"Finish the Story" Project. Another teacher who has taught migrants and other disadvantaged groups for many years is convinced that the primary problem of the disadvantaged is in the area of language development. Her curriculum reflects this belief, with practically all of her youngsters' school experiences built around tasks that will increase their ability to use standard English. She is also aware of these children's imaginative abilities.

Over the years this teacher has collected dozens of stories that depict the lives of persons (either real or fictional) with whom disadvantaged youngsters can readily identify. She uses them in creative and interesting ways. Sometimes the stories are used as the basis for playlets; other times the children may make puppets and retell the stories through the puppet.

Many of the stories she uses are appropriate for the social studies. For example, she used *Blue Willow,* the touching story of a little migrant girl, and encourages the youngsters to create their own ending to the story. The teacher affirms that she has gained a great amount of insight into the feelings of her students through this one story. Another story that she uses is *Down, Down, the Mountain,* the story of two mountain youths, their desire for new shoes, and the way in which they go about obtaining them. Once when I was visiting her classroom, the youngsters were dramatizing how they thought the two mountain children might have gotten their shoes. The students were expressing their ideas through paper bag puppets.

Such experiences give the disadvantaged chances to become more aware of the socialization processes. Even though they will not be able to verbalize the concept, they will have greater self-insight and be more sensitive to their own social situation. This is a first step to self-improvement.

The Explorers Project. One very successful social studies project grew out of the interest shown in a recent televised moonshot. After a follow-up discussion of the event, the teacher asked her students where they would like to go if they had their choice of going where no man had traveled before. The suggestions were varied. Some preferred the moon, others the bottom of the ocean, and so on. A second question was asked: "How would you get there and what kind of difficulties would you expect?" The teacher reported she had never had such response. The several groups immediately went to work planning the means of transportation, as well as preparations for overcoming expected difficulties at their imaginary destinations. Information was needed by these children and the librarian was brought in to help identify materials. The youngsters were seeking purposeful goals. The slower students seemed to be making as great a contribution as the accelerated ones. For example, one nonreading fifth grader was the person responsible for his group's mural. His art talents were being utilized for the first time. He needed to have information about the project, so he too was in the library seeking information with his friends. There is a high probability that this young man may have learned more than anyone in his class, for he learned many good things about himself that he did not know before.

The teacher said: "From this unit my children learned a lot about the difficulties encountered by the early explorers of our country." This alone is a most worthy objective, but it is suspected they learned even more about themselves and how to anticipate the problems of the future.

Summary

1. Adequate migrant education has not been accomplished because of the mobility of the migrant and the inappropriateness of traditional curricula.

2. The social studies can equip the migrant with valuable knowledge and skills needed for his future. To do this, the strategies for teaching him will have to be retooled.

3. When selecting social studies content for migrant children, the teacher should assess the social lives of the students and choose content based upon the weaknesses discerned. This means coverage of traditional topics may not be appropriate.

4. It is the responsibility of the social studies teacher to translate content into learnable tasks. A teacher who recognizes that the migrant youngster has certain learning strengths derived from his environment can be more discriminating when choosing her teaching methodologies.

5. A teacher who combines appropriate social studies content and teaching methods will be more likely to help migrants acquire the skills necessary for them to control their destiny.

References

1. Cheyney, Arnold B. *Teaching Culturally Disadvantaged in the Elementary School.* Columbus, Ohio: Charles E. Merrill Books, 1967.

2. Fenton, Edwin. *The New Social Studies.* New York: Holt, Rinehart & Winston, 1967.

3. Garvey, Dale M. *Stimulation, Role-Playing, and Sociodrama in the Social Studies.* Emporia, Kansas: Kansas State Teachers College, December 1967.

4. Jarolimek, John. *Social Studies in Elementary Education.* New York: The Macmillan Company, 1967.

5. Joyce, Bruce R. *Strategies for Elementary Social Science Education.* Chicago: Science Research Associates, Inc., 1965.

6. Muessig, Raymond H., and Rogers, Vincent R. *Social Science Seminar Series.* Columbus, Ohio: Charles E. Merrill Publishing Company, 1965.

7. National Council for the Social Studies. *Bringing the World Into Your Classroom.* Washington, D.C.: Curriculum Series Number Thirteen, 1968.

8. Riessman, Frank. "The Strategy of Style," in A. Harry Passow, Miriam Goldberg, and Abraham J. Tannenbaum, eds., *Education of the Disadvantaged.* New York: Holt, Rinehart & Winston, 1967.

9. Smith, James A. *Creative Teaching of the Social Studies in the Elementary School.* Boston: Allyn & Bacon, 1967.

10. Taba, Hilda. *Teachers' Handbook for Elementary Social Studies.* Palo Alto: Addison-Wesley Publishing Company, 1967.

11. Taba, Hilda, and Elkins, Deborah, *Teaching Strategies for the Culturally Disadvantaged.* Chicago: Rand McNally & Company, 1966.

CHAPTER 10

Measurement and Evaluation of the Migrant Child

JOHN J. BIBB, JR.

Dr. Bibb develops a frame of reference from which to view objectively the use of standardized tests. He discusses several types of standardized tests and what can be expected of them in terms of becoming more knowledgeable about children. The second half of the chapter deals with teacher-made tests and illustrations of test items.

Dr. John J. Bibb, Jr., has had wide experience as a consultant to teachers of disadvantaged children. Formerly a school psychologist and director of Psychological Services and Guidance in Charlottesville, Virginia, and associate professor of education at the University of Miami, he is now Supervising Psychologist of the Washington, D.C., office of American Management Psychologists, Inc.

IN COMMON with other teachers of the culturally disadvantaged, teachers of the migrant child often comment disparagingly on the results of standardized testing programs in which their schools participate.

"Why bother spending time, effort, and money to get results showing what you already know—that the migrant child receives scores placing him at the bottom end of the class?"

"There are results from three different intelligence tests included in Elaine's cumulative record. Since each IQ is different, which one gives me the best estimate of her ability?"

"The tests do not measure experiences which the migrant children have had. Why not devise a test which is fairer culturally to them so they can get high scores?"

These comments, somewhat representative of those made by teachers of migrant children, reflect the confusion, misinforma-

tion, and lack of information concerning measurement and evaluation which this chapter seeks to eradicate.

The teacher is expected to interpret the contents of each child's
cumulative record, including data from standardized testing, and
to provide a prescriptive program of education experiences meaningful to each child. Society expects the teacher to evaluate the
extent to which each child he teaches has demonstrated having
profited from the exposure to educational experiences, with letter
grades used to attest and to communicate the teacher's evaluation
of the child's proficiency in each area in which he has received
instruction. As evaluation is concerned, the teacher is in the best
position to report each child's progress in relation to the objectives
established by the teacher for each child's program of educational
experiences. It is, therefore, incumbent upon the teacher to identify where each child presently functions, to plan educational experiences out of which the child can derive meaning, to guide the
learning experiences, and to evaluate the attainment or mastery of
those learning experiences which the child can demonstrate.

Measurement and Evaluation Defined

As stated by Stanley (9), measurement refers to the administration
and scoring of tests while evaluation designates summing-up processes that involve value judgments. When value judgments are
related to the interpretation of test scores, evaluation is involved.
Pointing out the extreme in test interpretation, Cronbach (3) suggests that the objective reporting of the results of measurement is
a psychometric approach to test interpretation, while an impressionistic approach is followed when the teacher or examiner seeks
to evaluate the test score giving his impressions on its representa-
tiveness or investigating its meaning. When test scores from a standardized test are cumulated to determine a class average, the
psychometric approach is illustrated. In examining the pattern of
performance on subtests of an achievement test by an individual
student, the impressionistic approach is used. Regardless of the
approach used in test interpretation, because it involves interpretation it is evaluation.

Using Test Results

Before a teacher can put test results to use, it is necessary to establish what the test measures. The mere reporting of a score is not necessarily meaningful, fair, accurate, or representative of what the score is assumed to represent. In selecting a standardized test or in developing a teacher-made test, the teacher needs to know what measure is being sought and yielded from its use, if any relevant evaluation is to occur.

In this chapter, the treatment of "test" follows the definition given by Cronbach (3, p. 21): "A test is a systematic procedure for comparing the behavior of two or more persons." This definition is broad enough to include teacher-made tests as well as standardized tests, with the emphasis on following a systematic procedure for making such behavioral comparisons. It is important that the comparison be made on a sample of behavior that reflects experiences typical or representative of the persons tested.

In the classroom, the teacher is mindful of the experiences provided or structured as learning experiences with the children, but the child must perceive the experience and give it personal meaningfulness before that experience is grasped and communicated or observed as a learning experience. As for standardized test results with migrant children, often the results indicate the level at which the children presently function. Most definitely the content of the standardized test, any standardized test, reflects cultural bias to a greater or lesser degree. The migrant child typically enters his school experience with a language handicap when compared with the level of attainment representative for his age or grade group. The results of the standardized tests can be examined to indicate where the child stands, what he knows, what he can handle, what it is indicated that he does not know and cannot do when compared with the level of attainment that is representative for his age group or grade placement group. The results of the standardized test do not reveal any more, but no less, than a fragment of the total picture of his total performance. The results may be viewed as a photograph, revealing where he was ranked at the time he was tested on the materials included as a sample of whatever the test attempted to measure. The results are subject to change, and the teacher can be instrumental in providing experiences out of which the child can close the gap between his level of functioning and the level that is representative of his age or grade level. This statement is not intended to suggest teaching the content of the test, but it does suggest that a child's school experiences can be structured to parallel the kinds of expectations made of others at his age level or at his grade placement.

The teacher can use the results of standardized testing to provide for a prescriptive program of educational experiences. A prescriptive, individualized program requires an analysis of the child's strengths and weaknesses to establish a basis for formulating educational objectives out of which he can perceive and derive meaning. With personally meaningful educational experiences provided at a pace he can handle, the migrant child, like any other child, can then be led into concept formation and concept attainment. To facilitate academic growth the learning experiences must be relevant, meaningful, and related to his previous experiences. The teacher must remember that the child is the one who must perceive the experience as meaningful; this necessitates continuous evaluation of the extent to which the objectives are being attained.

Once the child can communicate a factual mastery of the subject content, he may be moved forward to engage in comparing and in contrasting this new knowledge with his previous learnings. Reasoning, comprehension, judgment, problem solving, and abstract generalizations become possible once meaning is associated with a concept by the child. Through such effective teaching, the migrant child's level of operation increases to approach a level of attainment more in keeping with his ability and more in keeping with subsequent expectations made of him in school and in life as a member of the total society. The systematic procedures known as testing, whether standardized tests or teacher-made tests, have their uses, but each also has its abuses.

Standardized Tests

When a test instrument is standardized, it is standardized with respect to its format, content, instructions for administration, timing, scoring, and interpretation of results in relation to the level of attainment that is representative or typical of those for whose use the test is intended. Each of these areas is set forth and explained in the test manual provided by the author and publisher of the instrument, and directions set forth in the test manual must be followed exactly. Unless each testing condition is followed precisely, there is no basis for comparing the sample of behavior measured by the test. As decisions are made on the basis of test scores, these test scores must reflect each child's representative performance under the same conditions, having been given the same directions, the same amount of time, and the same treatment and interpretation of the objective data.

Classification of Standardized Tests

The classification of standardized tests is admittedly arbitrary. In popular use, tests are classified as:

1. intelligence tests
2. educational achievement tests
3. aptitude tests
4. personality tests

The so-called intelligence test is based on an individual's achievement, his performance on items and tasks usually presented to him in a test booklet, and the results are used to predict his aptitude for success in a verbal-centered school curriculum. The intelligence test was initiated in the emergence of psychological testing to identify children who could not profit from regular classroom instruction, and the tests that are marketed as intelligence tests seek to report high correlations with the well-established individually administered intelligence tests that tend to follow Binet's approach to measuring intelligence. Anastasi (2) presents a section on the history of psychological testing that notes the contributions to the rise of intelligence testing in the tradition such testing continues to follow. In this treatment, it is sufficient to report that even the most widely known and used individually administered intelligence tests measure only some six to eight of the 120 aspects of intelligence made known through the three-dimensional model of the structure of intellect by Guilford (7, p. 63).

The Intelligence Quotient

When units of credit are administered for the successful completion of an item in months of mental age development, the total number of months of credit in mental age is then divided by the child's age in months since his birth. The product is multiplied by 100 to remove the decimal, and the intelligence quotient, IQ, is yielded. This approach to determine IQ is termed the developmental ratio approach. More recently, an individual's points of credit are translated into scaled scores reflecting his performance in relation to the level of achievement that is typical of his own age group. This approach, called the deviation IQ, is actually a standard score rather than a ratio between mental age and chronological age, a point elaborated on by Anastasi (2, pp. 52-58).

Different students can receive the same IQ from the administration of an intelligence test. Even with the same IQ, entirely different patterns of responses for which credit was given may occur. Thus, their resulting IQs may be the same without being equal to each other. The IQ concept is a relative one, and a fluctuation of several points from the obtained IQ on a subsequent administration is somewhat to be expected. Differences among IQs on different tests are perfectly logical, although they generally fall into the same general location with respect to the group for whose use the test was standardized. Assuming the student has done his own work without outside assistance, the highest IQ should be taken to indicate his aptitude for success in a school setting, other things being equal.

Achievement Test Results

Educational achievement tests may report their results in the scaling unit stanine. For educational purposes, generally, stanines 1-3 represent low achievement, stanines 4-6 represent average achievement, and stanines 7-9 represent high achievement; such achievement ratings are related to the group on whom the test was standardized and for whose use the test is intended. When use is made of the scaling unit "grade equivalent," caution should be exercised to preclude misinterpretation by improperly reversing the concept to suggest equivalent grade, which it does not express. With respect to the amount and direction of his grade equivalent, a student who scores high seems to have mastered well what is representative for his grade placement, and one who scores low indicates that when compared with the level of achievement typical for his grade content. A process item, for example, may instruct a child to fill in boxes with symbols of responses to the test items to determine through an impressionistic interpretation of the data why his scores are as they are in order to make appropriate professional use of the test results.

Aptitude and Personality Tests

Aptitudes do not tend to crystalize until around the age of 16, and use is not generally made of aptitude tests in the elementary grades. Similarly, widespread use of personality tests is not made in a school testing program. Included among the selected references at the end of the chapter are textbooks providing more detailed coverage of these topics.

Educational Implications

The teacher is urged to examine the responses made by a child to the items on an intelligence test or on an achievement test to understand the child's functioning level of operation. The child's functional level may be analyzed by noting those responses to items dealing with samples of behavior depending upon the mastery of subject content as contrasted with those responses to items which test intellectual and learning processes. Cronbach (3, pp. 26-27) presents a brief treatment of product versus process in test interpretation in which the emphasis on product is associated with the psychometric approach in test interpretation, and the emphasis on process is related to the impressionistic extreme in test interpretation.

The behavior being sampled on a test has to be identified before evaluating a child's performance. Does the sample reveal what you want measured? How does it do so? Is it a fair and appropriate approach through which to measure? Are the experiences common to the child? Is the vocabulary appropriate? Is the level of readability fair? Are you gaining a measure of the content or a reflection of inadequate experiences in world knowledge, word meaning, or reading?

The migrant child, who is culturally disadvantaged, has not had the opportunity for experiences that are typical of advantaged children. The results from testing the migrant child should be treated as an indication of the child's level of functioning at the time of testing. The results, when taken at face value, do not indicate the child's ability to profit from instruction.

When the results are examined to note the migrant child's response pattern of success on items dealing with *product,* an indication of his ability to handle educational expectations appropriate for his age or grade level is noted. When the child's response pattern of success on items dealing with *process* are examined, the teacher gains information on the child's ability to engage in reasoning, judgment, problem solving, and abstract generalizations. The process items do not require specific instructional content. A process item, for example, may instruct a child to fill in boxes with symbols according to a given code. The product items, or content items, require the child to answer specific questions such as identifying the capital cities of specified states of the United States of America. With this type of information, taken in conjunction with what is already known about the child and his level of functioning in the day-to-day operation in the classroom, the teacher is more able to plan for and to provide a prescriptive educational program of learning experiences.

It is largely up to the teachers of the migrant child, or, for that matter, of any culturally disadvantaged child, to serve as an intervening variable between the level at which the child functions and the level at which he could function. Such an approach to teaching would enable the migrant child to advance to a level more in keeping with his ability to profit from instruction, illustrating the competent and professional uses to which the results of standardized testing may be applied as an instructional aid.

In the course of instructional activities each day, the teacher may evaluate continuously the extent to which the objectives of each lesson are being attained. An intensive involvement through communication with members of the class enables the teacher to establish the extent to which the children perceive the learning experience personally and can deal with it effectively. An emphasis on student involvement, the exchange of ideas, intensive questioning, and structured exercises calling for the application of the new knowledge are procedures through which the teacher can guide learning. Through structuring the learning experiences to verify that the experiences are meaningful to the children, the teacher can establish that learning is taking place. Against each student's previous level of achievement, newly learned material can become meaningful to him. Probing questions seeking to establish why and how the new knowledge can be applied can lead into finding reasons, solving problems, exercising sound judgment, and generalizing. Based on the awareness of the extent to which the students can handle the instructional content on a daily basis, the teacher is advised to evaluate the effectiveness of methods, materials, procedures, activities, and techniques in attaining each lesson's objectives with each child as a learner.

Teacher-made Tests

Since the teacher seeks to sample learning experiences in order to evaluate each child's attainment of the instructional objectives, it is recommended that several test items be prepared each day. In preparing teacher-made tests, test items prepared daily following the awareness of what the students are able to demonstrate having understood will aid the teacher in making formal evaluations of each child's level of measured learning. In writing teacher-made test items, the teacher must bear in mind the reading ability of the students. For some students, oral examinations may be necessary, and in certain areas of instruction, performance tests may be called for to have students demonstrate the ability to perform a dance step, to operate a drill press, or to present a dramatized report. A detailed treatment of teacher-made tests has been presented by J. A. Green (6).

Constructing Teacher-made Tests

In constructing a teacher-made test, the teacher may be guided by some of the points listed below:

1. Determine the most effective testing technique through which the child's attainment of the lesson's objectives may be evaluated.
2. Attempt to focus attention on what is expected of the student; eliminate irrelevant or misleading content which may confuse him.
3. Make use of language which the student being tested can understand; seek to evaluate his understanding of the instructional content rather than his reading rate or comprehension.
4. Write the items in a clear style, with sufficient structure to enable him to understand the expectations made of him.

5. Provide an attractive format or appearance in presenting the test items.

6. Give clear directions or instructions for taking the test.

7. Allocate sufficient time for the student to complete the test without rushing.

8. Specify clearly the manner in which the responses are to be made, noting factors which affect the evaluation (such as spelling, English usage).

9. On any test, use no more than two objective test types, each type organized together as a unit.

10. Seek to have the test serve as a learning experience rather than a mere recall of factual information in accordance with reasonable expectations for the maturity, sophistication, and academic abilities of the students being tested.

In determining which test type to use, consideration needs to be given to the depth with which the students are expected to handle the content. Factors such as the amount of time to be spent both by the student in taking the test and by the teacher in evaluating his performance must be considered. The objective test types of teacher-made tests have an advantage in ease and objectivity in scoring, but they ordinarily do not enable the teacher to establish the ability of the student to analyze, synthesize, or organize his responses to reveal his level of comprehension or ability to communicate in depth.

The Essay Test

The essay test is notoriously low in reliability among different graders. In part, this lack of consistency among ratings by different graders is due to the lack of specific criteria by which the essay is to be evaluated. One grader may disregard misspelled words and English usage while another grader may associate his evaluation heavily on those areas. One grader may expect the student to set forth an abundance of factual detail while another grader places emphasis on the student's ability to synthesize the factual information into a meaningful organization centered around a central theme through which factual support is given less emphasis. Despite the lack of consistency among graders, the essay test does enable the teacher to structure what is expected of the student, to specify the criteria by which the essay is to be evaluated, and even to limit the amount of pages, words, or space which may be taken to develop the essay. The essay test permits the student to demonstrate his understanding of the topic, to communicate his ideas, and to submit a work sample of his own work, covering the assignment in depth. By structuring and communicating expectations, the teacher may present to the student through the essay test a medium wherein his resourcefulness, imagination, creativity, writing style and ability, and ability to communicate in depth may be determined through evaluation.

Objective Test Types

Of the objective test types, the most commonly used are: matching, true-false, completion, and multiple choice.

Matching. The matching form of test item is widely used to have the student form associations by pairing a response choice with each item. It emphasizes the recall of factual information, enabling the teacher to cover a wide variety of items in the area of instructional content in a minimum of time. It is relatively easy to construct and to score. Ordinarily, a test containing the matching form of test item should contain no fewer than five items to be matched, and the response choices should be a longer alphabetized list than the items to be matched. Green (6, p. 40) suggests that a single test contain no more than fifteen matching items. This suggestion is especially well taken when all fifteen items are to be matched from a longer listing of alphabetized response choices.

Example: Put the letter next to the color of the vegetable at harvest time in the space by the vegetable.

_____ 1.	pole beans	A. brown
_____ 2.	carrots	B. green
_____ 3.	ripe tomatoes	C. orange
_____ 4.	crookneck squash	D. red
_____ 5.	peanuts	E. white
		F. yellow

True-False. For the true-false form of test item, the teacher should not use "dead giveaway" statements or irrelevant information. Care should be exercised to leave out of the statements words such as "all," "never," "only," "always," and "none." The emphasis should be on statements that are entirely true or entirely false, rather than a misleading or ambiguous element within the statement. Unless attention to details in reading are being emphasized, it is better to avoid making use of negatively worded statements or misleading statements, such as "It is not uncommonly assumed that . . ." Ebel (4, pp. 138-143) illustrates use of the true-false form of test item dealing with factual recall, computation, application, and interpretation. Ebel (4, pp. 146-147) also states that "false statements tend to make more discriminating test items than true statements," and that the teacher may include as many as 60 percent false statements on a true-false test.

Examples: Put T if true and F if false in the space by each item.

( ) 1. One pound of tomatoes weighs the same as one pound of beets.

( ) 2. It takes more tomatoes to make a dozen than it does heads of cabbage.

Completion. The completion form of test item may be used to have the student fill in the word(s) missing in a blank in a statement, to answer a question, to give an identification, to complete a statement, or to restrict the amount of space to be used in responding to an item. One of the related uses of the completion form of test item is that the answers given by the students may aid the teacher in providing plausible answers for use in the multiple-choice form of test item. One of the disadvantages of the completion form of test item is that it requires the teacher to read all of the responses made by the students, being ready to give credit for answers other than what the teacher has expected or sought in phrasing the item. This condition poses a problem in devising a scoring key. Looked at as an advantage, however, the completion item form permits flexibility for the student in responding. In constructing the completion type of test, the teacher seeks to avoid grammatical contextual clues and to avoid giving a clue as to the length of an expected response by providing blanks of uniform length for all items to be completed. Pertinent information should be sought, and the number of blanks should be kept at a minimum in each item. Ordinarily, credit is awarded for the successful completion of each blank. To aid in scoring, the blanks may be num-

bered with instructions given the student to indicate his comple-
tions on a separate answer sheet with numbers corresponding to
the numbered blanks.

Examples: Supply the missing word to complete each statement.

1. If you average 50 miles an hour, it will take you ____hours to travel
   250 miles.
2. John has three older brothers, one younger brother, one older sister, and
   one younger sister, which means he has _____ brothers and sisters.

Example: Write your answer in the space at the end of the question.

3. If Tina's mother and father both work eight hours each on Saturday and
   make $1.75 per hour, how much money will they make? _____ .

Example: Write your answer in the space given at the end of each statement
or question.

4. Donna should get back $____ in change from the $5.00 she gave the
   cashier to pay for $3.54 worth of groceries.   (_____)

Example: Write your answer in the space given at the end of each statement
or question.

5. If Sam's father left home to go pick tomatoes at six o'clock in the morning and will be back home at seven o'clock in the evening, the number of
   hours he is away from home is   (_____)

Example: In the space below, explain why tomatoes are picked before they
are ripe on the vines.

6. _____
   _____
   _____

Multiple-Choice. The multiple choice form of test item is the
most widely used and most popular of the objective test item
types. Through its use the teacher can emphasize factual recall of
information, recognition, reasoning, judgment, problem-solving,
and abstract generalizations. When the teacher does not emphasize
the trivial, and when honest efforts are made to preclude ambigu-
ity, it can enable the teacher to cover a wide area of instructional
content in a minimum of time while also calling upon the student
to engage in higher order mental processes. In addition to avoiding
words such as "all," "never," and "only," and avoiding negatively
worded statements or questions, the teacher has to pay attention
to the structure, organization, and format of each item. Care
should be taken to provide item choices, or distracters, that are

plausible answers. Choices should be of nearly the same level of readability, of complexity, and of length. When use is made of distracters such as "all of the above" or "none of the above," the answer for which credit is given should not always be clearly "all" or "none." If two of the distracters are "all of the above" and "none of the above," the choice, "all of the above" must occur before the choice, "none of the above." As with true-false items, there should not be any discernible pattern of correct responses. Actually, there should be an equal number of items for which the correct choice is 1, 2, 3, 4, and 5, but this stipulation does not suggest that all five choices should occur in every five items. Ordinarily, there are five possible (and plausible) choices for each item. Just as "dead giveaway" choices are to be avoided, there should be only one correct, best answer for each item. While some specialists in measurement take an emphatic position that a question must introduce the item, in popular usage statements and incomplete statements are also used.

Example: Write the letter of your answer in the space next to each Question.
_____ 1. If it costs ten cents a mile to drive a truck, how much will it cost to drive the truck on a 267 mile trip?
    a). $ .03.
    b).   .27.
    c).   2.67.
    d).   26.70.
    e). $267.00.

Example: Write the letter of your answer in the space next to each item.
_____ 2. Spinach, kale, and pole beans are to green, as carrots are to orange, and as ripe tomatoes are to
    a). blue.
    b). brown.
    c). red.
    d). white.
    e). yellow.

In summary, the teacher is challenged with the responsibility for the education of the nation's youth. The teacher can facilitate, guide, structure, promote, and direct learning, but each individual has to do his own learning. In the course of evaluating pupil growth, the question might also arise, "If there is limited learning, what might be said of the teaching?"

References

1. Adams, G. S. *Measurement and Evaluation in Education, Psychology, and Guidance.* New York: Holt, Rinehart & Winston, 1965.

2. Anastasi, A. *Psychological Testing.* Third edition. New York: The Macmillan Company, 1968.

3. Cronbach, L. J. *Essentials of Psychological Testing.* Second edition. New York: Harper & Bros., 1960.

4. Ebel, R. L. *Measuring Educational Achievement.* Englewood Cliffs, New Jersey: Prentice Hall, 1965.

5. Freeman, F. S. *Theory and Practice of Psychological Testing.* Third Edition. New York: Holt, Rinehart & Winston, 1962.

6. Green, J. A. *Teacher-made Tests.* New York: Harper & Row, 1963.

7. Guilford, J. P. *The Nature of Human Intelligence.* New York: McGraw Hill, 1967.

8. Lindvall, C. M. *Measuring Pupil Achievement and Aptitude.* New York: Harcourt, Brace & World, 1967.

9. Stanley, J. C. *Measurement in Today's Schools.* Englewood Cliffs, New Jersey: Prentice-Hall, 1964.

10. Thorndike, R. L., and Hagen, E. O. *Measurement and Evaluation in Psychology and Education.* Second edition. New York: Wiley, 1961.

CHAPTER 11

Assessment Tests
for Elementary School
Migrant Children

RICHARD H. WILLIAMS and ARNOLD B. CHEYNEY

Drs. Williams and Cheyney discuss the construction of assessment tests for use with migrant children. The tests discussed were devised to help teachers place migrant children quickly into reading groups and to find out something of the children's social and educational backgrounds. This chapter is designed to give teachers ideas for developing instruments for their own classes.

Dr. Richard H. Williams has worked with the Head Start project in planning and development of statistical procedures and is presently teaching courses in statistical methods, experimental design, research, tests and measurements, and psychometrics as an associate professor of education at the University of Miami. He received his Ph.D. in Educational Psychology from Indiana University.

Dr. Arnold B. Cheyney has directed several federally funded programs in the area of migrant and inner-city disadvantaged. The author of numerous books and articles on several phases of education, he is a professor of education at the University of Miami where he teaches language arts and children's literature and where he received an outstanding teacher award in 1970. He received his Ph.D. from The Ohio State University.

THE DIFFICULTY in assimilating migrant children into an ongoing curriculum is at once obvious and frustrating. Not only are the children forced into a new and often incomprehensible environment, but school administrators and teachers have very little, if any, dependable information regarding experiences, interests, and abilities of the newly arrived migrant child.

The migrant child seldom enjoys the luxury of a full school year attendance. He typically begins the school year late and is forced to leave before it is concluded, his attendance between these times being at best irregular. In Florida, for instance, migrant children average about six months in school and move twice during this curtailed stay.

Since the usual standardized testing is conducted early in the fall and late in the spring, test information useful in placing and teaching the migrant child is often not available. Furthermore, children of migratory farm workers typically bring to school no record of previous schooling other than that which they or their parents can recall.

There is clearly a need to gather immediate and pertinent information about migrant children soon after their arrival in the classroom. The purpose of this chapter is to describe the construction and preliminary field testing of a set of assessment tests designed to give elementary school teachers of migrant children insights into the children's intellectual and social backgrounds.

The basic ideas for test construction described in this chapter can be used by classroom teachers of migrant children. Teachers can construct their own instruments by modifying the assessment devices presented here to produce tests that are consistent with their own teaching needs and the backgrounds and cultural characteristics of their students.

The specific purposes of the research described here were to develop instruments:

1. with which the the children could feel immediately at home,
2. which would give a rapid but fairly accurate estimate of interests and abilities,
3. which would leave the teacher free as much as possible during the testing period, and
4. which would not duplicate tests that are presently doing an adequate job.

These purposes necessitated that the tests utilize concepts familiar to migrant children. That is, the tests would contain cultural aspects which were understandable to the children and would, therefore, elicit from them the best responses they were capable of giving.

The research was divided into two phases. In Phase 1 five outstanding elementary teachers* of migrant children from South

*Jean C. Bennett, Angela D. Humphrey, Hazel Lambert, Maxine M. Ollis, and Jeanne Romine.

Dade County, Florida, were chosen to brainstorm tests ideas within the framework of their knowledge and understanding of migrant children. The teachers met with the test developers for several hours and began determining testing areas and kinds of tests that would merit their consideration. These meetings resulted in the development of five assessment devices: (1) *A Picture of Me*, (2) *Readiness for Reading*, (3) *Picking Tomatoes*, (4) *Arithmetic Readiness*, and (5) *Arithmetic Grouping*.

These assessment tests were field tested in a summer program for teachers of migrant children. As a result, the arithmetic tests were dropped because it was found that teachers could determine where children stood in arithmetic concepts without such instruments.

In the reading and social concepts tests problems arose, such as length of time required to complete the testing and vocabulary difficulties. Nevertheless, on the basis of the positive responses from teachers and children to the instruments, together with other information collected during the summer testing, these three assessment devices were revised for Phase 2.

Two University of Miami professors* with expertise in reading and social studies were engaged to help restructure the reading assessment devices with the authors. On the basis of their recommendations, which included changes in vocabulary and other information, the tests were revised.

A Picture of Me

A Picture of Me (figure 1) was designed to provide the teacher with information regarding children's perceptions of their experiential background which might aid the teacher in involving the children in the classroom curriculum. This instrument was also designed to help migrant children feel more at ease when entering a strange academic environment by engaging them in activities related to their own interests and experiences.

This assessment device requires that the child draw and write whatever he wishes within a loosely structured framework. The

*Dr. Charles T. Mangrum and Dr. Lucille B. Strain.

teacher then analyzes the child's responses as they relate to five basic areas:

1. *Providing Rapport*—What has the child drawn or written that could be used to involve him in the classroom activities?

2. *Breadth of Social Concepts*—What has the child drawn or written that indicates his understanding of geographic, historical, or agricultural concepts?

3. *Understanding of Familial Occupations and Relationships*—What has the child drawn or written that indicates his knowledge of his family's occupational role and his relationship to the other family members?

4. *Assessing Oral and Written Abilities*—What has the child said or written that would indicate the extent of his abilities in the area of expressive language? Cursive, manuscript, sentence construction, punctuation, spelling, dialect, bilingualism?

5. *Insight into Perceptual Abilities*—Are body parts complete or missing? Hands, feet, torso, eyes, mouth, hair, fingers, arms, nose, etc.? Is the cumulative effect one of maturity or immaturity?

The teacher and the migrant child gain the most benefit from *A Picture of Me* when the teacher analyzes the four drawings in the light of the five areas named and lists in words, phrases, or sentences the information she has ascertained under the five specific objectives. Educational strategies can then be developed from the total insights the teacher has gathered.

The pictures in the booklet are in outline form and serve as a frame of reference. The migrant child is encouraged to form associations that will stimulate thinking and recall. The writing within the "balloons" gives the teacher some evidence of the child's handwriting and written language abilities. If a child has difficulty with a word, the word is written for him on a piece of paper. He may then copy it into his booklet. In the case of a child who cannot write or does not wish to do so, the balloons are filled in by the teacher or an aide as the child dictates.

After the migrant child begins to feel at ease in the classroom, the teacher discusses *A Picture of Me* with him. On page 1 he is encouraged to make a drawing of himself under the balloon. A variety of colored crayons should be available.

On page 2, "My Family and What They Do," the migrant child is encouraged to draw pictures of the members of his family and the kinds of activities they engage in. This would not only include his mother and father but also his brothers, sisters, and other relatives. The balloon at the top can include names, conversation, or any kind of information the child wishes to divulge.

On page 3 the caption is "Where We Have Been." The child illustrates experiences he has had in other sections of the country. He may label these illustrations with the names of towns or states, or he may wish to draw a picture of the kind of vehicle he rode in.

"What I Like to do," page 4, has two aspects. The child is encouraged to express his desires in terms of what he likes to do at home and what he likes to do at school. Again, he may wish to write this information.

When the explanations are over, the child proceeds to "make his book." The teacher should answer any questions the child might ask but is encouraged to use discretion so that the responses in the booklet reflect the child's thinking rather than the teacher's.

In order to systematize and structure the responses to *A Picture of Me* so they will provide the teacher with pertinent information that will help him to do a better job of instruction, it is necessary to analyze the drawings as objectively as possible in terms of the five basic areas. The obvious danger in such a subjective approach lies in the fact that misinformation may be read into the accumulated data. This possibility must be guarded against. Teachers are not equipped to provide in-depth clinical interpretations. Judgments should be made on the basis of the use this material supplies for classroom strategies.

Where time, facilities, and abilities permit, children can role play scenes from their booklets. Tape recordings of this activity may be useful for the teacher who wishes to get more information about the children.

Readiness for Reading

Readiness for Reading is designed to provide teachers a rapid, gross assessment of the migrant child's ability to begin formal reading instruction. Format and content have been selected for their special appeal to migrant children, although specific skills

Figure 1. A Picture of Me

and abilities assessed are those generally pertinent to any child's readiness for reading.

Readiness for Reading consists of four activities by which the child can demonstrate his proficiency in performing tasks closely related to those required in the process of reading. Successful performance of all activities indicates that the child has achieved a reasonable degree of maturity in relationship to the following:

1. recognizing likenesses and differences
2. left-to-right progression
3. comprehending oral language
4. knowledge of relative terms
5. ability to follow directions
6. motor control
7. perceiving names and forms of the letters of the alphabet auditorily and visually
8. perceiving relationships
9. distinguishing colors
10. understanding a sequence of thought

The activities included in the test are designed to show children's development in relation to those abilities and skills generally expected of beginning readers. From a list of those abilities and skills which are pertinent, a selection was made of those most closely related to the sensory or mechanical aspects of the reading process. Activities were then designed to permit observation of children's performance in relationship to each aspect selected. A sample of these four readiness activities is given in figures 2, 3, 4, and 5.

Readiness Activity Number 1 is designed to assess a child's ability in recognition of likenesses and differences and left to right progression. The child "works" in the potato field by matching the letter in the first column with those to the right. The directions also call for drawing a line from the first letter in the row through all the others in the boxes to the right.

Readiness Activity Number 2 is designed to assess a child's ability to perceive names and forms of the letters of the alphabet auditorily and visually, follow directions, and comprehend oral language. The child is directed to find the cat and draw a circle

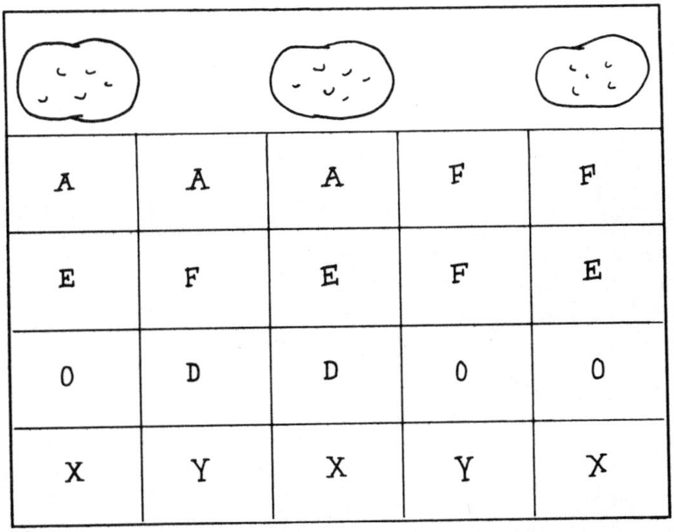

A	A	A	F	F
E	F	E	F	E
0	D	D	0	0
X	Y	X	Y	X

Figure 2.   Readiness Activity Number 1

| | L   P   C |
| Z   N   D |
| G   E   A |

Figure 3. Readiness
Activity Number 2

Figure 4.   Readiness Activity Number 3

Figure 5.   Readiness Activity Number 4

around the P, et cetera. After the activity is completed he is directed to cut out each picture.

Readiness Activity Number 3 is designed to assess the ability to comprehend oral language, determine knowledge of relative terms, appraise ability to follow directions, and judge motor control. To assess these areas the child is instructed to cut out the animals and place the cat on the step, the chicken under the house, and the pig beside the fence. Other prepositions can be used to further assess these abilities.

Readiness Activity Number 4 is designed to assess a child's ability to perceive relationships, sense a sequence of thought units, and distinguish colors. He is instructed to draw a red circle around each of the animals, a blue circle around each of the things found at school, and a green circle around each of the fruits and vegetables.

Readiness for Reading is not intended to be a complete and final evaluation of a child's readiness for beginning reading. It is intended as a means by which a teacher might acquire a quick assessment of a child's probable ability to profit from reading skill instruction. It is a set of convenient aids which can be used as initial activities for the migrant child who enters the primary grade classroom at various times during the school year. A child's performance of these activities should offer substantiation, or repudiation, of the teacher's own direct observation.

Each activity is greatly simplified in comparison with the usual reading-readiness tests. Therefore, it might be expected that the child should complete, satisfactorily, a large proportion of each of the activities. Performance considerably below this level might suggest that the child should be given experience with other similar activities to develop strengths in the areas tested before he is given formal instruction in reading printed material.

Picking Tomatoes

Picking Tomatoes (figures 6-8) is designed to determine initial reading placement of children who are to be instructed from standard reading texts. This instrument covers preprimer 1 through third grade reading levels. The child is given a sheet of paper with "rows of tomatoes" which can be flipped up at the "stem" (figure

6). On the sheet underneath appears a word. If the child can say the word correctly he marks it with a crayon or pencil (figure 7). Another child or teacher aide checks to see if he is correct and then marks a crate on a "truck" accompanying the test if the migrant youngster gives the correct response (figure 8). When the migrant child misses five in a row or does not wish to continue, he hands in his tomato field and word list and colors his truck. The teacher then scans the word list column by column to determine the child's initial reading grade placement.

This test was constructed using the standard Scott-Foresman Basic Readers, sixth edition, from the preprimer through third grade but a stratified random selection of the word lists from the basic readers or other reading materials used by any school system might be substituted. Each of the specified basic readers in the Scott-Foresman Basic Reading Program was examined to determine the new words introduced at that book level. Every new word was examined in light of the following criteria before being accepted as a test item:

1. Words that were forms of words introduced at a previous level were omitted from the lists.
2. All proper nouns were omitted from the lists.
3. Words with a single specialized meaning were omitted from the lists.
4. Words with highly irregular phoneme-grapheme relationships were omitted from the lists.

New words ranged in number from approximately 20 in the preprimers to approximately 350 at the book three level. Vocabulary was so loosely controlled starting with the book four level that no estimate of new words was possible.

Word lists were selected for determining reading levels for preprimer through third reader level, because it had been observed that reading deficiencies at these levels were most often in reading mechanics rather than in reading comprehension.

The following directions are given orally by the examiner when administering the test:

Underneath each of these tomatoes is a word. Some of the words are easy and others are not so easy. I would like you to lift up the tomato and try

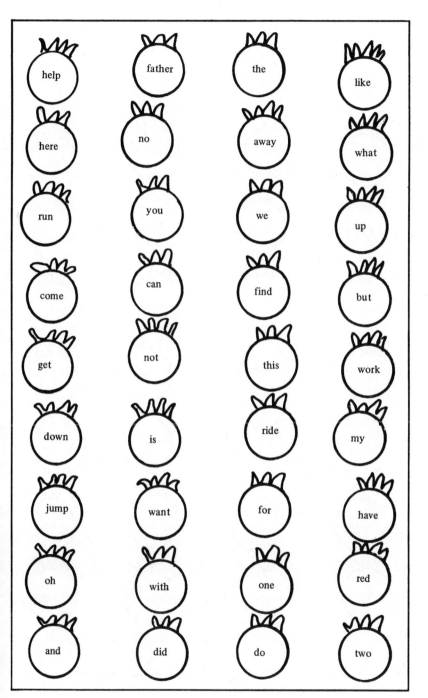

Figure 6. Picking Tomatoes, Game I. (The words shown are those which would be underneath the tomatoes on the second sheet of the actual test.)

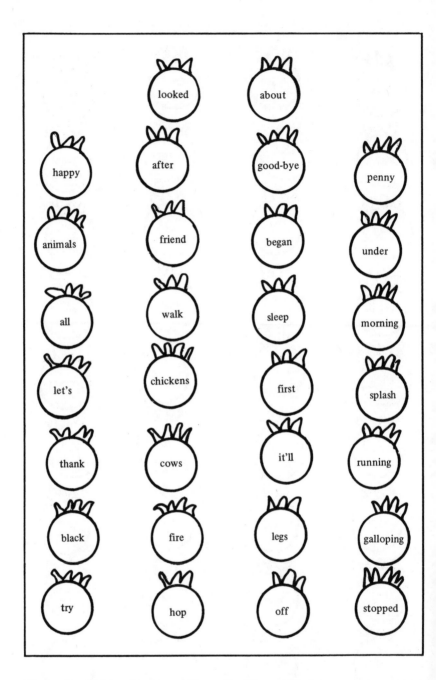

Figure 7. Picking Tomatoes, Game II. (The words shown are those which would be underneath the tomatoes on the second sheet of the actual test.)

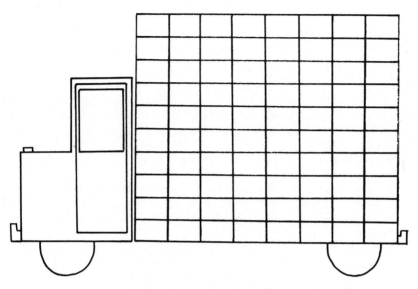

Figure 8. Picking Tomatoes

to say the word you see. If you are correct, you may mark an X on the word, and I will put the tomato in your truck. After this part of the game is over, you may color the truck and tomatoes. Now, let's begin at the top of the page.

It should be stressed that classroom teachers can modify an instrument such as *Picking Tomatoes* to suit their own needs. If the migrant child is more likely to be familiar with grapefruit, then an assessment device called *Picking Grapefruit* can be constructed.

Field Testing Results. Redland Elementary School, which educates large numbers of migrant children, was chosen for the bulk of the Phase 2 testing. Teachers involved in an NDEA Institute for Teachers of Migrant Children, directed by Dr. Arnold B. Cheyney, also tested children and evaluated the tests. Mrs. Jean Bennett, a teacher in Redland Elementary School, a member of the Institute and one of the teachers involved in Phase 1 of this study, acted as coordinator of the Phase 2 testing in the schools.

A Picture of Me was administered to 116 children from levels one through six over a two month period. In its present form this instrument does not lend itself readily to psychometric or statistical evaluation. Therefore, Mrs. Bennett's observations are most pertinent and valuable because of the close contact she had with the children and teachers during the administration of this instrument.

A Picture of Me was given on all grade levels with varying responses. In the first year classes, the teachers wrote what the children said. On other levels the children did their own writing, if any. Many of the figure drawings showed the immaturity of the children, as if they had never looked at people. Houses, trucks, planes, etc., were apt to be more accurately drawn. For some of the children the drawings were not true. I visited the home of one boy and found that he did not have nearly as large a family as he had drawn. He had given names to most of his "family" in the drawing. Used correctly, this booklet, more than the other two games, helps to establish a rapport between teacher and child. In looking at it and talking with the "artist," he can begin to feel your interest in him as a person and to realize that he can make a contribution to the class.

A subjective consensus analysis of the responses of children and written comments of teachers regarding *A Picture of Me* indicated the following:

1. (providing rapport) This objective was apparently met. In one instance this was the only way a teacher could get a response from a migrant child. Many of the nonmigrant youngsters were apparently jealous of the fact that the instrument was not for them. One of the teachers wrote: "I found this test useful for opening a discussion of what the child has done, where he has been, and interests. It gave us something to talk about or gave me some idea of the child's experiences."

2. (breadth of social concepts) There seems to be a lack of experience here although the children have traveled widely. Apparently they do not "see" much during their travels.

3. (understanding of familial occupations and relationships) This portion of the test appears to be more valid with the older children because they (e.g., the ten-year-olds) have gone out to the fields and have seen their parents work (and worked with them in a number of instances). The younger children were at home. One primary teacher commented: "They are very conscious of family members. The father was frequently left out of the picture for he was working. The brothers and sisters have a close relationship."

4. (assessing oral and written abilities) The instrument has potential for assessing these abilities. Their ability to construct sentences was indicated.

5. (insight into perceptual abilities, i.e., maturity level) The teachers indicated they were able to get a gross estimate of maturity. On the primary level, the majority of migrant children show immaturity as one

would expect. In terms of dress, for instance, no distinction was made between brothers and sisters.

Readiness for Reading did not meet purposes three and four (freeing the teacher during testing and not duplicating present tests) to the satisfaction of the teachers and test developers, although a subjective analysis based on teacher responses indicates that the device samples behavior which is related to later success in reading. It was found that the instrument could be given to small groups efficiently but it does take teacher direction and time.* There is no statistical information available for this assessment device at the present time. Mrs. Bennett's analysis of her experience with the instrument gives an indication of why it was decided that purposes two, three, and four were not satisfied (see p. 200).

> *Readiness for Reading* was used by teachers on the first and second year levels of the primary block, usually given to a group of children at the same time. During the testing, when the group was over five, the teachers found it difficult to check on some individual activity, such as drawing a line from left to right. It was easier to observe the ability to use scissors, paste, crayons, and pencil, as this was done over a longer period of time. One teacher noticed a difference in the children following oral instructions that followed a pattern. A few understood the first time, a few more on the second time, and others, finally, later.
>
> It was suggested that the test be given in two sittings. In the testing situation, it was found that if the tests were given on two successive days, there was some difficulty in completing the tests because of absenteeism of the migrant.

Picking Tomatoes was administered to 49 migrant children over a two-month period. The frequency distributions listed in Table 1 show the age and ethnic composition of the sample.

Since the majority of the children tested with *Picking Tomatoes* found Game III (grade levels 2 and 3) too difficult, Game III was not used in the statistical analysis. Game I and Game II have been combined for all of the analyses which follow. These games represent levels ranging from preprimer I through Book I. Throughout these analyses both omissions and wrong responses were marked

---

*The authors would encourage teachers to try the items illustrated in the readiness section as well as the other tests partially described here.

Table 1
Frequency Distributions for Age and Ethnic Groups
(Picking Tomatoes)

Age	f	Ethnic Group	f
6	1	Mexican-American	44
7	6		
8	13	Negro	3
9	18		
10	8	Puerto Rican	2
11	2		
12	1		N=49
	N=49		

Table 2
**Frequency Distribution, Reliability,* Mean, Standard Deviation,
and Range for the Total Sample of Migrant Children**
(Picking Tomatoes)

Score Interval	f
65-69	1
60-64	5
55-59	1
50-54	2
45-49	7
40-44	3
35-39	3
30-34	2
25-29	4
20-24	2
15-19	0
10-14	0
5- 9	7
0- 4	12
	N=49

$$r = .98 \qquad S = 22.55$$
$$\overline{X} = 28.16 \qquad R = 65 - 0 = 65$$

*Kuder-Richardson formula 21 was
used to estimate reliability

"wrong." Game I contains 36 vocabulary words and Game II contains 30.

Table 2 shows a frequency distribution, together with the mean, the standard deviation, the range, and a Kuder-Richardson formula 21 estimate of reliability.

Since there is large variability among the scores and since the reliability coefficient is unusually large, separate analyses were carried out for the eight- to ten-year-old children. Although smaller variation might well be expected for the separate age groups, this was not the case. The standard deviations for the eight-year-olds, the nine-year-olds, and the ten-year-olds were 23.87 to 23.26, and 23.19 respectively, the corresponding reliability coefficients being .99, .98, and .98. These coefficients are rather startling when it is recalled that KR-21 gives a lower bound on test reliability.

Table 3 presents further descriptive measures for the children who were administered *Picking Tomatoes.*

Table 3
Means and Ranges
for the Age Groups Comprising the Total Sample
(Picking Tomatoes)
(N = 49)

Age	Mean Score	Range
6	62.00	0
7	26.67	48 - 4 = 44
8	24.15	65 - 1 = 64
9	28.61	64 - 0 = 64
10	31.75	58 - 0 = 58
11	37.50	38 - 37= 1
12	0.00	0

The following four points may be useful in explaining the extremely high reliability coefficients obtained with this instrument. While the first two points describe properties inherent in the physical structure of the test, the last two points are a function of the particular group tested, as well as the test itself.

1. The test is long and, therefore, gives a large enough sample of a child's vocabulary so that repeated measurement would be likely to produce similar results.

2. There is small chance for guessing error.

3. The obtained mean score is close to $k/2$ (k = number of items = 66), which allows for maximum variation.

4. The obtained score standard deviation is unusually large. This is in part a function of the preceding point 3.

Mrs. Bennett, coordinator of testing in the schools, made the following comments:

> *Picking Tomatoes* was used on the third year level. A few of the children looking at the cover sheet did not recognize the drawings as tomatoes. They thought they were crowns. Coloring the drawings would help their identification. Some children were hesitant to lift up the cut-out, but, on being assured it was the expected and right thing to do, they quickly began to lift and try to read. For a few children who were the right age to be placed on the third year level, it was rather disconcerting not to recognize any of the words. Spanish-speaking children had difficulty in saying endings and some vowel sounds.
>
> They all seemed to enjoy having the truck picture, which is their score card, to keep. Most of them colored it right away. Some added X's in addition to the ones I had placed on it. One little boy said it wasn't a very good truck. He added fenders, another wheel at the back and made the tires bigger. He also thought it important to have a driver.
>
> This game was administered by the classroom teacher and a sixth grade student. Results were apparently the same. Each child took about ten minutes if he was able to do more than the first page of words.
>
> On our level we had reading groups corresponding to those on the test and the children were grouped accordingly. We feel that they have been placed in groups where they are attaining success in reading and learning the accompanying skills.

Picking Tomatoes appears to be a reliable measure of the vocabulary level of the migrant child. Evidence bearing on predictive validity will be determined in the future, when independent measurements are taken and compared with this test's placements. The construction of *Picking Tomatoes* was done in such a way that emphasis was placed upon content validity rather than upon correlation with some external criterion.

These assessment tests are at this time purely experimental so by their very definition they are open to further modification and refinement. We believe that *Picking Tomatoes* and *A Picture of Me* have a great deal of potential for helping teachers and children in the classroom setting while *Readiness for Reading* does not appear to have as much potential.

Recommendations

The recommendations we would make for assessment devices basically call for teachers of migrants to create their own tests from these ideas in action research settings.

We believe further investigation of these instruments is desirable as they appear to have pedagogic value for the teacher of migrant children. A larger sample of migrant children is needed and independent measurements need to be taken to further investigate psychometric and other properties of these instruments.

These assessment devices can easily be modified by the classroom teacher to fit the backgrounds of the children he teaches. For instance, *Picking Tomatoes* could just as easily be *Picking Oranges, Grapefruit, Watermelons,* or *Strawberries.* Vocabulary for the *Picking Tomatoes* test can be chosen from any basic reading series the school might be using and content validation can then be built into the test. We would encourage teachers to construct such modifications.

Finally, those of us involved in this study became increasingly aware that these instruments could be used with any child regardless of background. In fact, nonmigrant children expressed great interest in them. We hope that teachers of children of other cultures and backgrounds will try creative testing of these ideas.

The experimental assessment tests described in this chapter were developed through a grant from the State Department of Education (Floyd T. Christian, Commissioner) to the Florida Migrant Survey Project, University of Miami.

PART III

Future
Considerations

CHAPTER 12

National Goals
for Migrant Education

HERBERT W. WEY and ARNOLD B. CHEYNEY

Drs. Wey and Cheyney make a plea for education that is relevant to the migrant child. Among the national goals they recommend pursuing are: Begin aiding migrant children at the point where they enter this world; Give migrant children the opportunity to make the choice of staying in the migrant stream or leaving it; Develop coordination/cooperation at all levels; and Maintain a constant evaluation of objectives.

Dr. Herbert W. Wey has been a consultant to the United States Office of Education on migrant education, a member of the National Commission on Education and Human Rights and Responsibilities, a consultant for the Office of the Attorney General of the United States, a consultant for IDEA (Innovation in Education), and the director of the President's National Conference on Innovation, among many other distinguished positions. He received his Ed.D. from Indiana University. He is now president of Appalachian State University, Boone, North Carolina.

THE MAJOR RESOURCE of our country is the potentiality of all our children. What we do to encourage and free their possibilities may well determine the future of our nation as a stronghold of the democratic process and life. Children are not so unintelligent that they cannot make comparisons between a one-room dirt floor shack and a modern three-bedroom bungalow. Children see differences in the clothes they wear and those of their classmates. The differences are polarized in the minds of children in the migrant streams: affluence and poverty; hot lunch and peanut butter sandwich; supermarket and company store; tile lavatory and privy; playgrounds and fields.

We cite research that indicates the first five years of life are crucial to wholesome adult development and then we begin our educational offensive when children reach the age of six. We believe that emotional stability is best nurtured in the early years and yet we wait until adolescence to organize guidance programs and hire personnel for children long gone psychologically, if not physically, from the school setting. We ask questions and seek answers that are not relevant to the basic needs of all human beings.

We should be asking questions relating to these basic needs of all human beings:

Food, sleep, air, shelter, and protection from danger.

A chance to be loved and to love.

An opportunity to be an independent person, but able to depend on others also.

A feeling of importance and value as an individual.

Freedom to explore, to grow, to learn, and to create. (10)

Our questions belie, perhaps inadvertently, our true concerns for migratory youth. One central criterion should concern us as we seek to develop fundamental questions—as we pursue national goals—"Will what we are doing affect positively the potentiality of all children whether migratory or stationary, Negro or Anglo-American, Spanish-speaking or nonstandard dialect?"

The problems attendant to migrant children cannot be divorced from their innercity peers. The complexities of our present day make every man his brother's keeper regardless of the reluctancy or hesitancy of any one person to be so. Listen to Senator Javits (4): "The crisis of the core city is also a crisis for rural America, whose people are taking flight to the cities as farm manpower needs diminish. No program or effort which seeks to resolve the problems of the city slum can stand alone. . . . "

Let us aim at the problem in its totality and focus on our children in their individuality, and let this focus be adjusted by the criterion of what will affect in a positive way their potentialities.

In an allegorical sense, we can ask, as did the prophet Isaiah,

"Who hath believed our report?" Opulent Americans cannot believe because they do not see these people who are crowded in camps away from the mainstream of our society. We see the reflections of the sun on rockets encircling our earth and the work of man in outer space blinds us to the needs of man in his inner space at the price tag of four to one. It is not a matter of being unable to believe the report of poverty in the midst of plenty—it is that we do not wish to believe.

Perhaps it is as Isaiah wrote, and again we take poetic license to make this point, "For he [the migrant child] shall grow up . . . as a tender plant and as a root out of dry ground; he hath no form nor comeliness; and when we shall see him, there is no beauty that we should desire him." Until we have the fortitude to take the part of this migrant child, no matter how unlovely he may be, we cannot say we are truly interested in the well-being of all children.

At least 150,000 migrant children, according to the National Committee on the Education of Migrant Children, make the trek from South to North and back again as their parents follow the harvests in search of employment. Another report states: "An estimated 50,000 are on the road between October and May when other children are in school and larger numbers miss school time at the beginning and end of school semesters" (1).

Migrant Children—Our First Consideration

We delude ourselves by thinking we can solve the education problems of migrant children by waiting until they are school age to assist them. They must be helped even before they are born.

An inadequate diet in the early years of life can impair mental development, language skill, and physical development (7). Regardless of the competency of the teacher, he cannot under any circumstances overcome prenatal and early childhood deficiencies.

Therefore, as a national goal, we must *develop and extend medical, nutritional, child care, and educational assistance to migrant mothers and their children from conception into the early school years.*

The *Florida Health Notes* details the life of "a typical migrant family—the Miggs."

The Miggs suffer from lack of proper foods. They don't know about balanced diet, nutrition, etc. Many of them have no experience in cooking the vegetables they harvest. Shortage of space and limited equipment in their quarters make adequate preparation of food almost impossible. Mrs. Miggs usually serves fried fish, grits, collards and bread for breakfast. Food in the fields may consist of a meat sandwich and a bottled soft drink purchased from a lunch truck. When she returns from the fields in the evening, Mrs. Miggs usually is so tired that the late meal consists of canned food and soft drinks.

The children, if they are not in school, eat breakfast leftovers or have nothing between breakfast and supper. Daily trips to the store are necessary because of the lack of a refrigerator; the only cooking utensils are a couple of frying pans; and the stove is a two-burner hotplate or kerosene stove. If the Miggs do not have money to buy food when in the Belle Glade area, they live on fish from the canals and abandoned vegetables from the fields. (2)

The effect on the child due to an inadequate diet is incalculable. Dr. Phillip L. White states:

To delay until a child has reached school age to institute dietary alterations to correct malnutrition is to wait too long. Correction must begin well before the child reaches school. . . . The critical period for the realization of the ultimate potential of central nervous system development and brain development is during the last trimester of pregnancy and during the infant's life. The brain achieves almost its normal size in the first four years and the most rapid development occurs during the first two years. . . . So it is at this time optimum nourishment is extremely critical for establishing the appropriate conditions for optimal growth of the brain and the central nervous system. It has been well established in studies in most every country of the world that interference with growth and development during the first four years will produce very significant stunting, stunting of growth in all probability and also stunting of mental development. (12)

A staff instructor at the Child Development Center of the University of Miami School of Medicine commented: "I can personally document numerous cases of children who are mentally retarded, not because of prenatal or birth injury, but solely because their mothers did not have the money to provide them with adequate nutrition. The large numbers of children with malnutrition in our state should shock us from our complacency."

And a final documentation for this goal, Senator Harrison A. Williams, Jr., chairman of the Subcommittee on Migratory Labor Hearings:

> In 1964 the infant mortality rate among migrants was at the level of the country as a whole for 1949. The maternal mortality rate in 1964 was the same as the national level of a decade ago.
>
> Mortality from tuberculosis and other infectious diseases among migrants in 1964 was two and a half times the national rate, approximating the national rate of more than a decade ago.
>
> Of the more than one million migrants, including workers and their dependents, 750,000 still live and work outside the areas served by existing migrant health projects. This group includes, by conservative estimates:
>
> 1. Over 6,500 persons with diabetes who are without adequate medical care.
>
> 2. Over 5,000 migrants with tuberculosis who are traveling and working with their disease undetected and untreated.
>
> 3. Over 300 children under the age of 18 who have suffered cardiac damage as a result of rheumatic fever. These children are unlikely to receive treatment for prevention of reinfection and further cardiac damage. Such treatment is ordinarily readily available to most nonmigrant children in their communities.
>
> 4. Approximately 9,800 children who have undiagnosed and untreated iron deficiency anemia. This increases their susceptibility for childhood infection and interferes with their normal growth and development.
>
> 5. Over 250 infants who will die in the first year of life as a result of congenital malformation or disease. Early, adequate medical care will not be available for these infants.
>
> 6. Over 16,000 expectant mothers who will find it difficult to obtain prenatal care. Infant and maternal mortality can be expected to be significantly higher under such conditions.
>
> 7. Between 20,000 to 30,000 individuals who have enteric parasitic infestations—resulting in most cases from poor sanitation. Such a problem is almost nonexistent in the general public.
>
> Just two months ago, in one of the wealthiest states in the nation—a migrant with an emergency illness was rejected by four hospitals because he could not assure payment of the bill. At the fifth hospital, where he obtained attention, doctors said the patient had only about two hours left to shop around for hospital treatment. (9)

Given conditions such as these for developing mentally and physically, it would not be difficult for most of us to decide whether we would prefer this type of life. We would not. The migrant youngster should be given the opportunity to make such a judgment also.

Therefore, as a national goal, we must *order conditions in such a fashion that migrant youth can make a decision to leave or stay in the migrant stream.*

A review in *Time* magazine of *No Harvest for the Reaper,* filmed by National Educational Television, points out the inability of some migrants to be able to leave the stream.

> The Long Island story begins in Arkansas where a crew chief, himself a Negro, recruits his workers ("All you've got to do is get on my bus"). He barely mentions the $30 fare that begins the treadmill of debt. Sometimes, in picking strawberries at 10¢ per quart, the migrants earn only $2 for their day's work but the crew chief deducts $1.25 a day for transportation to the fields. He also overcharges them for their filthy accommodations, for their food (a concession controlled by his wife), and the 51¢ a-pint payday wine that he sells for $1. As a result, at the end of the Long Island harvest, the migrant will have no choice but to bus along with the crew to the next stop: Florida—and then back to Long Island—perhaps for a lifetime of latter-day slavery. (6)

Implicit in this second goal is the understanding that children will receive the educational wherewithal to actually take such action. This decision would be based on an adequate educational background, including vocational training that would lead to worthwhile, satisfying employment. Since our present information reveals that most migrant youngsters withdraw from school after the elementary grades and very few ever go beyond junior high school, it is mandatory that we include vocational guidance and training early and report whether this has any effect on retaining migrant students in the classroom.

Organizational Cooperation and Commitment

As a national goal, we must *develop a projection of migrant needs and culture as they would appear to be in the next ten, twenty, or thirty years.*

We are all acquainted with the move from rural to urban areas. We know that small farmers are not the prime employers of migrant help. Actually "the top nine per cent of all farms pay more than 70 per cent of the total annual farm wage bill. More than 30 per cent of all expenditures for hired farm labor is made by one-half of one per cent of the very largest farms" (5). This should portend some future developments as they relate specifically to the education of migrant children.

Some questions come quickly to mind. Will automation deprive the migrants of a livelihood as they now know it? What will life be like in the agricultural areas in the years ahead? If they were not to migrate, how would they be best assimilated? In the rural areas? In urban areas? Should we attempt to keep them from migrating? What does all this mean in terms of developing school plants? Curriculum? Employment opportunities?

There are, of course, no ready answers to these questions. If military men in our defense establishment play war games on the basis of what might happen under given holocaust situations, why cannot we, looking to develop a brighter, more meaningful life for children, do much the same kind of conjecturing? To implement this projection attempt, there needs to be a standing committee of knowledgeable persons from the various government departments —Labor, Commerce, Health, Education and Welfare, Agriculture, Transportation, et cetera—state departments—citizen advisory groups—growers—university personnel—and the migrants them-selves. These groups would look into the future, report on trends, and keep the nation advised on possible events that would affect us all. Too long we have locked the gate after the horse has strayed.

One of our problems, at present, is inadequate data and knowl-edge about the migrant in terms of size of population, density, and distribution; health, housing, and sanitation; educational and skill development.

Therefore, as a national goal, we must *collect pertinent data concerning migrant children and the families from which they come.*

Careful studies of diverse migrant populations are now being made in the states of Louisiana, Florida, South Carolina, and Vir-ginia. These studies will be coordinated and it is hoped that the instruments and collected data will be of use not only to these states but to other states concerned about the migrant population.

The Florida study involves a total state look at the migrant populace including the determination of the major unmet needs of migrant children. Interviewers were selected and trained to gather information in the counties that migrants tenant.

In addition to general information concerning present trends in the migrant population and information concerning the needs of migrant children, more data are needed regarding what is now happening to migrant youth as a result of the millions of dollars we are spending on programs to improve migrant education. To do this will involve an objective, longitudinal study of at least three or four years. A possibility might be a research design involving the home base states of California, Texas, and Florida. Once the migrant student population is adequately determined, then, by use of sampling techniques, 100 migrant children in each of the three states could be selected and carefully studied over a three or four year period. A study of this type would be designed as an attempt to determine changes in areas, such as, student self-image, vocational aspirations, communication skills, physical strength and health, school attendance, et cetera. This research of a carefully selected sample of migrant children could serve as a basis for evaluating the many new programs being undertaken. Concurrently, this study should furnish information that would help us develop educational programs of higher validity for migrant children.

The need for up-to-date information about migrant children is desperate. Documented evidence must be gathered so that appropriate action can be taken. For example, site visitors to migrant programs in 30 counties in Arizona, California, Georgia, Florida, New Mexico, and Texas reported that "In one area, observers were informed that only 10 percent of eligible school children were attending school" (8). If this is true, and it certainly can be checked, then it is unforgivable. The need for information is great.

The need for data demands coordination among various individuals, groups, agencies, and states. Because the migrant community is nationwide, our concern must generate from a cooperative, united heartbeat.

Therefore, as a national goal, *coordination/cooperation of efforts must be pursued, developed, and maintained among the various directors, advisory committees, and agency representatives of groups within and among the states concerned with the welfare of migrants.* Among these groups are state and local boards of health, education, and welfare, educational associations, regents, labor organizations, federal government agencies, growers, and the migrants themselves.

Time and again at conferences and meetings where the educatory problems of migrant and other disadvantaged children are discussed, the cry is voiced, "We cannot do thus and so because of state policy or local regulations," but let it be recognized that anything that will improve the educational and social status of these youngsters can and must be done. It is incredulous to think we would beat down an idea that has potential for improving the status of migrants with the excuse that "policy" will not allow us to do so. If we want to, we can change policy and even laws if necessary. Perhaps it is necessary, as Dr. B. Frank Brown of Melbourne, Florida, says, to use "craft and low cunning" in order to do what is needed for boys and girls.

Implicit within this goal of coordination is the concept of support for migrant education through local, state, and national resources. We have been and are continuing to become more and more dependent on the federal government for the education of the deprived, especially migrant children. We are prone at the local and state levels to say, "Let the federal government do it." It is unforgivable that so little was done at the local and state level until federal funds forced us to take action.

Federal funds have now motivated us to take notice of migrant children and so we must also accept the fact that a large share of the responsibility for their education must be borne by local and state educational agencies and this means the use of local and state tax funds.

Within the programs at all levels, attention should be given to how funding can meet the changing conditions brought about by weather, crop increase or failure, automation, and those circumstances that will increase or decrease the number of migrants in an area at any given time. For want of a better expression a "program escrow account" should be built into the budget of migrant programs so the unforeseen can be implemented quickly and positively and children will not be prey to the whims and vagaries of man and nature.

To facilitate this goal of cooperation/coordination, it is again proposed, as was done earlier (11), that state departments of education and the United States Office of Education establish at least three or four major regional migrant centers for purposes of research, dissemination, consultative service, and development and evaluation of present and future programs of migrant education. These centers could, in a functional way, develop programs for interagency and interstate cooperation involving coordination of all education programs for migrants.

These centers, university based and located in the states considered home base for the majority of migrant workers, would receive support from monies allotted to the states for work with migrants under Title I, ESEA. The staff of each center would include persons with an expertise and experience in working with migrants.

To act positively on the preceding suggestions demands an end to provincial interests. Coordination/cooperation as words have been fused together in this discussion. They cannot be dichotomies; they must be partners.

Educational Program Development

The need for highly trained, qualified teachers for migrant children is great. Even after training them the problem of locating teachers in areas where migrant children live is difficult. So far the efforts and results have been negligible. The training of new teachers must be done in the context of retraining or upgrading the skills of present instructors of migrant children.

Therefore, as a national goal, we must *develop preservice and inservice education programs for teachers of migrant children.*

The migrant centers discussed could be deeply involved in the training and the retraining of educational personnel for work with migrant children. During their early instruction undergraduate students could be given tutorial and small group experiences with migrant children and thus develop understandings and skills that would make their professional course work such as student teaching more profitable. The centers, being depositories and generators of migrant education research, would be available to these students also.

Inservice teachers would not only be able to upgrade their techniques through the centers but would also be able to develop special competencies as diagnosticians, language development instructors, and in master teacher classifications. Teacher aides could also be trained, drawing from the migrant population itself as is being done presently in a number of localities.

The education of teachers of migrant children cannot be done in three or four widely separated centers, but these centers can be the depositories and disseminators of films, video tapes, kinescopes, and other media which could be on loan to other educational institutions and would, therefore, enhance the instruction of many.

Teacher Corps and Education Professions Development Act funds should be used to sponsor inservice training programs for teachers of migrants. Certainly, the Teacher Corps program has proven its value in upgrading and preparing teachers to work with migrants who are at the bottom of the disadvantaged groups.

The farther program implementation gets from the local problems, the more loss—educationally, materially, and financially—is incurred. We need to return again to the criterion for stating our goals—how will this affect positively the individual potentialities of migrant children?

Therefore, as a national goal, we must *initiate and implement at the local level answers which are of personal concern to migrant children and teachers.*

One of the authors, while visiting a principal and some of her teachers in a school whose student population was fifty percent migrant, brought up the subject of additional federal funds that had become available to assist them in their work. The remark was greeted with laughter. The author was told in no uncertain terms that the staff of this school had not been consulted nor would they be consulted as to how the money might be used. The principal confided that she would probably have to do some financial juggling so that at least some of the money was allocated beneficially for the children. This is just one case but even if true in only this instance, it is certainly an indictment in using available funds.

Officials at the state level have long accused the federal government of dictating programs to the states on the basis of incomplete information at best or a complete lack of understanding of the problems. Lately the money has been flowing generously but all too often it is not filtering down to the grass roots where it is desperately needed. There is no apparent growth, because the water is too often siphoned off for consultants and conferences (good things) but not for those needs expressed by people who work directly with migrants.

The basic problem is the children in the classroom: this is the taproot which needs soaking. Unfortunately, we content ourselves with spraying the leaves and not saturating (with money) the root.

The responsibility for this situation lies with all of us. For a certainty, we can no longer blame the federal government since the money is presently turned over to the states and the state agencies have the responsibility for determining problems and finding their solutions. If we are not careful, we are going to commit the same sin at the state level we wrongfully or rightfully accuse the federal government of committing. It is heard around the country, voiced by teachers, principals, and local school administrators: "We are having more trouble now in working out programs and getting our money than we did when we dealt directly with the federal government." This should not be true. As we plan and develop new programs for migrant children, we must get down to the basics and involve teachers and other personnel who are in daily contact with migrants. And is there any really valid reason why migrant children and parents could not be involved?

Unfortunately, we are so anxious to get the money and to see that it is spent that there is a tendency to forget the basic purpose for which the money was appropriated.

Dr. Jack Frymier of The Ohio State University illustrated this problem rather succinctly in a recent speech, "We presume that people who are higher up know more than those who are further down. That's almost never true. Almost no secondary school principal knows as much about teaching biology as the biology teacher" (3). And this is true in finding consultants with migrant expertise to help develop meaningful programs. Perhaps we need to go directly to the source. The care and education of migrant children can only be as good as those at the local level make it.

Evaluation

Each of the preceding goals can be evaluated. How rigorously evaluation will be pursued and how much the results will be heeded will determine whether migrant children will be given a real chance to develop their potentialities.

Therefore, as a national goal, we must *maintain a constant evaluation of our objectives in their specificity and totality.* Tools and techniques must be developed which actually tell us where we are going and how we are doing. Insignificant problems cannot be attacked with significant research and evaluation designs because we will only validate insignificant problems. We must evaluate our large problems truthfully and be man enough to admit that what we tried was found wanting when the results so indicate.

Up to the present time our evaluation of the migrant programs, except in a few rare instances, has been an after-the-fact evaluation. Usually this evaluation has consisted of sending some observers into an area where a migrant program has been under way and having them talk to the recipients or directors of the program. There is certainly nothing wrong with this type of evaluation; if properly controlled it can give vital information needed to evaluate the success of a project as well as make recommendations for improvement. This type of evaluation would be better, however, if it were planned in advance of the undertaking of the project to be evaluated. For an evaluation to be truly effective, it should be designed at the same time a project is planned and developed. A proposal for a new program for migrant youngsters should include not only the major objectives of that program but also an evaluation design. Only in this way can the administrators of the program know what data they need in advance of the beginning of the project in order to do an adequate job of evaluation at the end of the project. It is difficult to tell how far we have gone if we do not know where we started. Likewise, it is very difficult to tell whether we have arrived at a place if we do not know where we are going. Most good programs have well-defined objectives that are specific enough to be measured. Evaluation is not difficult if it is adequately planned for previous to actual day-to-day operation.

All too often the wrong questions are asked in evaluation procedures. Frymier says the wrong kind are frequency and efficiency questions such as "How many school buses do migrants ride?" or "How much will it cost?" The correct questions would deal with effectiveness: "Is what we propose to do likely to make a significant change for good in the lives of migrant children and youth?"

In this context, let us consider the matter of record keeping as it relates to migrant youngsters. We have placed much importance on this topic. If we undertake a program to develop an effective traveling record for migrant youngsters, and this should be our aim, then we will want to evaluate the success of this project. It would be very easy to measure whether or not we are able to establish a traveling record for a large proportion of migrant children. We can decide that if we end up with a traveling record for ninety percent of our migrant children, that we were highly successful in this program. However, a more important objective would be: "Does the traveling record make teaching and learning more effective?" This objective is not so easily measured but it can be if we plan for the evaluation of the objective in advance of the project. After we have completed our program, we would again measure it to see whether we have moved forward or backward. All of us know there are more complicated ways of measuring the effectiveness of certain techniques, such as different teaching procedures. Often this type of research gets so complicated that the actual goal of improving instruction is lost in the pure delight of doing a research study. This is not the type of an evaluation that we are advocating. We are advocating the type of evaluation where we carefully think through our objectives, and then, before we undertake the project, try to determine our present status, then proceed with the new program, and somewhere along in the program and at the end we determine what has been accomplished. If we know what our objectives are, know what our status is when we start the project, determine how we are going to measure the objectives before and after the project is undertaken, then our project is not only simplified but also reliable and valid.

Congress requires the commissioner of education by law to see that there is coordination of effort among the states. He is also charged with seeing that proper evaluation is made of the goals that are set. Even so, our motivation must not be in the tenor of "requirements"—we must do all we can in the spirit of what is best for children.

Thoreau once said: "If you have built castles in the air, your work need not be lost; that is where they should be built; now put foundations under them."

References

1. Bennett, Fay. *The Conditions of Farm Workers and Small Farmers in 1967.* National Sharecroppers Fund, 112 East 19th Street, New York, New York 10003.

2. Florida State Board of Health. "Better Health for Migrants." *Florida Health Notes,* 57 (September 1965), 127-150.

3. Frymier, Jack. "The Teacher is the Key." *Curriculum Innovation for Desegregated Schools.* Edited by Harry O. Hall and Michael J. Stolee. Coral Gables, Florida: University of Miami, South Florida School Desegregation Consulting Center, August 1966.

4. Javits, Jacob K. *New York Daily News,* November 22, 1967.

5. National Advisory Committee on Farm Labor. *Farm Labor Organizing, 1905-1967: A Brief History.* 112 East 19th Street, New York, New York 10003, July 1967.

6. "No Harvest for the Reaper." *Time,* 91 (February 16, 1968), 51-52.

7. Scrimshaw, Nevin S. "Infant Malnutrition and Adult Learning." *Saturday Review,* 51 (March 16, 1968), 64-66f.

8. "Site Visits to Migrant Education Projects–Title I." ESEA: January and February 1968. (Mimeographed.)

9. United States Congress, Senate, Committee on Labor and Public Welfare. *Migrant Health Services.* Hearings before Subcommittee on Migratory Labor, 90th Congress, lst Session, on S. 2688, December 7 and 13, 1967. Washington: Government Printing Office, 1968.

10. United States Department of Health, Education and Welfare. *Your Child from 6 to 10.* Washington: Government Printing Office, 1966.

11. Wey, Herbert W. "Coordination of Programs for Migrants." Paper distributed at the National Meeting on Migrant Problems, University of Miami, Coral Gables, Florida, January 8, 1968. (Mimeographed.)

12. White, Phillip L. "Nutrition and Genetic Potential." *The Journal of School Health,* 36 (September 1965), 337-340.

Bibliography

Books

Agee, James, and Evans, Walker. *Let Us Now Praise Famous Men*. Cambridge: Houghton Mifflin, 1960.

Allen, Steve. *The Ground Is Our Table*. Garden City, New York: Doubleday, 1966.

Anderson, Nels. *Men on the Move*. Chicago: University of Chicago Press, 1940.

Benedict, Murray R. *Can We Solve the Farm Program?* New York: Twentieth Century Fund, 1955.

Blanchard, John. *Caravans to the Northwest*. New York: Houghton Mifflin Company, 1940.

Browning, Robert H., and Northcutt, Travis J. *On the Season*. Jacksonville: Florida State Board of Health, 1961.

Cash, W. J. *The Mind of the South*. New York: Knopf, 1941.

Coles, Robert. *Uprooted Children: The Early Life of Migrant Farm Workers*. New York: Perennial Library, 1970.

Coles, Robert, and Clayton, Al. *Still Hungry in America*. New York: The World Publishing Company, 1969.

Collins, Henry Hill. *America's Own Refugees: Our 4,000,000 Homeless Migrants*. Princeton, New Jersey: Princeton University Press, 1941.

Dollard, John. *Caste and Class in a Southern Town*. Garden City, New York: Doubleday, 1957.

Erikson, Erik H. *Childhood and Society*. New York: Norton, 1963.

Erikson, Erik H. *Insight and Responsibility*. New York: Norton, 1964.

Fisher, Lloyd Horace. *The Harvest Labor Market in California*. Cambridge: Harvard University Press, 1953.

Good, Paul, and Clayton, Al. *Poverty in the Rural South*. Atlanta: Southern Regional Council, 1967.

Greene, Shirley E. *The Education of Migrant Children: A Study of the Educational Opportunities and Experiences of Agricultural Migrants.* Washington, D.C.: National Council on Agricultural Life and Labor, 1954.

Hanna, A. J., and Hanna, K. A. *Lake Okeechobee.* New York: Bobbs-Merrill, 1948.

Hogarty, Richard A. *New Jersey Farmers and Migrant Housing Rules.* Indianapolis: Bobbs-Merrill, 1966.

Hurston, Zora N. *Their Eyes Were Watching God.* Philadelphia: J. B. Lippincott, 1937.

Kardiner, A., and Ovesey, L. *The Mark of Oppression.* New York: Norton, 1951.

Kleinert, E. John. *Migrant Children in Florida: The Phase II Report of The Florida Migratory Child Survey Project, 1968-1969.* Two volumes. Coral Gables, Florida: University Of Miami, Florida Migratory Child Survey Center.

Koos, Earl L. *They Follow the Sun.* Jacksonville: Florida State Board of Health, 1957.

Lange, Dorothea, and Taylor, Paul S. *An American Exodus: A Record of Human Erosion.* New York: Roynal and Hitchcock, 1939.

Lewis, Oscar. *The Children of Sanchez.* New York: Random House, 1961.

Lewis, Oscar. *Five Families.* New York: Basic Books, 1959.

Malzberg, B., and Thomas, S. *Migration and Mental Disease.* New York: Social Science Research Council, 1956.

Matthiessen, Peter. *Sal Si Puedes—Escape If Your Can: Caesar Chavez and the New American Revolution.* New York: Random House, 1970.

McGehee, Florence. *Please Excuse Johnny.* New York: Macmillan, 1952.

McWilliams, Carey. *Factories in the Field.* Boston: Little, Brown and Co., 1939.

McWilliams, Carey. *Factories in the Field: The Story of Migratory Farm Labor in California.* Hamden, Connecticut: Archon Books, 1969.

McWilliams, Carey. *Ill Fares the Land: Migrants and Migratory Labor in the United States.* Boston: Little, Brown and Co., 1942.

Moore, Truman. *The Slaves We Rent.* New York: Random House, 1965.

Myrdal, Gunnar. *An American Dilemma.* New York: Harper's, 1944 and 1962.

National Committee on the Education of Migrant Children. *Wednesday's Children: A Report on Programs Funded Under the Migrant Amendment to Title I of the Elementary and Secondary Education Act.* New York: National Committee on the Education of Migrant Children, 1971.

Nelson, Lawry. *American Farm Life.* Cambridge: Harvard University Press, 1954.

Nelson, Lowry. *Migratory Workers: The Mobile Tenth of American Agriculture.* Washington, D.C.: National Planning Association, 1953.

Nicholson, Clara K. *Anthropology and Education.* Columbus, Ohio: Charles E. Merrill Publishing Company, 1968.

Orwell, George. *The Road to Wigan Pier.* New York: Harcourt, Brace and World, 1958.
Porter, Pearl. *Children of the Harvesters.* Privately published, 707 Buchanan Avenue, Lehigh Acres, Florida 33936, 1969.
Samora, Julian. *Los Mojados: The Wetback Story.* Notre Dame, Indiana: University of Notre Dame Press, 1971.
Sandage, Shirley M., and Stewart, Jo Moore. *Child of Hope.* New York: A. S. Barnes and Company, 1968.
Schultz, Theodore W. *Transforming Traditional Agriculture.* New Haven: Yale University Press, 1964.
Schwartz, Harry. *Seasonal Farm Labor in the United States with Special Reference to Hired Workers in Fruit and Vegetable and Sugar-beet Production.* New York: Columbia University Press, 1945.
Shannon, Fred A. *The Farmer's Last Frontier.* New York: Holt, Rinehart and Winston, 1963.
Shotwell, Louisa R. *The Harvesters–The Story of the Migrant People.* Garden City, New York: Doubleday, 1961.
Steinbeck, John. *Grapes of Wrath.* New York: Viking, 1939.
Steiner, Stan. *La Raza, The Mexican Americans.* New York: Harper and Row, 1970.
Sunderlin, Sylvia, ed. *Migrant Children: Their Education.* Washington, D.C.: Association for Childhood Education International, 1971.
Sutton, Elizabeth. *Knowing and Teaching the Migrant Child.* Washington, D.C.: Department of Rural Education of the NEA, 1962.
Taylor, Paul S. *Adrift on the Land.* New York: Public Affairs Committee, 1940.
Taylor, Paul S. *Mexican Labor in the United States.* Berkeley: University of California Press, 1928.
United States Department of Agriculture. *The Farmer's World: The Yearbook of Agriculture.* Washington, D.C., 1964.
Vance, Rupert B. *Human Factors in Cotton Culture.* Chapel Hill: University of North Carolina Press, 1929.
Vance, Rupert B. *Human Geography of the South.* Chapel Hill: University of North Carolina Press, 1935.
Williams, Richard H., and Stewart, Elizabeth E. *Project Head Start, Summer 1966: Some Characteristics of Children in the Head Start Program (Section 1).* Princeton, New Jersey: Educational Testing Service, 1967.
Wright, Dale. *They Harvest Despair: The Migrant Farm Worker.* Boston: Beacon Press, 1965.

Periodicals

"AFL–CIO Organizers Go After Farm Labor." *Business Week* (September 24, 1960), 50-52.
Alman, E., and Stephenson, R. T. "Douglas College Migrant Worker Program." *The American Teacher Magazine,* 47 (February 1963), 8.

"American Outcasts." *Christian Century,* 78 (May 3, 1961), 548.

Andrews, Dorothea. "Moppets Who Migrate." *Children,* 1 (May 1954), 85-91.

"Another Bad Year." *Commonweal,* 76 (April 6, 1962), 29.

Armitstead, Austin H. "Learn About Migrants." *International Journal of Religious Education,* 33 (December 1956), 16-17.

Barton, B. "Uprooted People." *Children,* 5 (November 1958), 233.

Bennett, Fay. "Still the Harvest of Shame." *Commonweal,* 80 (April 10, 1964), 83-86.

Blackwood, Paul E. "Migrants in Our Schools." *Educational Leadership,* 14 (January 1957), 207-213.

Blair, Harry E. "Human Relations Problems of Migratory Students," *National Association of Secondary School Principals Bulletin,* 39 (March 1955), 63-70.

Buchan, Gerald, and Potter, Robert E. "Helping Migrants Communicate." *Instructor,* 78 (April 1969), 84.

Burnham, Philip. "A Million Migrants." *Commonweal,* 71 (February 19, 1960), 572.

"California Farm Labor." *Commonweal,* 70 (September 18, 1959), 508.

"Charity Ends at Home; Proposal to Improve Living Conditions in South Jersey Stalemated." *New Republic,* 156 (February 18, 1967), 9.

"Children of Migrant Workers Pose a Problem for Schools." *The Saturday Evening Post,* 232 (May 28, 1960), 10.

"Churches and Braceros." *America,* 104 (March 25, 1961), 810-811.

Close, Kathryn. "Combining Forces for Migrant Children." *Children,* 1 (July 1954), 148-152.

"Coke's Migrants Get a New Deal." *Business Week,* Number 215 (November 14, 1970).

Coles, Robert. "Social Struggle and Weariness." *Psychiatry,* (November 1964).

Coles, Robert. "Southern Children Under Desegregation." *American Journal of Psychiatry,* 120 (October 1963).

Coles, Robert. "Uprooted Children." *National Elementary Principal,* 50 (January 1971), 6-14.

Coles, Robert. "What Migrant Farm Children Learn." *Saturday Review,* 48 (May 15, 1965), 73-74.

Compton, N. "Green Valley Isn't So Jolly: Migrant Labor Camp Conditions, Yakima." *New Republic,* 159 (September 7, 1968), 19-20.

Conde, Carlos. "A School for the Migrant Child." *American School and University,* 36 (June 1964), 34-36.

Corker, Jeanne L. "Our Brother the Migrant." *Christian Century,* 82 (September 29, 1965), 1192-1193.

Croker, Eleanor Cartwright. "Child Welfare Worker in a Program for Migrants; Tri-County Citizen's Committee on Migratory Labor, Camden County, North Carolina." *Children,* 10 (May 1963), 87-92.

Davis, Billie. "And Here is Your Desk." *NEA Journal*, 45 (September 1956), 337-338.

Davis, Billie. "I Was a Hobo Kid." *Saturday Evening Post*, 225 (December 13, 1952), 25f. Condensed in *Reader's Digest*, 62 (April 1953), 13-16.

Davis, Billie. "Life that is Better than Beans." *National Parent-Teacher*, 50 (October 1955), 4-7.

Delgado, G., Brumbeck, C. L., and Deaver, M. B. "Eating Patterns Among Migrant Families." *Public Health Reports*, 76 (April 1961).

"Dispute in the Cabinet." *Commonweal*, 70 (September 25, 1959), 534.

"Do Your Own Thing This Summer: Teaching Migrants." *Instructor*, 78, (June 1969) 62-67.

Dougherty, Sarah E. "A School Health Program for the Children of Migrant and Seasonal Agricultural Workers: Progress Report 1970; New Jersey." *The Journal of School Health*, 41 (March 1971), 115-118.

Dougherty, Sarah E., and Uhde, Madeline. "School Health Program for Children of Seasonal Agricultural Workers." *The Journal of School Health*, 35 (February 1965), 85-90.

Dreher, Barbara B. "Language Training in a Preschool for Spanish-Speaking Migrant Children." *The Speech Teacher*, 20 (January 1971), 64-65.

"Drudgery and Despair." *Newsweek*, 58 (October 23, 1961), 68.

Edwards, Esther P. "Children of Migratory Agricultural Workers in the Public Elementary Schools of the United States: Needs and Proposals in the Area of Curriculum." *Harvard Educational Review*, 30 (Winter 1960), 12-52.

"Employment and Earnings of New York Migrant Farm Workers." *Monthly Labor Review*, 84 (April 1961), 393-394.

Evans, J. Claude. "Discord Along the Rio Grande: TCC and Mexican American Farm Workers." *Christian Century*, 86 (March 26, 1969), 397-400.

Ferrar, E. "Student's Reaction to the Project." *The American Teacher Magazine*, 47 (February 1963), 19-20.

First, J. M. "Educationally Deprived." *Michigan Educational Journal*, 39 (October 1961), 194-195.

"Followers of the Crops." *International Journal of Religious Education*, 36 (March 1960), 7-10.

Fowler, Bob. "Those Migrants in Our Midst; Westside School, Fresco County, California." *Farm Journal*, 81 (June 1957), 43-44.

Fransecky, Roger B. "Visual Literacy and Teaching the Disadvantaged." *Audiovisual Instruction*, 14 (October 1969), 28-31.

Friedland, William H. "Labor Waste in New York: Rural Exploitation and Migrant Workers." *Trans-Action*, 6 (February 1969), 48-53.

Friedman, Milton. "Migrant Workers." *Newsweek*, 76 (July 27, 1970), 60.

Gagen, Joseph F. "Invisible Poor of the Garden State: Conditions in New Jersey." *Commonweal*, 86 (September 8, 1967), 540-541.

Givens, R. A. "Report on Migratory Farm Labor." *Labor Law Journal*, 18 (April 1967), 246-248.

"Going to Market." *Economist,* 224 (September 2, 1967), 816.

"Government is Responding to Migrant Needs." *National Council Outlook,* 8 (December 1958), 15-16.

Groom, P. "Report from the National Farm Labor Conference." *Monthly Labor Review,* 88 (March 1965), 275-278.

Harnishfeger, Lloyd. "Desk for Ignacio." *Ohio Schools,* 43 (April 1965), 30-33.

Heffernan, Helen. "Migrant Children in California Schools." *California Journal of Elementary Education,* 30 (May 1962), 228-236).

"Helping Helpless Migrants: Florida Migrant Ministry." *National Council Outlook,* 8 (March 1958), 17-18.

Howard, H. "Toll Road Tommy." *Michigan Education Journal,* 35 (February 1958), 224-225.

Howard, Ruth Boring. "Better Health for Colorado's Migrant Children." *Children,* 3 (March 1956), 43-48.

Hudson, Lois Phillips. "Children of the Harvest." *The Reporter,* 19 (October 16, 1958), 35-38.

Karraker, C. "Can We Afford Misery? " *The Journal of Nursery Education,* 19 (January 1964), 88-95.

Karraker, C. "Right to Have Fun." *Recreation,* 55 (November 1962), 435.

Kavanaugh, S. "Can We Afford Misery? " *The Journal of Nursery Education,* 45 (September 1967), 50.

Kavanaugh, S. "Statewide Help for Migrants." *Michigan Education Journal,* 45 (September 1967), 50.

Keisker, Sue. "Harvest of Shame." *Commonweal.* 74 (May 19, 1961), 202-205.

Kell, Leone, and Alsup, Beth. "One Cup of Sugar: Home Economics and Migrant Families." *Journal of Home Economics,* 55 (October 1963), 642-644.

King, Lawrence T. "Blight in Our Fields." *Commonweal,* (November 24, 1961), 227-230.

Kirby, Helen. "Children of Mexican-American Migrants—Aliens in their Own Homeland." *Today's Education,* 58 (November 1969), 44-45.

Kleinert, E. John. "The Florida Migrant." *Phi Delta Kappan,* 51 (October 1969), 90-93.

"Lady Doctor to Migrant Workers." *Ebony,* 17 (February 1962), 59-60.

Laing, James H., and Austin, David E. "Migrant School Helps Children Catch-Up; Merced County Migrant School Project." *The Nation's Schools,* 79 (February 1967), 67-68.

LeBerthon, Ted. "At the Prevailing Rate." *Commonweal,* 78 (November 1, 1957), 122-125.

"Legal Umbrella for Farm Workers." *America,* 101 (June 13, 1959), 426-427.

Lopez, Frances. "Regional Program for Migrant Education." *Childhood Education,* 45 (September 1968), 22-27.

McDonald, Thomas F., and Moody, Earl. "A Basic Communication Project for Migrant Children." *The Reading Teacher,* 24 (October 1970), 29-32.

McFadden, Davis L. "Stepping Stones for the Stranded." *The Journal of Industrial Arts Education,* 28 (March 1969), 7.

McGreal, Sister Mary Nona, O.P. "Apostolate in a Sugarbeet Camp." *Religious Education,* 51 (March 1956), 107-111.

Markoff, S. "Sweatshops Under Blue Skies." *American Federationist,* 64 (October 1957), 18-19.

Maxwell, G. N. "Opening New Doors for Children of Migrants Through a Girl Scout Program." *Social Service Review,* 29 (June 1955), 148-152.

Mayer, Arnold. "Grapes of Wrath, Vintage." *The Reporter,* 24 (February 2, 1961), 34-36.

Mercer, Blaine E. "Rural Migration to Urban Settings: Educational and Welfare Problems." *The Social Studies,* 55 (February 1964), 59-66.

Metzler, W. H., and Sargent, Frederic O. "Problems of Children, Youth and Education among mid-Continent Migrants." *Southwestern Social Science Quarterly,* 43 (June 1962), 29-38.

"Migrant Children Will Benefit from Innovative Projects." *The Catholic School Journal,* 67 (September 1967), 84.

"Migrants: Conference on Education of Migrant Children and Their Families." *School Life,* 39 (May 1957), 3-4.

"Migrant Workers; Ignorance is Fear." *Economist,* 224 (July 15, 1967), 238.

"Migrant Workers to be Trained for Aircraft Production Jobs." *Aviation Week and Space Technology,* 87 (August 14, 1967), 127-128.

"The Migratory Farm Labor Problem in the U.S." 1969 Report, Committee on Labor and Public Welfare, U.S. Senate, U.S. Government Printing Office, Washington, D.C.

Milani, E. J. "New Breed of Gypsy Technicians." *Personnel,* 44 (November 1967), 56-60.

"Miserable Migrants." *America,* 108 (March 23, 1963) 386.

"Misery on the Move." *Economist,* 225 (December 30, 1967), 1292.

Molinari, R., and Bove, R. A. "Helping the Migrant Child." *New York State Education,* 56 (May 1969), 26-27.

Moore, Truman. "Migrant Children will Benefit from Innovative Projects." *The Catholic School Journal,* 67 (September 1967), 84.

Moore, Truman. "Slaves for Rent: the Shame of American Farming: Excerpt from Slaves We Rent." *Atlantic,* 215 (May 1965), 109-122.

Morales, H. "From Their Hands, A Feast; Meadow Wood Acres, Texas." *American Education,* 1 (November 1965), 1-5.

Morgan, Edward P. "Forgotten People." *The Reporter,* 20 (March 5, 1959, 4. .

Naylor, N. L. "Nursery Education and the Children from Nowhere." *The Journal of Nursery Education,* 18 (January 1963), 89-97.

"New Deal for the Mexican Worker." *Look,* 23 (September 29, 1959), 54-56.

"New Grapes; El Teatro Campesino (the Farm Workers' Theater) Performs for Migrant Workers." *Newsweek,* 70 (July 31, 1967), 79.

"Nine Cents an Hour." *Newsweek,* 57 (June 5, 1961), 31.

Northcutt, T. J., Browning, Robert H., and Brumbeck, C. L. "Agricultural Migration and Maternity Care." *Journal of Health and Human Behavior,* 4 (Fall 1963).

Ogle, Alice. "Plight of Migrant America." *America,* 115 (July 9, 1966), 33-34.

Palley, Howard A. "Migrant Labor Problems, Its State and Interstate Aspects." *The Journal of Negro Education,* 32 (Winter 1963), 35-42.

Parmar, S. "Unemployment or Exile: Is There a Third Choice for the Migrant Worker?" *UNESCO Courier,* 22 (July 1969), 32-34.

Pfeil, Mary Pat. "Computer Harvests Migrant Records." *American Education,* 6 (November 1970), 6-9.

"Plan Three Year Citizenship Program Among Migrant Workers." *National Council Outlook,* 7 (March 1957), 27.

"Possible Turning-Point." *Commonweal,* 70 (April 17, 1959), 68-69.

Postelle, Yvonne. "Migrant Youngsters: Our Forgotten Children." *Parent's Magazine,* 45 (May 1970), 60-63.

"Poverty Spurs Ecumenism." *America,* 112 (April 10, 1965), 475.

"Prosperity's Outcasts." *Senior Scholastic,* 79 (November 29, 1961), 12-14.

Rapping, Leonard A. "Unionism, Migration, and the Male Nonwhite-white-Unemployment Differential." *Southern Economic Journal,* 32 (January 1966), 317-329.

Raskin, A. H. "Misfortune's Children on the Move." *The New York Times Magazine* (August 6, 1961), 8-9.

"Report on our Migrant Workers." *America,* 114 (March 12, 1966), 346.

Reul, M. R. "Communicating With the Migrant." *Child Welfare,* 49 (March 1970), 137-145.

Reyes, R. "School Days Come for the Migrant Child." *CTA Journal,* 64 (May 1968), 14-17.

Rivera, Vidal A., Jr., "Forgotten Ones: Children of Migrants." *National Elementary Principal,* 50 (November 1970), 41-44.

Rogers, A. "Regression Analysis of Interregional Migration in California." *Review of Economics and Statistics,* 49 (May 1967), 262-267.

"Roots for the Rootless." *Christian Century,* 80 (May 15, 1963), 635-636.

Sartain, G. "New Approach to the Migrant Problem." *International Journal of Religious Education,* 40 (July 1964), 18-19.

Sawyer, Richard P. "Wanderer: Profile of a Migrant Child." *National Elementary Principal,* 49 (April 1970), 41-44.

Scholes, William E. "Our Migrant Neighbors." *International Journal of Religious Education,* 32 (May 1956), 4-6.

Scholes, William E., "Who are these Migrants?" *International Journal of Religious Education,* 32 (April 1956), 6-7.

Shannon, L., and Morgan P. "Prediction of Economic Absorption and Cultural Integration Among Mexican-Americans, Negroes, and Anglos in a Northern Industrial Community." *Human Organization,* 25 (Summer 1966), 154-162.

Sheridan, Marion L. "Family Day Care for Children of Migrant Farmworkers." *Children,* 14 (January 1967), 13-18.

Shotwell, Louisa R. "Harvesters." *Commonweal,* 75 (January 12, 1962), 417-418.

Sutton, Elizabeth. "The World of the Migrant Child." *Educational Leadership,* 14 (January 1957), 221-228.

Sutton, Elizabeth. "When the Migrant Child Comes to School." *NEA Journal,* 50 (October 1961), 32-34.

Taylor, Paul. "Migrant Mother: 1936." *American West,* 95 (June 8, 1970), 41-47.

Teilman, Mrs. I. H. "For Migrant Families." *The Child,* 18 (November 1953), 38-42.

Thomas, D. R. "Migrant Labor Laws: Now and Then: Texas-Mexican Farm Labor." *Social Education,* 24 (May 1960), 205-206.

Thomas, D. R., and Stueber, Ralph K. "No Desk for Carmen." *Teachers College Record,* 61 (December 1959), 143-150.

Tobin, Richard L. "The Revolution is Not Coming. It is Here." *Saturday Review,* 51 (August 17, 1968), 12-15.

Turner, W. "No Dice for Braceros: Imported Farm Labor, California." *Ramparts Magazine,* 7 (January 25, 1969), 37-40.

"Two Approaches to Problems of Migrant Workers." *Christian Century,* 76 (June 3, 1959), 660.

Ulibarri, H. "Education of the Adult Spanish-Speaking Migrant and Ex-Migrant Worker." *Adult Leadership,* 15 (September 1966), 80-82.

"Vagabond Kings." *The Reporter,* 28 (May 9, 1963), 12-14.

Vance M. "Church Pilot Project Helps Migrants; New Jersey Program." *The Interchurch News,* 1 (September 1959), 1.

Velie, Lester. "Poverty at the Border: Mexican Labor Brought in by Greedy U.S. Employers." *Reader's Digest,* 97 (August 1970), 92-97.

Vera, Josefina. "Essentials First for Migrant Students." *The Texas Outlook,* 51 (November 1967), 28.

Von Hilsheimer, George. "Child Care and the Migrant Farm Hand." *The Journal of Nursery Education,* 18 (September 1963), 262-266.

Weaver, Dortha Ann. "Migrant Children in Vacation Schools." *International Journal of Religious Education,* 33 (April 1957), 20-21.

Weber, Lin. "Learning Readiness for Migrant Children." *Grade Teacher,* 88 (December 1970), 36-38.

Wills, Clarice. "Families on the Move." *International Journal of Religious Education,* 35 (October 1958), 20-21.

Winters, Marjorie Tolman. "Towns Organize to Help Migrants." *International Journal of Religious Education,* 39 (May 1963), 14-15.

"Women You'd Like to Know; Day Care Center." *Farm Journal,* 94 (May 1970), 60-61.
Wood, H. D. "Children Who Move With the Crops." *NEA Journal,* 47 (March 1958), 107.
"Workers and Migrant Firms." *America,* 108 (January 5, 1963), 4.
"Workers Remain All Season On This Farm." *Farm Journal,* 81 (July 1957), 64.

Miscellaneous Papers

"Basis for a Plan of Action for Improving the Education of Migrant Children." California State Department of Education, Sacramento, California. 1967.
"Bibliography Relating to Agricultural Labor." Departmental information report number 69-1, Texas Agricultural Experiment Station, Texas A. & M. University, College Station, Texas 77843, March 1969.
"Catalog of Educational Films and Filmstrip Sets." Migrant Media Center, Region I, Education Service Center, Box 307, Edinburg, Texas. 1969,
"Child Labor Standards and School Attendance as they Relate to Rural Youth." National Committee for Children and Youth, Washington, D.C. 1963.
"Children in Migrant Families: A Report to the Committee on Appropriations of the United States Senate." United States Department of Health, Education and Welfare, Washington, D.C. 1961.
"Curriculum Materials for Teaching the Migratory Pupil." Richland School District, Shafter, California. 1967.
"Disadvantaged Mexican-American Children and Early Educational Experience." Southwest Educational Development Corporation, Commodore Perry Hotel, Austin, Texas. 1968.
"Educating Migrant Children." State Education Department, Albany, New York. 1968.
"Educating Migrant Children in Colorado." Colorado State Department of Education, Denver, Colorado. 1961.
"Education for Migrant Children." Texas Education Agency, Edinburg, Texas. 1962.
"Education on the Move—Report of a 1960 Demonstration Summer School for Migrant Children in Manitowoc County, Wisconsin." Governor's Commission on Human Rights, Madison, Wisconsin. 1962.
"Evaluation of Migrant Education in Texas." Southwest Educational Development Laboratory, Austin, Texas. June 1968.
"Facilitating the Learning of the Migrant Child." Bucknell Conference, Bucknell University, Lewisburg, Pennsylvania. 1968.
First Papers on Migrancy and Rural Poverty: 1. "Attitudinal Characteristics of Migrant Farm Workers"; 2. "The Mexican-American Heritage: Developing Cultural Understanding"; 3. "Agencies and the Migrant: Theory and

Reality of the Migrant Condition." Teacher Corps, School of Education, University of Southern California, Los Angeles. 1968.

"Good Food to Grow On." Menus for well-balanced meals and recipes for one-pot dinners. Florida Atlantic University, Boca Raton, Florida. n.d.

"Guide and Curriculum for Migrant Preschool Children." Florida Atlantic University, Boca Raton, Florida. n.d.

"Guide for Programs for the Education of Migrant Children." Texas Education Agency, Austin, Texas. 1968.

"Handbook for Teachers of Migrant Children in Wyoming." State Department of Education, Laramie, Wyoming. 1968.

"Identifying, Locating and Knowing the Migrant Child Eligible for Programs Under the Migratory Amendment to Title I, P189-10." Southeastern Education Laboratory, 5440 Mariner Street, Tampa, Florida 33609. 1967.

McCanne, Roy. "A Study of Approaches to First Grade English Reading Instruction for Children from Spanish-Speaking Homes." Colorado State Department of Education, Denver, Colorado 80203. 1966.

"Migrant." State Department of Education, 301 W. Preston Street, Baltimore, Maryland 21201. 1968.

"Migrant Children Summer School Pilot Program." Washington Office of Public Instruction, Olympia, Washington. 1962.

"Migrant Education: A Comprehensive Program." Report of 1968 Program, State Education Department, Albany, New York 12224. 1968.

"Migrant Education Handbook." Monterey County Office of Education, 132 W. Market Street, Salinas, California. n.d.

"Mini-Corpsmen." Migrant-Teacher Assistant Mini Corps, Project Report, State Department of Education, Sacramento, California. 1968.

"Ohio Conference on Migrant Education." Department of Education, Columbus, Ohio. 1968.

"Opening Doors." 1967 Educational Program for Children of Migrant and Seasonal Families in New Jersey. Department of Education, 225 West State Street, Trenton, New Jersey 08625. 1968.

"Our Young Visitors." Department of Public Instruction, Dover, Delaware. 1968.

Ponce, Carlas, and Powell, LaFayette. "Teaching Migrant Children: The Problem and an Approach." Kutztown State College, Pennsylvania. 1968.

"Preventive Approach to Problems of the Low-income Child." San Jose State College, California. December 1966.

"Programs and Services Benefitting Migratory Farm Children: A Directory." State Department of Education, Tallahassee, Florida. 1967.

"Promising Practices in Summer Schools Serving the Children of Seasonal Agricultural Workers." California State Department of Education, Sacramento, California. 1964.

"Proposed Curriculum for Texas Migratory Children." Texas Education Agency, Austin, Texas. 1963.

"Reading, Games and Activities." Broward County Board of Public Instruction, Fort Lauderdale, Florida. 1968.

"Report of Title I, ESEA Migrant Coordinators Meeting." December 1968, Office of Education, USDHEW, Washington.

"Schools for the Families of Seasonal and Migrant Workers." New Jersey, 1968, Department of Education, Trenton, New Jersey 08625.

"Scott, Ellis Bryan. *A Survey of Educational Programs for Agricultural Migrant Children During 1967.* A dissertation. New Mexico State University, Las Cruces, New Mexico. May 1968.

"The Somerton Story." State Department of Public Instruction, Phoenix, Arizona. November 1968.

"Something Started, Something Achieved." Department of Public Instruction, Helena, Montana 59601. 1968.

"Summer Programs for Migrant Children." Special issue: *Your Public Schools.* Department of Public Instruction, Olympia, Washington. July and August 1968.

Taylor, Paul S. "Migratory Laborers in the Wheat Belt, Second Half of the 19th Century." Harvard University Library. Unpublished report. 1951.

"Texas Child Migrant Program." Texas Education Agency, Austin, Texas. February, 1969.

"Those Who Remained: A Study of Migrant Agricultural Workers Who Did Not Follow the Migrant Stream." Florida Atlantic University, Boca Raton, Florida. 1967.

Wages, Sherry, Thomas, Katheryn, and Knolesky, William P. "Mexican-American Teen-Age Dropouts: Reasons for Leaving School and Orientations Toward Subsequent Educational Attainment." Texas A. & M. University, College Station, Texas. Mimeographed. April 1969.

Bibliographies With Migrant References

Booth, Robert E., et. al. *Culturally Disadvantaged: A Bibliography and Keyword—Out-of-Context (KWOC) Index.* Detroit, Michigan: Wayne State University Press, 1967.

Charles, Edgar B. "Mexican-American Education: A Bibliography." 22 pp. Las Cruces, Mexico: ERIC/CRESS, 1968.

Charles, Edgar B., and Bruch, Russell A. "Bibliography: Early Childhood Education." 29 pp. Las Cruces, New Mexico: ERIC/CRESS, 1968.

Charles, Edgar B., Nygard, Wilbur A., and Loomis, Charlotte Ann. "A Bibliography of Clearinghouse Documents Pertaining to Agricultural Migrants." 12 pp. Las Cruces, New Mexico: ERIC/CRESS, 1967.

Heathman, James E. *Migrant Education, A Selected Bibliography.* Las Cruces, New Mexico: ERIC/CRESS, 1969.

Mangalam, J. J., and Morgan, Cornelia. *Human Migration: A Guide to Migration Literature in English, 1955-1962.* Lexington: University of Kentucky Press, 1968.

Potts, Alfred M. *Knowing and Educating the Disadvantaged: An Annotated Bibliography.* 460 pp. Alamosa: The Center for Cultural Studies, Adams State College, Colorado, 1965.

Ross, Frank Alexander, and Kennedy, Louise Venable. *A Bibliography of Negro Migration.* New York: Burt Franklin, 1969.

"Teaching English to Non-English Speaking Children." 6 pp. Las Cruces: ERIC/CRESS, 1967.

Tuttle, Lester E., Jr., and Hooker, Dennis A. *An Annotated Bibliography of Migrant Related Materials.* Boca Raton, Florida: Migrant Education Center, Florida Atlantic University, 1969.

Index